The New Economy

The New Economy

ROGER ALCALY

FARRAR, STRAUS AND GIROUX

New York

Farrar, Straus and Giroux
19 Union Square West, New York 10003

Library of Congress Cataloging-in-Publication Data
Alcaly, Roger E., 1941–
    The new economy / Roger Alcaly.— 1st ed.
        p.   cm.
    Includes index.
    ISBN 0-374-28893-3 (alk. paper)
        1. Information technology—United States.   2. Technological
innovations—United States.   3. United States—Economic
conditions—20th century.   4. United States—Economic conditions—
2001–   I. Title.

HC110.I55 A43 2003
330.973—dc21   2002042599

Designed by Robert C. Olsson

www.fsgbooks.com

1   3   5   7   9   10   8   6   4   2

For Helen, David, and Mara

Contents

Contents

Contents

The New Economy

Introduction

IN THE SPRING and summer of 2002, as the economy and stock market struggled to recover from the declines resulting from their earlier excesses, the long boom of the 1980s and 1990s seemed a distant memory. Gone too was the reigning hopefulness, overwhelmed by a "crisis of confidence" brought on by the collapse of stock prices and economic growth and by accumulating evidence that many favored companies had deceitfully exaggerated their performance. But if one took a longer view and considered what had happened over the preceding decades, it was clear that the economy had changed enormously—and for the better. Spurred by remarkable new technologies as well as by growing global competition and financial innovation, it had virtually reinvented itself, fashioning a record-setting stretch of economic growth and stock market gains and creating for a while a sense among many that they were living in a new era of limitless prosperity. And while the euphoria of the late 1990s, like the melancholia that displaced it, was far overdone, there was always a more fundamental sense in which the economy of the 1980s and 1990s truly was new, a characterization that has not been undermined by the corrections that inevitably, and temporarily, slowed its growth in the first few years of the twenty-first century.

This book is about the ways in which the economy has changed over the last generation and why they are real, substantial, and likely to persist long beyond any short-term slowdowns or retreats—why, in short, the last few decades of the twentieth century marked the beginning of a period of great innovation and revitalization whose impact is likely to be felt for at least another generation, and probably even longer. As happened with the transformation based on electric power and mass production in the early twentieth century, and with the industrial revolution a century earlier, such periodic bursts of exceptional creativity and productivity have combined to produce the seemingly steady progress we have come to expect. And although their motive technologies differ markedly—now computers, telecommunications, and "lean" production, as opposed to electricity and mass production, which provided the spark for most of the twentieth century, or steam power and the shift from a craft-based system to a factory mode of production, which dominated the nineteenth century—their impact has been comparably large. Moreover, each of these spurts has been accompanied by unrealistic expectations and stock market bubbles—not to mention scandals and shady dealings—whose deflating was painful but never fatal to the bigger changes under way.

Even when considered in this restrained sense, much is new about this new economy, particularly its signature information technology, the broad combination of technical equipment and know-how that enables us to process, store, and transmit information more efficiently. There have also been significant changes in the ways businesses operate, in the extent of trade and economic integration among nations—globalization—and in the influence and inventiveness of financial markets, including the stock and junk-bond markets. All were reflected in the long economic expansions, rising share prices, and intense merger activity that lasted for most of the 1980s and 1990s and in the extravagant expectations that accompanied them, particularly in the last half of the 1990s, when both the economy and the stock market grew at rates that could not be sustained. The stock market peaked in March 2000, while business activity crested about a year later, and their declines and weakness during the following two years deflated the most extreme claims about the information age, the ideas that the future was limitless, that the business cycle was a relic of the past, and that there were new ways of valuing a company's shares other than credible estimates of its future earnings. The economy's softness in the early years of the new millennium, which was accentuated by the effects of the terrorist attacks of September 11, 2001, by the corporate scandals that surfaced a few months later, and by the likelihood of war with Iraq, also highlighted some of the outstanding questions about the lasting significance of the new economy. Could it survive the radical contraction in economic growth, and if it does, will the ongoing benefits of information technology measure up to those of the great inventions of the past, such as electricity and the internal combustion engine?

Although complete answers to these questions will not be known for several decades, there are good reasons to believe that the developing new economy will justify its name. The force of its underlying innovations may even strengthen during subsequent upturns in the business cycle, but though their impact is likely to be long-lasting, it will not carry on forever. As has happened in other prolonged periods of robust growth and productivity gains, the impetus provided by the propelling technologies will eventually wane, and since restorative new advances are unlikely to spring up on cue, the pace of progress may slow for a time, only to pick up again when some comparably far-reaching discoveries are made. Because technological and organizational leaps are so important to economic growth yet are by their nature irregular and unpredictable and tend to come in bursts, economic progress has tended to be episodic rather than smooth and continuous, except when looked at over very long spans of time. Even the lengthy process of refining, improving, and applying major new discoveries, a process that is still going on in the case of the computer and transistor, which are so important to today's new economy, is not steady or foreseeable. Indeed, the extended and irregular nature of

this improvement process helps to explain both the long delay in realizing the benefits of these inventions and why their potential was so
vastly underestimated when they were first introduced in the late
1940s.[1]

FROM THE NEW INDUSTRIAL STATE
TO THE NEW ECONOMY

Keeping in mind the uneven nature of economic progress enables us
to better place the new economy in perspective. Hopes of an enduring new era of unlimited prosperity flourished several other times in
the last hundred years, most notably in the 1920s but also at the turn
of the century and in the 1960s. All were times of unusual prosperity,
great optimism, and exuberant stock markets, perhaps even stock
market bubbles. Most important, all contributed significantly to the
grand sweep of twentieth-century economic growth, which was so
substantial that the worldwide production of goods and services during the century is thought to exceed all that was produced up to that
point. Looked at from afar, the ascent in living standards in the last
one hundred years seems inexorable and continuous—if anything, a
bit too gradual to have produced the tenfold gains achieved in the
United States and other advanced economies. (Such is the power of
compounding that an economy that grows at a seemingly modest rate
for a long time increases spectacularly, much like investments whose
returns are reinvested and continue to grow along with the initial
principal.) But we don't have to look much more closely to see that
there were also many bumps in the road, particularly the Great Depression of the 1930s that ended the 1920s boom and wiped out a
generation's growth in living standards.[2]

Most immediately relevant to appreciating our present prosperity
and the innovations that have made it possible, and are likely to propel it further as they continue to evolve and ripen, are the two other
phases the economy has gone through since the end of World War II,
the "golden age" of the 1950s and 1960s and the "tarnished" 1970s

that followed.[3]* This was a time in which the economy was hobbled by the unusual combination of inflation and recession, the result, in turn, of inept economic policy, oil price spikes engineered by the major oil-producing countries, and an economy grown old, one that could not withstand the pressure of growing international competition. It now is clear that the 1970s, and much of the 1980s, were essentially a transitional period between the prosperous postwar years—which marked the culmination of an era of high productivity growth based on exploiting the opportunities created by the development of electric power, the internal combustion engine, and mass production—and the emergence of the new economy, a stretch in which the reigning industrial state was dismantled and another, more dynamic one began to develop. The makeover was aided significantly by superior economic policy and financial innovation that enabled, and encouraged, companies to adopt the new information and communications technologies and stimulated them to become more efficient.

Except for the mild recession in 1990–1991 and the one that began in March 2001, the economy has been growing since the early 1980s, but the significance of its new features, especially the growing influence of computers, high-speed telecommunications, and other technological advances, was not clear until the mid-1990s. The rates of economic growth and productivity growth had been unimpressive until then, when they both surged, in large part because of the new technologies and the business innovations they induced and facilitated. They now are comparable to the rates of growth achieved in the golden age, giving essential backing to the idea that we are living in a new era of great prosperity and potential. Before the acceleration in productivity and economic growth became apparent in the data,

---

*As these labels are typically used, the "golden age" of the 1950s and 1960s really extends from about 1948 until 1973, and the "tarnished age" of the 1970s, a term suggested by Moses Abramovitz and Paul David, runs from the late 1960s or early 1970s through at least the mid-1980s, and by some reckonings, until the mid-1990s, when productivity growth began to accelerate.

it was hard to counter much of the skepticism, particularly among economists, about the likely impact of information technology. That it took so long for the effects to kick in, however, should not have been surprising. As was also true of electric power in the early part of the century, and is generally true of important innovations, it took time for the technologies to develop and spread widely throughout the economy and for businesses and people to learn how to use them effectively. Economic growth and productivity may also have been mismeasured; indeed, the nature of the acceleration became much clearer after the Commerce Department revised its data in October 1999, about four years after the pickup actually began.[4]

Another way to gauge the significance of the transformation now under way, and its likely staying power, is to contrast today's economy with that of the postwar years as portrayed, for example, in John Kenneth Galbraith's 1967 best-seller, *The New Industrial State*. The comparison also contains, at least implicitly, a warning about how wrong it can be to extrapolate existing tendencies too aggressively. Galbraith described an economy dominated by large bureaucratic corporations, which seemed more like socialist planning bureaus than the competitive firms of economic theory. But instead of languishing, this industrial colossus, he believed, would continue to grow and prosper, largely because of the abilities of the bureaucracies that ran the major corporations—the "technostructure"—to plan effectively and thus control the markets in which their companies operated. He also thought the system would continue to drift toward socialism. Rather than confirming its ongoing success, however, Galbraith, it turns out, was writing an epitaph for institutions that were too ossified to respond effectively to growing international competition or to more assertive and demanding shareholders. In less than a generation, an economy grounded in stagnant, highly concentrated, unionized manufacturing industries such as steel and automobiles was transformed into a highly competitive one led by the technology, finance, and media industries. Like Galbraith, and for much the same reason, many pundits missed the changes under way in the developing new economy. Even in the late 1980s and early 1990s, for example, writers such as historian Paul Kennedy and economists Lester Thurow and Alan Blinder badly overestimated Japan's recent success and, by comparison, America's decline. Some of the same people missed the post-1995 productivity surge and remain skeptical that it will last. And until recently, new-era extremists seemed to be making a similar mistake, albeit one that pointed in the opposite direction, a consequence of extrapolating the late-1990s gains too aggressively.[5]

Although information and communications technologies are the heart of the new economy, its strength and vitality are also due to complementary changes in the way businesses operate, as has been true of all other significant economic transformations. These new business methods have evolved over the last thirty years in response to the pressures and opportunities presented by not only the new technologies but also increased global competition, deregulation of many industries, and important financial innovations, including the development of the junk-bond market and the spread of hostile corporate takeovers. Compared to the rigid hierarchical operating structures of the Galbraithian economy, the business arrangements of the new economy are leaner, more flexible, and more entrepreneurial. Modeled initially on the example of Japanese firms such as the Toyota Motor Company, the new practices began to be adopted in the late 1970s and early 1980s and have continued to evolve, incorporating the latest technological advances and spreading to more and more firms throughout the economy. Rather than producing mass quantities of relatively standardized products, companies employing the new approach try to respond more directly to customer demands and orders, a seemingly simple change in perspective that has had far-reaching consequences. It entails producing a greater variety of goods in smaller batches; coordinating operations closely with suppliers, designers, and distributors; giving workers more responsibilities to make decisions; and supporting and encouraging them with more training and with pay that is linked to their performance, such as profit sharing and stock ownership.

Such lean and flexible operating methods have helped to reduce business inventories dramatically, improve the quality of goods and services, shorten production cycles, speed up distribution, and raise productivity and profitability, but they took time and effort to implement effectively. By making the economy more responsive and adaptable, they may also have helped to moderate swings in the business cycle, making recessions relatively mild. Symbolized by companies such as Dell Computer, the new arrangements have been enhanced by rapidly improving information technology and the Internet. But although the surge in economic growth and productivity coincides with its explosion, the Internet, because it is so new that businesses are still learning how to use it effectively, is unlikely to have been a major contributor to the productivity acceleration. On the other hand, its relative lack of development suggests that future gains for the economy, if not for Internet stocks, are yet to come.

Euphoria about the new economy was probably reflected most clearly in the stock market. From 1982 to early 2000, the compound annual return from owning shares was about 18 percent, significantly above the return since World War II and roughly double the yearly return over the last two centuries. Even more astonishing was the market's rise after 1995, when productivity and economic growth began to take off, particularly the rise in technology and Internet stocks traded on the Nasdaq stock market, which rose by almost 40 percent a year on average. Their explosion between October 1998 and March 2000, when the Nasdaq Composite Index rose roughly twice as rapidly as it did in the preceding two and three-quarters years, was so extreme that it clearly constituted a speculative bubble, an increase in prices so divorced from reasonable estimates of the companies' future prospects that it could not be sustained—and it wasn't. In the following twelve months, the Nasdaq fell roughly 60 percent, wiping out all its gains since 1998 and harming particularly those investors who got in toward the end of its run-up. Many of these were relatively inexperienced investors who bought stocks on-line, using the very technology—computers, high-speed telecommunications, and the Internet—in which they were investing.

The stock market not only reflected the changes under way in the economy and the excessive expectations that frequently accompanied them; it also helped to bring them about. If anything, the stock market in the 1980s and 1990s played an even bigger role in the economy than it normally does, helping first by rooting out bureaucratic waste and pushing companies to become more efficient and later by providing ready financing for innovative companies. Inevitably, both these pursuits were carried too far, beyond financially responsible bounds and legal and ethical standards; nevertheless, their overall impact remains largely beneficial. In concert with the developing junk-bond market, the stock market in the 1980s enabled aggressive firms and investors to acquire stodgy, poorly performing businesses, hoping to improve their operations or sell their assets to other firms that could use them more effectively. Because these hostile takeovers became so pervasive, the threat of being acquired impelled corporate managers to focus more intensely on reducing unnecessary expenses and boosting productivity and profitability. As a result, despite the excesses and abuses, corporate raiders and leveraged-buyout firms operating in the stock and junk-bond markets in the 1980s were important constructive forces in reconfiguring the old industrial economy.

In the 1990s the stock market played a somewhat different role, financing newly public companies at rates comparable to those of the 1920s, when many of today's major firms first went public, and enabling others to merge and raise capital for expansion and modernization. Unlike the hostile takeovers of the 1980s, which were so effective in breaking up ill-conceived and inefficient conglomerates and in shaking up the established order, the mergers of the 1990s generally were amicable arrangements, negotiated among firms in related lines of business, and typically paid for in shares that were never cheap and were sometimes seriously overvalued. In these and related respects—heightened rates at which firms entered the stock market or left it through mergers, frothy share prices that couldn't be maintained, and deceitful accounting and underhanded deals that accompanied the stock market's wild ride—the stock market of the 1990s was similar to that of the 1920s, the period in which electric power and mass-production methods began to boost productivity growth significantly.

Despite the many similarities between the 1980s and 1990s and the 1920s, there are important differences, particularly the fact that while the stock market crash of 1929 soon became the Great Depression of the 1930s, the stock market collapse that began in the spring of 2000, like that of the junk-bond market in late 1989, resulted in only a relatively mild recession, notwithstanding the sharp fall in business spending on technology equipment, which plunged along with share prices, and the uncertainties created by the terrorist attacks of September 11, 2001, and the corporate scandals that came to light a few months later, both of which reinforced and accentuated existing anxieties about the economy's recovery. We have not had a recession severe enough to be deemed a depression since the 1930s, largely because of the lessons learned from the monetary policy errors of that period, when the Federal Reserve Sysytem (the Fed), notoriously, failed to contain the 1929 crash. Beyond this fundamental advance, the relative mildness of the current recession is due in part to the operating flexibility and financial innovations of the new economy that have allowed companies to better control their operations and diversify and manage their risks, thus helping to maintain productivity growth at rates high enough to prevent the sustained decline in economic activity that is typical of most recessions.

The Business Cycle Dating Committee of the National Bureau of Economic Research (NBER), a private, nonprofit research organization that has been the recognized judge of U.S. business cycles since 1961,* has emphasized that even though employment, industrial pro-

---

*The NBER was founded in 1920 and has always had a strong interest in business cycles, thanks in part to Columbia professor Wesley Clair Mitchell, a key figure in establishing the organization and in focusing its early research on quantitative studies of

duction, and wholesale and retail sales have fallen much as in other recessions, neither personal income nor overall economic activity has declined in a significant or sustained way. The group attributes some of the economy's unusual strength to "the continuation of rapid productivity growth," which has boosted wages and personal in come and kept the gross domestic product (GDP) from falling as much as it generally does. "Output fell less than employment during the recession," the committee wrote in August 2002, "and currently is rising faster than employment because of unusual productivity growth."[6]*

In addition to abnormally strong productivity growth, firm and sensible monetary policy has contributed to the relative tameness of the most recent recession. In sharp contrast to the 1970s, when problems were allowed to get out of hand, the economy in the 1980s and 1990s benefited from unusually good monetary policies enacted under two exceptionally effective Federal Reserve chairmen, Paul Volcker, who became chairman of the Federal Reserve Board in August 1979, and Alan Greenspan, who replaced him in 1987. These policies did not create the new technologies and business methods that are the foundations of the productivity revival and impressive expansions of the last two decades, but they helped to establish an environment in which these innovations could develop and spread throughout the economy. Some of the Fed's most visible and acclaimed successes

---

business cycles. His student Simon Kuznets, who won the 1971 Nobel Prize in economics for his "empirically founded interpretation of economic growth," did much of his work at the NBER from the late 1920s through the early 1960s. The group became the quasi-official judge of U.S. business cycles in 1961, when the Commerce Department announced that it would publish the organization's determinations.

*While a common rule of thumb defines a recession as a period of at least two consecutive quarters of falling GDP, the NBER Business Cycle Dating Committee thinks of recessions more broadly, as periods in which there is "a significant decline in activity spread across the economy, lasting more than a few months, visible in industrial production, employment, real income, and wholesale-retail sales." Thus it concluded in November 2001 that a recession had started in March, and it continued to maintain that judgment through April 2002, even though the GDP had "declined by only 0.3 percent and only for a single quarter." Subsequent data revisions showed that the GDP had fallen in the first three quarters of 2001, although the declines were not severe.

were achieved in defusing potential crises, including those that might have resulted from the sharp fall in share prices in the fall of 1987, or from the collapse of the emerging Asian and Russian economies and from the failure of a prominent hedge fund in the fall of 1998. Similarly, if less dramatically, at the start of 2001, three months before the acknowledged beginning of the recession, the Fed moved aggressively to confront softening economic conditions. Between January 3 and August 17, it lowered interest rates seven times, cutting the federal funds rate from 6.5 percent to 3.5 percent over eight months. Then, in the wake of the September 11 terrorist attacks, it accelerated its intervention, lowering the funds rate to 1.75 percent in four steps over just three months. And about a year later, with the economy still struggling, the Fed lowered interest rates once again, hoping to prevent further softening and to leave the economy in relatively good shape to resume its rise once the remaining effects of the bubble were worked through.

SCHUMPETER'S VISION

This book elaborates the idea that the American economy is now in the early stages of a new epoch of superior productivity growth and prosperity propelled by pervasive new information and communications technologies and complementary changes in business practices. Such a new economy will not produce unlimited prosperity or fully tame the business cycle, but it is remarkable nevertheless and extremely rare, a once-in-a-lifetime phenomenon. Its emergence after a lengthy period of subpar economic performance is consistent with historical experience, with both the broadly cyclical, or wavelike, way in which living standards have grown over the last two centuries and with the prominence of technological and organizational advances in producing this pattern, a growth trajectory that essentially ebbs and flows around a pronounced upward trend.

That the dynamism of capitalist economies is primarily the result of the innovations and technological advances they encourage, and, as a consequence, that the pace of progress is uneven, are the critical insights of the Austrian economist Joseph Schumpeter, who called the process "Creative Destruction." In contrast to most economists of his time (and today), who focused on analyzing "how capitalism administers existing structures," Schumpeter was concerned with how those structures changed over time, with how capitalism "creates and destroys them." "Capitalism," he wrote in his best-known book, *Capitalism, Socialism, and Democracy*, first published in 1942, "is by nature a form or method of economic change," a system that "not only never is but never can be stationary." Economic change, in turn, is driven by innovation, a process "that incessantly revolutionizes the economic structure *from within*, incessantly destroying the old one, incessantly creating a new one." "This process of Creative Destruction," he emphasized, "is the essential fact about capitalism."[7]

Not surprisingly, Schumpeter is now very much in vogue. Born in 1883, he taught at the Universities of Graz and Bonn, served briefly as Austrian minister of finance in 1919, and was president of a Viennese bank that went bankrupt in the mid-1920s. In 1932 he became a professor at Harvard, where he remained until his death in 1950. Fifty years later, he is probably "receiving far more attention," one scholar has written, "than he did in the last decade or so of his life." Even so, much of that interest is one-sided, celebrating his emphasis on the importance of technological advance and innovation but ignoring the accompanying discontinuity that he also stressed, the fact that while the "capitalist process . . . progressively raises the standard of life of the masses," it does so not continuously but "through a sequence of vicissitudes, the severity of which is proportional to the advance." The general process—surely one weakness of Schumpeter's theory is that it is so broad and imprecise, but that may be endemic to grand theories—is one in which major technological advances or discoveries, and associated refinements, improvements, and extensions, create long periods of prosperity that are accompanied by great optimism and speculative euphoria. Their influence ultimately "ebbs away," however, only to be restored eventually, but not without some downtime, by new breakthroughs. The effects of this process can be seen, Schumpeter believed, in the "long waves in economic activity, analysis of which reveals the nature and mechanism of the capitalist process better than anything else."[8]

Schumpeter's view of economic growth and development as a process of creative destruction explains why extrapolating a given tendency too aggressively—whether it be the success of the new industrial state of the 1950s and 1960s, the failure of the tarnished economy of the 1970s, Japan's remarkable rise in the 1980s, or the record-setting expansion of the 1990s—is so frequently dreadfully wrong. It also helps to make clear why it is so hard to build models of the economy that can anticipate its turning points and why, in setting economic policy, we cannot rely on simple rules or formulas. And, ironically, it explains why Schumpeter, and later Galbraith, who seems to have adopted the least insightful part of Schumpeter's work, were so wide of the mark in suggesting that capitalism would evolve into socialism. What is not clear, however, is why, in making this prediction, Schumpeter ignored his own emphasis on the transforming forces of innovation and "industrial mutation," forces that once again have led an extraordinary renewal of the American economy.

Is There a New Economy?

IN THE WAKE of the stock market collapse and economic slowdown of 2000–2002, there has been little talk of a new economy, but in the second half of the 1990s the idea was very much alive, much as it had been in the 1920s. "No one can examine the panorama of business and finance in America during the past half-dozen years without realizing that we are living in a new era," wrote John Moody, founder of Moody's Investors Service, a company engaged in the fundamentally conservative practice of evaluating the soundness of corporate bonds and other securities. The new era, he continued, was one in which "this modern, mechanistic civilization . . . is in the process of perfecting itself."[1] Moody was writing near the end of the 1920s but would hardly have been out of place in the late 1990s. As in the 1920s, the economy and the stock market, propelled in part by revolutionary new technologies—then electricity and the internal combustion engine, now computers and information technology—appeared to have broken all the old rules, unleashing throughout the country unbounded optimism about the future. The economic expansion, which began in April 1991 following a relatively mild recession, became the longest in our history in February 2000 and until the fall of that year still appeared impervious to external or internal pressures. In fact, both economic growth and growth in productivity had accelerated sharply in the last half of the 1990s, more like what happens at the beginning of a boom than the end. At the same time, wages began to grow more rapidly and unemployment remained near 4 percent, the lowest it had been since 1970, yet inflation did not take off. And probably most exhilarating for many people, the stock market continued to surge, defying all traditional methods of valuation, until it began to pull back toward the end of March 2000.

Neither the 1990s nor the 1920s were the first time in which large numbers of people came to think and act as if there were a new economy of unlimited prosperity. In 1873, for example, Walter Bagehot, editor of *The Economist*, wrote of the tendency of businessmen and investors to "fancy the prosperity they see will last always, that it is only the beginning of a greater prosperity."[2] Three decades later, the optimism that accompanied the stock market boom and merger wave at the turn of the twentieth century led the *New York Daily Tribune* to proclaim a "new era" based on a "community of interest." The euphoria was stimulated in part by the great efficiencies that were expected to result from the giant enterprises formed in this period, such as U.S. Steel, which was put together by J. P. Morgan in 1901 and instantly became the world's largest company. It was also inspired by the promise of new technologies, as suggested, for example, by Guglielmo Marconi's transatlantic radio transmission, but both hopes and share prices were carried too far. Looking back at the boom almost forty years later, Alexander Dana Noyes, a financial journalist and editor who had attacked the "speculative movement" in *The Evening Post* as it was occurring, called it "probably . . . the first of such speculative demonstrations in history which based its ideas and conduct on the assumption that we were living in a New Era; that old rules and precedents of finance were obsolete; that things could be safely done to-day which had been dangerous and impossible in the past." In 1901 "this illusion seized on the public mind," he continued, "quite as firmly as it did in 1929. It differed only in the fact that there were no college professors who preached the popular as their new political economy."[3]

Such bouts of speculative excess and new-era thinking have recurred repeatedly over the last two hundred years and probably much longer. It seems not to have mattered very much that their fanciful expectations have always been—and will always be—badly disappointed. The devastation was particularly severe at the end of the Roaring Twenties that Moody celebrated, when the soaring stock market crashed and, because economic policy was so ineffectual, crippled the economy for almost a decade. Yet despite such inevitable corrections, new-era wishfulness and financial bubbles will continue to be, as the MIT economist Charles Kindleberger has put it, "if not inevitable, at least historically common." This is so because outsize hopes and speculative euphoria are inspired by changes in the "economic outlook," often because of noteworthy innovations or discoveries whose likely impact is hard to evaluate precisely. These "new opportunities," Kindleberger writes, are then "seized and overdone, in ways so closely resembling irrationality as to constitute a mania."[4]

The American economy in the 1980s and 1990s basically followed such a course. After emerging in late 1982 from one of the most severe recessions since the 1930s, which did away with the crippling inflation of the prior decade, the economy recovered strongly and continued expanding for an unusually long time. It is well known that the 1990s economic expansion was the nation's longest; less well known is that the 1980s run was the second-longest peacetime expansion and the third-longest overall. Taken together, which seems appropriate since they were separated only by a very mild and short recession, they constitute what has been called "the long boom."[5] In addition to its longevity, the boom was marked by unusually robust stock markets and by the development of ever more exciting new technologies that were embodied in new goods and services that permeated everyday life. Although the presence of these new technologies was undeniable, it was extremely difficult to gauge the impact they were likely to have on the economy. With no good guidelines, at least none that people cared to consult, it was understandable that imaginations might run wild, particularly since the country's standing in the world seemed to be exploding along with the technologies, the economy, and the stock market. The growing prestige and economic strength of the United States were accentuated by the simultaneous collapse of Communism and of the Japanese economy and by the infiltration of American culture—music, movies, basketball, and on and on—into every corner of the world, no matter how poor or repressed. Moreover, the rapid diffusion of American goods and ideas, and their large impact on the world, were in part attributable to the new information and communications technologies, particularly fax machines, cell phones, personal computers, and the Internet. Together with growing individual control over retirement funds, these new technologies also drew many more Americans into the stock market.

All these developments, and many more, were reflected in people's euphoric view of both the future and company shares, especially technology stocks. After rising unusually rapidly for almost two decades, and incredibly in the last few years of the century, the stock market finally reached a peak in March 2000 and fell significantly over the next eighteen months. The economy crested about a year after the stock market did, and as in earlier hoped-for new eras, softening economic conditions, falling share prices, and corporate scandals, which emerged somewhat later, shattered the faith of all but the truest believers in the fanciful prospect of limitless prosperity. Nevertheless, there is a consequential, albeit more restrained, sense in which we can call today's economy "new." And ironically, evidence supporting this more limited notion of a new economy gathered force just as the optimism and confidence propelling the grander, more utopian vision were waning.

WHAT MAKES AN ECONOMY NEW?

Whatever else we might wish it were, a new economy is one that has changed significantly through the adoption of innovative new technologies and business practices, leading to a meaningful and sustainable increase in the rate of productivity growth. Such a new economy cannot overcome the fundamental limits with which all economies must contend, and it will not last forever, but it is extraordinary and hardly common. Thought of in this way, a new economy is not very different from an economic or industrial "revolution" or "age," terms also used to mark the development of pathbreaking new technologies and new organizations to exploit them, resulting in relatively long spans of higher productivity growth.

None of these notions of economic newness and large-scale change is very well defined, but faster productivity growth and unusual technological and organizational advance are central to all of them. The most commonly acknowledged sea change in economic life is probably the "industrial revolution," but, as the Harvard economic historian David Landes has pointed out, even this term is used in at least three different ways. When applied most specifically, it denotes the innovations and technological discoveries that were first applied in England in the mid- to late eighteenth century and brought about the "shift from handicrafts to manufacture," the first major step in the development of a modern economy. Throughout the last few centuries, this transformation took place at different times in all of the relatively advanced countries of the world, and a broader use of the term refers to this group of similar revolutions. Finally, and much more generally, the name can be construed, as it is in the preceding paragraph, as referring to an unusual and lasting increase in productivity growth resulting from "any rapid significant technological change." When used in this way, Landes writes, there are "as many 'revolutions' as there are historically demarcated sequences of industrial innovation."[6]

Judging which sequences of innovation and technological advance are important enough to be deemed a revolution, a new era, or a new economy, however, will never be unambiguous and, as is true of the standard proposed in this chapter, is likely to be based on historical comparisons. But using productivity growth as the fundamental gauge or measuring rod is straightforward. Productivity growth is probably the single most significant feature of an economy, the principal source of long-term growth in average living standards, a concept to which it is closely related. Productivity is most commonly measured as an economy's total output of goods and services per hour of labor expended. Because aggregate hours of work grow fairly slowly and steadily, productivity growth also is the major determinant of an economy's "speed limit," the rate at which its capacity to produce—its economic potential—is increasing. When an economy operating near "full employment" exceeds its speed limit, it risks serious inflation. Hours of work in the United States have been growing at about 1 percent a year; assuming that the productivity improvements of the late 1990s discussed later in this chapter are lasting, the economy can safely grow at more than 3.5 percent a year, 2.5 percent or more because of productivity growth and 1 percent reflecting the rise in hours worked. If, on the other hand, productivity grows even more rapidly once the economy recovers from the recession and sustains that pace for a while—a possibility that is at least as likely as a subsequent slowdown in productivity growth—then the economy's potential growth rate will increase apace.

While productivity is generally measured by output per hour worked, average living standards can be approximated by income per capita or output per person, identical concepts for the economy as a whole. Since hours of work tend to move with population over extended periods of time, living standards tend to grow in line with productivity over the long term. But these growth rates can diverge over shorter periods as working patterns change, and the differences between them can be substantial. For much of the nineteenth century, for example, population grew very rapidly, but the economy grew even faster and living standards rose by more than 1 percent a year. This was the period in which the industrial revolution took hold in America, when large numbers of people left farms and rural areas to work in the rising urban factories that were transforming the American economy much as the English economy had been revolutionized in the last part of the eighteenth century and the decades that followed. Improving transportation and communications networks, including roads, canals, steamboats, railroads, and the telegraph, increased mobility of both people and goods, making possible the extensive division of labor that distinguishes factory from craft production. Compared with artisanal shops, factories were much bigger and more mechanized, and jobs were far more narrowly defined and required limited skills, making them accessible to the migrants from the farms and other workers with little training. The new system was also more productive than the old one, but because hours worked grew more rapidly than population, productivity grew roughly half as fast as living standards. Average living standards also grew much more rapidly than productivity in the 1970s and 1980s as more women and baby boomers entered the labor force and their increased participation in market-based work partially made up for slower productivity growth. The influx of these inexperienced workers may also have depressed productivity growth below what it would have been were they more seasoned, thus muting the impact of their numbers. (Productivity growth and growth in living standards in the 1970s and 1980s, and in the first half of the nineteenth century, are shown in the table on page 28, which describes their evolution over the last two hundred years.)[7]

Despite such periodic differences, productivity and living standards have risen quite similarly, and remarkably, over the last few centuries, multiplying in the United States by ten to fifteen times in the last one hundred years, but they have not done so continuously. Rather, they have tended to grow particularly rapidly in sustained spurts of unusual prosperity, propelled by the adoption of especially powerful and far-reaching new technologies and innovations, while lagging or falling at times in between, sometimes disastrously, as in the Great Depression. That the dynamism of capitalist economies is primarily the result of the learning, innovations, and technological advances they encourage and, as a consequence, that the pace of progress is uneven in the short term but relatively steady and pronounced over the long term are, as we have seen, perspectives associated most closely with Joseph Schumpeter. Schumpeter epitomized a style of grand theorizing that fell out of favor in the postwar push toward greater precision in economics. In the excitement about the apparent emergence of a new economy, however, he practically became a cult figure, and "Creative Destruction," the evocative phrase he used to portray the process of innovation and economic change, seemed to be everywhere, an almost mandatory reference in commentary about the economy.

Although not formulated precisely, Schumpeter's general view of economic growth rests on two basic propositions that have been solidly established in the decades since his death in 1950. First, due largely to the work of the Nobel laureate Robert Solow and Moses Abramovitz, it is widely agreed that innovation and technological advance are the major determinants of long-term growth in productivity and living standards. Before that, most economists thought that growth depended mainly on capital investment and, as a result, that an underdeveloped economy with a large supply of potential workers could, Solow has written, "jack up its rate of industrial growth merely by increasing its investment." This one-sided view of the growth process influenced the policies of institutions such as the World Bank for a long time, perhaps because it is easier to boost stocks of physical capital than to establish institutions that are conducive to growth or to raise levels of "human capital" and technical skills that are now recognized as vital to sustained economic progress. But, as Solow emphasized, if economic development was as easy as the old perspective made it seem, "it would be hard to understand why more poor countries did not follow that route to rapid growth."[8]

Support for the second proposition underpinning the Schumpeterian vision has been developed by economic historians such as Abramovitz and his Stanford colleagues Paul David and Nathan Rosenberg, who have shown that the development of new technologies and innovations is highly uneven, unpredictable, and prolonged, even after the initial discoveries. In 1939 Schumpeter had pointed out that "major innovations hardly ever emerge in their final form or cover in one throw the whole field that will ultimately be their own." And, as if to emphasize his observation, although in this case it would not be clear for half a century, *The New York Times* in December 1947 reported the invention of the transistor in a minor story on an inside page and suggested only that it might be useful in developing better hearing aids. Similarly, in 1949 Thomas J. Watson Sr., president of IBM, could see only a small potential market for computers. As it turned out, the invention of the transistor was probably the critical element of the information revolution, leading over the next twenty-five years to the development of the integrated circuit and micro-processor, which made possible the design of increasingly powerful and efficient computers, greatly expanded data storage capacity, and, together with the laser and fiber optics, enabled information to be transmitted at incredibly faster speeds. Aspects of these stories are discussed in the next few chapters. Here the focus is on the trajectory of economic growth in the United States over the last two hundred years.[9]

PRODUCTIVITY GROWTH OVER THE LAST TWO CENTURIES

Both productivity and living standards have grown remarkably over the last two hundred years, especially during the twentieth century, when they rose by at least 2 percent a year on average, but such very long-term trends obscure the great variability in growth rates that is apparent when they are measured over shorter periods. In addition to being affected by the irregular pace of innovation and technological advance, productivity growth in the short term reflects the impact of factors such as wars and depressions and the recoveries that follow, creating further, and more pronounced, volatility. Although events such as these are relatively rare, productivity growth, when looked at over narrow spans of time, also varies with the phases of the business cycle, which is neither as regular nor as precise as its name implies.*

---

*Business-cycle dates are determined, as noted in the Introduction, by the NBER, a nonprofit organization that is the recognized arbiter of such matters. A cycle consists essentially of two consecutive phases: an expansion and a recession. An expansion runs

Productivity typically grows rapidly in the early years of an expansion as the economy recovers from recession and business picks up, and slows as the economy nears a peak and the onset of a new recession, but this general pattern did not hold in the 1990s, when productivity growth accelerated in the second half of the upswing. Moreover, since World War II, business-cycle contractions have gotten shorter and expansions longer, most notably in the 1980s and 1990s, when the expansions were exceptionally long and the recessions unusually brief and mild, at least in part because of the new technologies and business practices that enabled companies to better manage their operations and control their inventories. The expansion that ran from November 1982 through July 1990 lasted 92 months, and the recession that followed was only 8 months long, far better than the postwar averages of 43 months and 11 months, respectively. The subsequent expansion was even longer, continuing for a record 120 months from March 1991 through March 2001, and the recession that followed looks as if it, too, will be relatively mild if not less than average length.[10]

Establishing a clear and meaningful picture of how different historical eras have contributed to the seemingly steady rise of productivity over the last few centuries, and of the relationships, if any, between these contributions and the forcefulness of innovation in different periods, requires taking adequate account of the factors that may have caused temporary fluctuations in productivity growth. At the very least, adjustments should be made for the effects of the Civil War, the Great Depression, and World War II, and growth rates for the different historical periods should be calculated between points that span comparable parts of the business cycles that make them up.

from a trough in economic activity to a subsequent peak, which marks the onset of a recession. A depression is an unusually severe recession, while a growth recession is a period in which the economy grows much slower than its potential. It may encompass a recession but need not do so. In the five peacetime business cycles between 1919 and 1945, the average contraction lasted twenty months and the average expansion twenty-six months; by contrast, in the seven peacetime cycles from 1945 to 1991, the length of the average contraction fell to eleven months, while the average expansion increased to forty-three months.

One attempt to deal with these issues, a careful and comprehensive study of American economic growth over the last two centuries by Abramovitz and David, shows quite clearly that when productivity growth is compared across successive periods of fifteen to twenty-five years, each of which encompasses several smaller business cycles, it fluctuates unevenly from one such "long interval" to the next. On the other hand, when measured over longer periods of approximately fifty years, each spanning two long intervals, productivity growth appears surprisingly even, accelerating in a series of regular steps from one "long period" to the next.

More specifically, as shown in the main part of the table on page 28, which has been constructed from the data compiled by Abramovitz and David, the average rate of productivity growth over long periods more than doubled between the first and the second half of the nineteenth century, and doubled again between the second half of the nineteenth century and the first third of the twentieth century. It rose another 25 percent in the second third of the century, before falling precipitously in the 1970s and 1980s. Yet despite this relatively steady acceleration across successive long periods spanning more than 150 years, when these half centuries are split into shorter intervals of roughly 20 years each, there is substantial variation in the rate of productivity growth from one long interval to the next, a "succession of slowdowns and accelerations" that can be seen clearly in the first part of the table. Moreover, the authors point out, if the record were evaluated over even shorter spans, the fluctuations would be sharper still.[11]*

---

*Abramovitz and David call the fifty-year spans "long periods" and the fifteen-to-twenty-five-year intervals that make them up "long-swing intervals." As constructed, each long period consists of a pair of long-swing intervals, one in which productivity growth was relatively slow, followed by a second one in which growth rebounded from the depressed rates of the first. One such low-growth interval includes the years surrounding the Civil War; another encompasses both the Great Depression and World War II. In addition, productivity growth rates for the long-swing intervals were calculated between comparable points of the constituent business cycles, while growth rates for the longer periods were calculated between similar parts of their constituent long-swing intervals.

TABLE I. *Growth in Productivity and Living Standards, 1800–1989*

LONG INTERVALS	PRODUCTIVITY GROWTH (%)	LONG PERIODS	PRODUCTIVITY GROWTH (%)	PERCENTAGE DUE TO TECHNOLOGICAL CHANGE	GROWTH IN OUTPUT PER PERSON
1800–35	0.41				
1835–55	0.37	1800–55	0.39	51	0.87
1855–71	0.14				
1871–90	1.84	1855–90	1.06	35	1.47
1890–1905	1.36				
1905–29	2.45	1890–1929	2.01	69	1.74
1929–48	1.96				
1948–66	3.11	1929–66	2.52	83	1.73
1966–89	1.23			54	1.84
1990–1995	1.46				1.24
1996–2000	2.66				3.09
1990–2000	2.01				2.08
1967–2000	1.88				2.13

The main body of the table, which covers the years 1800–1989, was constructed from data developed by Abramovitz and David for the private domestic economy. See "Two Centuries of Macroeconomic Growth," especially Tables I:I, I:IV, I:IV–Addendum, and I:IA–I:IVA. The information in the lower part of the table, which covers the years 1990–2000 and 1967–2000, was calculated from Bureau of Labor Statistics data on productivity growth for the business sector, Bureau of Economic Analysis data on real GDP, and Bureau of the Census data on population.

The overall pattern that emerges from this study, one in which the fluctuations in productivity growth from one twenty-year interval to the next give rise to a much more regular stepwise acceleration across consecutive fifty-year periods, shows up even more clearly in Figure 1, which pictures the data from the table above. The jagged line that rises from the lower left to the upper-right-hand corner of

FIGURE 1. *Productivity Growth Across Long Intervals and Long Periods, 1800–1989*

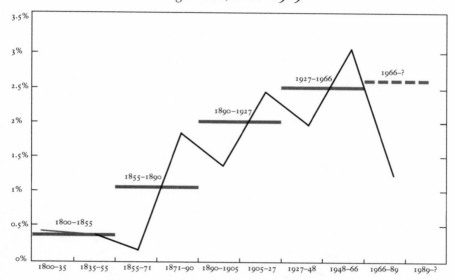

This figure was constructed from the data in the table on page 28.

the page connects productivity growth rates for twenty-year intervals, while the horizontal lines, which shift upward every fifty years or so, show them for successive long periods. When looked at in this way, there can be no question that the steady long-term trend in productivity growth has been established through a small number of jumps that were sustained over relatively long periods. But the long-period growth rates, like the century-long trends, also mask substantial volatility among their component long intervals. The steady progression of productivity growth from one long period to the next reflects the net effect of the fluctuations across these shorter intervals, whose growth rates themselves incorporate variations over still shorter spans.

The clarity of the image in the figure is partly a result of the specific way in which it was constructed. Dividing the last two centuries into shorter periods of significant length tones down many of the irregular features of American growth and development so that important aspects of the underlying pattern are more visible. The question is not whether something like this should be done; rather, it is whether this particular analysis of the data strikes the right balance between the longer- and shorter-term aspects of productivity growth; whether, in other words, it yields a useful picture of how the long-term trend of productivity growth has been generated. Abramovitz and David are relatively unique, for example, in dating the productivity slowdown of the 1970s and 1980s from 1966 rather than 1973, as is more typical, but that is a minor point. More important, their profile of economic progress in the United States is appealing because they followed sensible procedures and because the successive long periods of increasingly rapid productivity growth they uncovered roughly match the important waves of innovation that have occurred since the end of the eighteenth century.[12]

Even in retrospect, however, technological breakthroughs cannot be identified unambiguously, and some scholars reject the view that there have been a number of relatively discrete bursts of critically important innovations over the last two centuries. For example, Douglass North, a Nobel Prize–winning economic historian, thinks that modern productivity growth derives from a single economic revolution that began in the second part of the nineteenth century, one grounded in "the development of the scientific disciplines and the wedding of science and technology." In this regard he is not very different from Alfred North Whitehead, who thought "the invention of the method of invention" should be considered "the greatest invention of the 19th century."[13] More typically, though, historians believe there were two, or possibly three, main bursts of innovation in the century and a half before World War II, and the economic revolutions they produced match the long periods reasonably well: first, an industrial revolution based on steam power, iron machinery, and coal, which began in England in the 1780s and took hold in the United States during the nineteenth century; and second, a revolution based on electric power, the internal combustion engine, and petrochemicals, which began to affect the American economy significantly after

World War I and continued, with notable interruptions, through the 1950s and 1960s.

The relationship between these major economic transformations and Abramovitz and David's long periods is at best approximate, however, primarily because the revolutions are impossible to define and date precisely. Profound economic changes do not occur evenly or neatly; rather, these fundamental makeovers tend to build unevenly over prolonged periods as the underlying innovations evolve and spread and businesses learn how to use the new technologies effectively and make necessary changes in their operating methods. Moreover, as Schumpeter observed more than sixty years ago, major economic upheavals are propelled by large "clusters" of innovations for which "the periods of gestation and absorption of effects by the economic system will not, in general, be equal," making some advances more important in certain phases of the process and others more prominent at different times. Thus some people think there was a third significant jolt to the American economy, the so-called railway age of the second half of the nineteenth century, when advances in railroad technology made possible the building of a nationwide rail system in which larger trains would eventually carry passengers and freight across longer rail lines spanning the entire country. In the 1880s alone, for example, seventy-five thousand miles of railroad tracks were laid, a record amount for any country in any prior decade.[14]

The last half of the nineteenth century also witnessed the commercialization of telegraph service, the development of networks for gathering and transmitting news and financial information, and the emergence, as Alfred Chandler has emphasized, of large multidivisional companies capable of managing large flows of goods and information across broad geographical areas. These innovations reinforced and supported one another, and grew together. Modern transportation and communications systems were "built, operated, enlarged, and coordinated," Chandler writes, "by large hierarchical firms." Because telegraph service, which first became available in the late 1840s, was so important in enabling the large and growing railroads to control their far-flung operations, the railroads helped the telegraph companies extend and maintain their lines and operated telegraph offices in their stations and depots. By providing the means for disseminating news and financial information as well as for transporting raw materials and finished goods, these growing telegraph and rail networks also stimulated the development of grain exchanges and commodity futures markets and expanded the reach of the New York Stock Exchange. Nationwide news-gathering services grew up, too, including the New York Associated Press, precursor of the AP, which was formed in 1848 and was capable of distributing news stories throughout the country by 1859. Mail service improved as the postal system, using the expanding transportation and communications networks to overhaul and streamline its operating methods, began sorting and dispatching mail from moving trains rather than first taking it to central hubs. And by the early 1880s, a decade after the telephone was invented, the Bell Company had established service in most major cities and was moving to construct a nationwide telephone system. Even so, because much of what was new in this period resulted from further exploitation of the steam engine and iron machinery and further elaboration of products and services already available, it seems appropriate to think of it as an important phase of the first industrial revolution rather than an equivalent upheaval, as calling it an "age" rather than a "revolution" suggests.[15]

Now we think we are at the beginning of a fourth prolonged period of superior prosperity, a new economy based on information and communications technology. How should it be judged? For the emerging new economy to maintain the progressive acceleration in productivity growth across the last two centuries, it must be sufficiently forceful to make up for the collapse in the 1970s and 1980s and raise the long-term rate of growth. The problem is deciding which long-term rate to use as a standard. Because productivity growth has increased steadily from one long period to the next, the earlier we begin, the lower the average rate of growth, and hence the easier the test. If, for example, we use as the standard the rate of productivity growth from 1855 to 1973, the test is relatively easy: the new economy must be strong enough to boost productivity growth from 1973 onward to more than 1.9 percent a year, about a third above its average from 1973 to 1995. This could be achieved if productivity grows by roughly 2.5 percent a year for the next fifteen years, slightly slower than it grew from 1996 to 2000, but there are many other combinations of growth rates and durations that will yield the same result. If, on the other hand, we use the period from 1890 to 1973 as the measuring rod, productivity growth after 1973 would have to average more than 2.25 percent a year. This goal implies that productivity will have to grow by close to 3 percent a year for the next twenty-five years, a rate that is roughly double that of the 1970s and 1980s and comparable to the pace achieved in the golden age of the 1950s and 1960s, but not much faster than the tempo in the last three years of the 1990s expansion. Finally, for the yet-to-be-completed long period beginning in 1973 and extending at least through the first few decades of the twenty-first century, it would be far tougher to require that productivity grow faster than it did from 1929 through 1966 (or through 1973). Although this criterion would ensure that the new economy maintains the pattern described by Abramovitz and David, in which productivity growth accelerated across successive fifty-year periods spanning the last two centuries, it may be unfair. As they point out, the extraordinary productivity growth of the golden age, which constitutes the constructive half of this long period, was due in part to "many quite special conditions . . . in both the US and international economy," which were temporary in nature and thus wore out eventually, another reason that the subsequent decline in productivity growth was so severe. Indeed, by 1989 productivity was roughly half as great as it would have been had the golden-age growth path been maintained.[16]

The exceptional performance of the golden postwar years was in a sense the culmination of the economic transformation based on electric power, automobiles, chemicals, and mass production, which had been interrupted by the Great Depression and World War II. And when these constraints were finally lifted, the impact of the underlying economic forces was amplified by pent-up demands that could not be satisfied during the Depression or war years or by the recovery of the war-torn economies of Europe and Japan. In fact, a noted new-economy skeptic views the path of productivity growth since 1870 not as a secular progression but as "one big wave" that began to build after World War I, crested during the golden age, and then fell back toward the much lower rates of the late nineteenth century, which he thinks are more typical. Yet while a falloff from the rates attained during the golden age was inevitable—the consequence of the aging of the old mass-production regime and the exhaustion of the special stimulants that enhanced economic growth after World War II—it, too, may have been overdone, in part because the complacency and inertia of the bureaucracies that ran American companies made it especially hard for them to cope with new challenges, thus helping to make the tarnished age so tired and weak.[17]

Fifty years after the golden age, similar forces are at work in the economy, including powerful new information and communications technologies and complementary new business practices, as well as growth in world trade and investment resulting in part from the fall of Communism, the end of the Cold War, and the spread of market-based economies. Although we might wish it had happened sooner, it is hardly surprising that productivity growth eventually began to accelerate sharply, rising by more than 2.5 percent a year from 1996 through 2000 and by about 2.75 percent a year in the last three years of that span. Productivity rose by 3 percent in 2000 and has held up extraordinarily well during the recession, growing by 1.1 percent in 2001, not much below its average from 1973 through 1995, and by slightly under 5 percent a year in 2002. Although it is still too soon to know for sure whether a lasting new trend of productivity growth has been established, or how powerful it will be, the depth and importance of the changes over the last twenty-five years strongly suggest that a truly new economy has begun to emerge. And since we are still in the early stages of its evolution, there is reason to think that the best is yet to come.

THE PRODUCTIVITY PARADOX

Since at least the mid-1980s it has been apparent that something different has been happening in the economy, particularly in comparison to the 1970s, when the economy was hamstrung by stagflation, the unusual combination of high unemployment and high inflation. Between 1969 and 1983, there were four recessions, the rates of unemployment and inflation both averaged more than 6.5 percent annually, and pessimism reigned. Ronald Reagan captured the presidency in 1980 largely because the "misery index"—a measure he developed and trumpeted at every opportunity—the sum of the rates of unemployment and inflation, was more than 20 percent, a record by a large margin. In contrast, except for the unusually mild and short recession in 1990–1991, the economy grew almost continuously between the recession of 1981–1982, one of the harshest since the Great Depression, and the one that began in March 2001. Moreover, both unemployment and inflation fell significantly during the extended eighteen-year expansion, and while unemployment has risen more than usual in the latest downturn, productivity growth has been relatively strong, and personal income and total output have fallen less than usual, while inflation declined even further.

The long expansion benefited from unusually good monetary policy, but it was driven primarily by increased global competition, continuing diffusion of new information and communications technologies, adoption of new business practices capable of using them effectively, and the proliferation of new financial products and services that both reflected and encouraged these developments. Computers, pagers, cell phones, and other equipment for processing and transmitting information spread rapidly, and companies restructured their operations dramatically, reducing excessive inventories and wasteful layers of administration, focusing their efforts on those lines of business in which they had the greatest competitive advantages, and generally trying to operate more flexibly, which frequently involved allowing workers to make more decisions on their own and tying more of their pay to how well they performed. In making these far-reaching and difficult changes, corporations were aided, encouraged, and sometimes compelled by more assertive investors and more open financial markets, particularly the stock and junk-bond markets, which played such an important role in the efficiency-enhancing wave of mergers and acquisitions, leveraged buyouts, and hostile takeovers of the 1980s and funded many new and reconfigured businesses.

The advent of the Internet and on-line stock trading in the mid-1990s, together with the growth of incentive-based compensation, such as stock options and profit sharing, and of 401(k) retirement plans, in which employees exercise more control over investment decisions, involved a growing proportion of the population in the stock market, increasing its sway over people's lives and opinions. And at least until the collapse of technology stocks, and the accounting scandals and shady practices that subsequently came to light, it seemed that "attitudes about wealth" were changing, two *Wall Street Journal* reporters observed, "as more Americans either experience it, or hope to do so in the future." This may have helped to explain the breadth of support for issues such as repeal of the estate tax, cuts in the capital-gains tax, and privatization of Social Security. It may also have been a factor in the decline of unionization and the even sharper fall in strikes since the late 1970s. At the same time, the influx of so many new investors, together with a tendency to overestimate the immediate implications of wondrous new technology, undoubtedly helped create the bubble in technology stocks in the late 1990s.[18]

These mutually reinforcing changes in technology, business practices, and financial markets were further strengthened during the last two decades by deregulation of many industries and by growth in world trade and cross-border investments—globalization—that made competition more intense. The resulting vigor of the American economy, combined with the fall of Communism and the end of the Cold

War at the close of the 1980s, the dramatic decline of the Japanese economy that began at about the same time, and the continued stagnation of much of Europe, created in the world a growing sense of U.S. economic dominance. By the end of the century, even a Green Party member of Germany's parliament could say about the American economy, "In the current political debate, there is no other model," a judgment that cannot be attributed entirely to the effects of the bubble.[19]

Despite such gathering evidence of broad and deep changes in the economy, however, until the mid-1990s productivity continued to languish in the rut into which it had fallen in the early 1970s. And because it takes time for a new, higher trend to be established, it was not fully clear that productivity growth had picked up until the end of the decade. Until then, the emerging new economy seemed limited, perhaps even fatally, the victim of an apparent "productivity paradox," which was highlighted in Robert Solow's observation: "You can see the computer everywhere but in the productivity statistics." Solow made the comment in a 1987 book review, in response to the authors' contention that they did not have to show why new technologies were likely to "produce a break with past patterns of productivity growth" in order to establish their significance. "What this means," he wrote, "is that they, like everybody else, are somewhat embarrassed by the fact that what everyone feels to have been a technological revolution, a drastic change in our productive lives, has been accompanied everywhere, including Japan, by a slowing down of productivity growth, not by a step up."[20] Of course, in 1987 things were very different from how they are today. Japan was at the height of its economic powers, the envy of most of the developed world. Indeed, many pundits were suggesting that its future was almost unlimited, and America's bleak.

Japan's ascent lasted only a few more years, but it took almost a decade for productivity growth in the United States to accelerate significantly. It finally began to pick up after 1995, rising over the next five years at a rate of more than 2.5 percent a year, almost twice as fast as its pace between 1973 and 1995 and within striking distance of the rates achieved during the golden age of 1948–1973. The surge during the last half of the 1990s raised the average growth rates of productivity and living standards for the entire decade to roughly 2 percent a year, about the same as for the century as a whole. And because compounding magnifies small differences in growth rates, whether or not these faster rates can be maintained, or even rise, has large implications. If, for example, living standards continue to grow by 2 percent a year, they will double every thirty-five years, about a generation and a half. If, however, these growth rates fall back to 1.5 percent a year, roughly the pace at which they had been stuck from 1973 through 1995, it would take approximately fifty years for living standards to double.

WHAT CAUSED THE REVIVAL
OF PRODUCTIVITY GROWTH?

The most important questions about the productivity revival in the United States have to do with what caused it and whether it is likely to last. Since the late 1990s, a wide and growing body of evidence has shown that the revival is diffused throughout the economy, that it is largely due to the use of information technology and related improvements in the way businesses operate, and that much of it is likely to be long-lasting. Before reviewing these findings, however, we should highlight two general features of the data. First, as emphasized in the discussion of American productivity growth over the last two centuries, and shown even more clearly for the postwar years in Figure 2, productivity growth jumps around considerably from quarter to quarter and from year to year, making it hard to identify new trends or breaks in old ones. Identifying a new trend is particularly difficult for the period since 1995, because it is so short. Nevertheless, statistical tests based on data through late 2000 confirm the general impression of "structural breaks" in trend productivity growth both in 1973, when it fell, and in 1995, when it rose.[21]

Second, despite our advanced system of economic measurement,

FIGURE 2. *U.S. Productivity Growth, January 1948 Through September 2002*

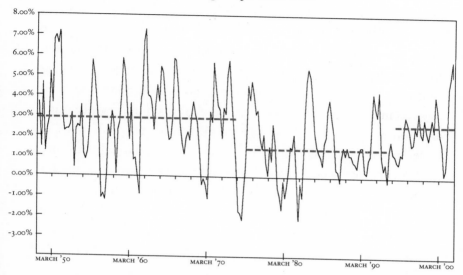

For each quarter of a year, the figure shows the annual percentage change in output per hour from the corresponding quarter of a year earlier. The horizontal lines show the average rates of productivity growth for the subperiods 1948–1973 (2.9 percent), 1974–1995 (1.4 percent), and 1996 through the third quarter of 2002 (2.6 percent). The data are for nonfarm businesses and are available at www.bls.gov.

many difficulties persist, especially in accounting for new and improved goods and services and for "intangible" investments, such as expenditures for reconfiguring plants, developing new operating methods, and training workers to perform effectively in the new environment. These problems are particularly acute in periods of great change such as the present one, and although they are addressed continually, they are far from solved. In fact, as discussed in the next chapter, some of the problems may be largely unsolvable. Even so, relatively modest improvements in the data can have important consequences. For example, in its last periodic revision of the national income and product accounts, the Commerce Department's Bureau of Economic Analysis made a number of changes that altered the pattern of productivity growth since the 1950s. The revised data were released in October 1999 and showed that since 1977 the economy had grown approximately 10 percent faster than previously thought. Most notable, the new procedures classified computer software purchases as investments rather than routine business costs, recognizing belatedly that software is useful over a period of years.* This change alone raised economic growth by approximately 0.2 percentage points a year (almost 10 percent) over the period 1987–1998. Although it did not help much in dating the productivity revival, it was useful in explaining it, thus putting the acceleration on a much sounder basis. A second important revision, one resulting from the annual review of the national income and product accounts in 2000, adjusted downward earlier estimates of economic growth in the years 1998–2000, largely because software investment was revised downward in each of these years. This lowered productivity growth in the late 1990s by about 15 percent but left intact the acceleration in the second half of the decade, even if it was less pronounced.[22]

In trying to explain productivity growth, economists typically use a procedure independently developed by Solow and Abramovitz in the late 1950s. This method of "growth accounting" attributes labor productivity growth to two basic sources, increases in the capital equipment that can be used by workers (capital equipment per hour of labor or "capital intensity"), and changes in the effectiveness with which workers use that capital, a concept called "total factor productivity" (TFP) or "multifactor productivity." Total factor productivity captures all improvements in the economy's ability to produce *beyond* those that can be explained by changes in the basic factors of production, labor, and capital. It is our best measure of technological

---

* The differences between expensing and capitalizing business expenditures can be large. In calculating corporate profits or "value added" in producing final products, the costs of raw materials and intermediate goods, such as steel used in making automobiles, are deducted fully from revenues as they are incurred—they are expensed. Costs of capital investments such as machinery and equipment, on the other hand, are capitalized and depreciated over the useful lives of the equipment. Thus, if the useful life of the equipment is thought to be five years, one-fifth of its cost would be deducted from revenues each year under the straight-line method of depreciation.

progress, organizational innovation, and gains in overall efficiency, but it is relatively crude and unsatisfying. Impossible to measure directly, it must be calculated as a *residual*, the increase in labor productivity that cannot be explained by greater capital intensity. Moreover, the distinction between productivity improvements due to technological advances and those due to greater investment in capital equipment is far from clear, because technical improvements are to a great extent "embodied" in new equipment and may, therefore, induce investment. In addition, the method assumes that all capital investment boosts productivity, even if it is not useful or not needed. For both these reasons, growth accounts tend to overstate the contribution of capital investment and understate that of technology. Even without these problems, however, total factor productivity would be, as Abramovitz pointed out when the concept began to be used, "a measure of our ignorance about the causes of economic growth." Identifying these causes, he emphasized, "will, no doubt, remain the central problem in both the history and theory of economic growth."[23]

Despite these difficulties, or perhaps because of them, there is a strong consensus about the critical role of information technology (IT) in the productivity acceleration in the second half of the 1990s. Computers and other equipment for processing, storing, and transmitting information contribute to overall productivity in three ways. First, because the technology sector is an expanding part of the economy, advances in producing IT equipment not only boost productivity directly but are increasingly important for overall productivity growth. Second, progress in producing IT equipment improves its performance and lowers its prices, further stimulating its use throughout the economy, thus raising capital intensity and productivity in other sectors. And third, because the new technology allows businesses to make deeper and more extensive improvements in the way they operate, it enables them to become even more efficient. In other words, productivity growth has risen because of increased productivity in the *production* of IT equipment *and* because of greater *use* of information technology throughout the economy. And while more than half of its overall increase can be attributed to these effects of information technology, productivity growth has also accelerated outside the technology sector, and efficiency gains in the rest of the economy account for about a third of the acceleration in economy-wide productivity growth. No less important, because its impact is likely to be longer-lasting, faster growth in total factor productivity throughout the economy contributed more to the revival of labor productivity growth than did growing capital intensity.

All of the major studies of productivity growth in the late 1990s used the same basic methodology and reached very similar conclusions. They found that compared with the slow rates of growth that persisted between 1973 and 1995, labor productivity growth increased by roughly 1.2 percentage points a year from 1995 through 2000, a rise of more than 80 percent. They also show that faster growth in total factor productivity accounts for approximately 60 percent of the acceleration, while greater investment in IT equipment accounts for the remainder. The studies differ mainly in allocating the rise in overall efficiency between the IT sector, primarily computers and semiconductors, and the rest of the economy. On average, however, they find that technological advances in the IT sector account for about half of the acceleration in TFP, while efficiency gains in the rest of the economy explain the other half or slightly more. Expressed somewhat differently, the overall acceleration in labor productivity growth can be attributed to three relatively equal factors: technological advances in producing computers and semiconductors; more rapid growth of total factor productivity in sectors that use the equipment; and greater investment in information processing and communications equipment.[24]

WILL IT LAST?

There are three good reasons for thinking that the acceleration of productivity growth in the last half of the 1990s marks the beginning of a new long interval of more rapid gains in productivity, one that is likely to persist for the next several decades or even longer. First, more than half of the acceleration is due to faster growth of total factor productivity. Unlike productivity gains resulting from greater capital intensity, which are sensitive to the ups and downs of investment spending and are ultimately limited by diminishing returns, those due to superior technology and better operating methods are more enduring. Second, the acceleration seems to have been widespread, not highly concentrated in narrow segments of the economy, making it less likely that it was caused by chance or by idiosyncratic improvements in particular sectors. It also makes the acceleration less vulnerable to reversals in any one area. Third, very little of the acceleration appears to have been cyclical, a consequence of the expansionary phase of the business cycle and thus relatively short-lived. Indeed, there is evidence that in the last part of the decade businesses had trouble coping with the rapid surge in technology investment, which grew so quickly that they could not absorb the new equipment effectively, thus depressing productivity growth below what it would have been had investment increased more gradually.

Investment in information-processing equipment and software grew by more than 20 percent a year in the late 1990s and by about 16 percent a year for the entire decade, almost three times as fast as all business investment. As a result, technology spending became increasingly important to the economy, rising over the decade from roughly 15 percent of all investment to more than 35 percent, and from about 2 percent of overall economic activity (GDP) to almost 7 percent. Technological advances, which were reflected in the sharply falling prices of semiconductor chips and computers, stimulated much of the growth in IT investment. Computer prices fell by more than 20 percent a year over the entire decade and by more than 30 percent a year in the second half, largely because microprocessors and memory chips improved so dramatically. These gains in semiconductor capabilities are consistent with Moore's law (see page 59), a fundamental force of the new economy, which now anticipates a doubling in chip capacity every eighteen months or so.

The rapidity with which IT investment expanded in the last years of the 1990s was due in part to the "exuberant" stock market. Technology-smitten investors financed many more Internet and telecommunications companies than could possibly survive and encouraged firms to boost their technology spending, even if not all the new equipment could be used effectively. Some investments were also induced by fears about potential "Y2K" computer problems, which stimulated precautionary purchases of new equipment and accelerated other spending that normally would have been delayed. By so speeding up the development of the Internet and the "wiring" of the economy, these special factors helped many companies satisfy their near-term technology needs and created substantial excess capacity in many sectors of the economy, thus limiting further growth in technology investments over the near term. The excesses were particularly noticeable in the telecommunications sector, where one analyst counted "16 different fiber-optic networks spanning North America," all of which "do the same thing." But the technology boom also affected more mundane companies such as the carpet maker Mohawk Industries, which cut back on its IT investments in 2001 after spending heavily for three years. "We're not spending as much," the company's chief information officer told *The Wall Street Journal*, "because we've already spent it." This drag on investment spending, like the much-noticed failures of Internet and telecom firms, was a predictable consequence of the late 1990s exuberance and has to be worked off before investment and economic growth can really pick up again.[25]

How much of the late 1990s surges in IT investment and productivity was due to cyclical influences and other distinctive features of the period is a principal issue in the small remaining debate about the revival of productivity growth and the existence of a new economy. Robert Gordon, a leading skeptic of the durability of the productivity revival, bases his lingering doubts on his judgment that productivity growth is "narrowly based in the production and use of computers," with "no acceleration" of total factor productivity growth outside durable manufacturing, especially computers.[26] However, his conclusion depends critically, as he acknowledges, on the procedure he uses for separating the cyclical components of productivity growth from the more lasting trends, a task that is especially difficult now because the new trend is so young. In addition, the technologies and business practices that have produced the productivity acceleration seem to have altered some of the old cyclical relationships, making his techniques more questionable, while the difficulty of measuring productivity growth in the expanding service sector may also have biased his results. Most telling, other researchers have found that the business cycle contributed little to reviving productivity growth; if anything, it may have slowed it. One important study found that by 1995 most of the cyclical boost to productivity that results from more intense use of factories and equipment had already been realized. It also showed that the extra costs incurred in trying to deploy unusually large inflows of new equipment and new workers in the second half of the decade depressed total factor productivity growth by more than 15 percent a year.[27]

Going further, studies of productivity growth in different industries and sectors of the economy show that the pickup was widely diffused and that the gains were related to technology investments and organizational innovations. Since 2000, when the Commerce Department's Bureau of Economic Analysis improved its measurements in the service sector, industry-specific data have indicated that productivity growth picked up after 1995 in roughly two-thirds of the sixty-odd industries covered, including wholesale and retail trade, personal, business, and health services, and finance, insurance, and real estate, all of which tend to be big users of information and communications equipment. More generally, the gains in productivity growth were greater in industries that were intense users of information technology equipment, accelerating up to two percentage points faster in those that used more than the norm. As a group, the twenty-six industries that invested heavily in information technology accounted for about 80 percent of the direct industry contributions to the acceleration in productivity growth, while the two IT producers were responsible for approximately 20 percent. These findings help to establish the depth and breadth of the productivity revival and to link it to the use of information technology. And because it is unlikely that cyclical effects would be concentrated in industries that use the new technologies intensively, they further undermine the contention that the revival was largely a cyclical phenomenon.[28]

A series of case studies assembled by the McKinsey Global Institute sheds more light on what caused productivity growth to accelerate in six industries—wholesale trade, retail trade, computer manufacturing, semiconductors, telecommunications services, and securities—and what caused it to stagnate in retail banking and hotels despite their heavy investments in information technology. The McKinsey analysis highlights the importance of organizational innovations that complement the new technologies in boosting productivity growth. Competitive dynamics were also critical, particularly the pressures placed on other companies by industry leaders that dramatically improved their operations by investing in IT and adopting new business methods. These influences were especially important in the semiconductor sector, where intense competition between Intel and Advanced Micro Devices, the two leading producers of microprocessors, the "brains" of personal computers and most workstations, pushed each of them to achieve the improvements in chip capabilities summarized in Moore's law (see page 59). Such rapid rates of advance, roughly 60 percent a year, also set a tough standard for potential competitors to meet.[29]

Similar pressures were evident in retailing, where Wal-Mart rose to dominance by creating a new business paradigm based on "big box" stores, "everyday low prices," and "logistical efficiency." To ensure that its stores were well stocked with fast-moving, high-margin goods without accumulating large stocks of inventories, the company established a new supply network, doing away with independent wholesalers, dealing directly with suppliers, and locating its stores in a "hub and spoke" pattern around its central distribution centers. This setup proved especially efficient because it was coordinated by advanced information systems, another area in which Wal-Mart has been a pioneer. In 1969 it was one of the first retailers to use computers to track inventories in its distribution centers, a capability that it upgraded and extended as new technology became available. It adopted bar-code scanning in its stores in 1980 and began using wireless scanning guns in the late 1980s, shortly after setting up an electronic data exchange with its suppliers, which it expanded dramatically in the 1990s. Over the years it has developed a commercial database thought to be the world's largest.

Although Wal-Mart's information systems were critical to its success, they alone were not sufficient to achieve it. Along with the innovative retailing model in which these systems functioned, other operational changes made by the company helped raise productivity. For example, Wal-Mart trained its employees broadly, enabling them to work in a variety of departments. It also taught its cashiers to keep customers flowing through the checkout lines and monitored how busy these positions were in order to avoid both bottlenecks and dead time, boosting checkout productivity by up to 20 percent. By the mid-1990s, Wal-Mart had become almost 50 percent more productive than its competitors, up from 40 percent in 1987, and had accounted for about 27 percent of all general-merchandise sales, compared with 9 percent in 1987. Competitors finally began to catch up in the mid-1990s, adopting many of Wal-Mart's innovations and focusing more intently on raising their productivity, which grew by 20 percent in the first half of the decade and by 28 percent in the second half, rates that were comparable to Wal-Mart's gains of 28 and 22 percent, respectively. The other companies' improvements help to explain why Wal-Mart's share of all general merchandisers' sales, which had tripled between 1987 and 1995, rose relatively slowly in the late 1990s, from 27 percent in 1995 to 30 percent in 1999.[30]

Overall, the McKinsey report is useful in providing a richer, more nuanced picture of how productivity growth accelerated in a diverse group of industries, but although its findings are consistent with those of other industry-specific studies, they are presented in a way that exaggerates apparent differences. The study downplays the complementarity between information technology and the other productivity-enhancing factors it identifies, and it emphasizes the weakness of the relationship it finds between an industry's productivity gains and its IT investments, even though the correlation is reasonably strong when specified somewhat differently.[31] The report is also concerned about the strength of the productivity gains in the six industries it considers in depth, worrying that the rest of the economy may not become significantly more productive in the future.[32]* But this concern, like Gordon's, ignores important historical evidence and thus seems premature. Given the magnitude of the changes involved, it makes sense that transforming "general purpose" technologies should affect the economy rather modestly at first, perhaps even disappointingly, and gain strength gradually, producing more robust benefits as the technologies and associated innovations mature and become more dispersed throughout the economy. The electric power revolution evolved in this way, not approaching its full potential for almost half a century, and during its gestation productivity gains in generating electric power and in manufacturing accounted for a large fraction of economy-wide productivity growth. Moreover, total factor productivity growth in the production of electric power remained greater than in any other sector throughout the first half of the twentieth century. The abrupt cessation in these gains in the 1960s, David Mowery and Nathan Rosenberg have pointed out, "raises intriguing

---

*McKinsey's findings have been misleadingly portrayed as showing that six industries, constituting less than one-third of the private sector, accounted for all of the acceleration in productivity growth. In fact, productivity growth in these six industries increased by 1.3 percentage points after 1995, but twenty-eight other industries had gains of about 0.5 percentage points, while productivity growth in the remaining twenty-five industries fell by about the same amount. Thus, it is more accurate to say that productivity growth accelerated in close to 60 percent of the industries in the sample, a finding consistent with other studies, and was especially strong in the six of them that account for about 30 percent of all employment in the private economy.

questions of its possible connection" to the slowdown in productivity growth in the 1970s.[33]

The new economy is just emerging, but even at this relatively early stage, its productivity improvements compare favorably with those in both the first and the second industrial revolution. According to Nicholas Crafts, a British economic historian who has written extensively about the first industrial revolution, information technology's contribution to productivity growth in the last 25 years "has exceeded that of steam and at least matched that of electricity over comparable periods." Seen in this light, the interesting question is not why the gains have not been more forceful, but, rather, "why more should have been expected." The new economy also compares well with the past in the extent to which total factor productivity growth contributed to the rise in productivity after 1995. Just as an abrupt drop in TFP growth in the 1970s accounts for virtually all of the productivity slowdown after the golden age, its rapid rise after 1995 accounts for most of the acceleration in labor productivity growth. Labor productivity growth rose by roughly 80 percent in the last half of the 1990s, but growth in total factor productivity increased threefold, bringing it more in line with the trends uncovered by Abramovitz and David. As shown in the next-to-last column of the table on page 28, technological change has been the most significant contributor to economic progress over the last 150 years, and its role has grown progressively from one long period to the next. Although total factor productivity growth still lags behind that in the golden age, its recent gains have boosted its contribution to labor productivity growth near that achieved in the first part of the century, when the effects of electric power and mass production began to be felt.[34]

Ironically, these findings substantiate most of what could realistically have been hoped for among the overblown expectations for the new economy, but they appeared just as public confidence was waning, undermined by slowing economic growth and the collapse of the Nasdaq. Even so, the results seem to have conquered much of the remaining skepticism among economists about the existence, strength, and durability of the new economy. Strong growth in total factor productivity in the late 1990s was critical to this reassessment, largely because it makes it likely that the gains achieved so far will continue for a while, perhaps even increase. The Internet is another reason that productivity growth is likely to increase further: although it has contributed very little so far, economists think that it may boost productivity growth by 20 percent or more a year over the next five years or so, mainly by making markets more competitive and by enabling companies to better manage their operations, particularly their supply chains. Even if this were not to happen, however, the continued operation of Moore's law (page 59) would still support high rates of productivity growth for a long time.[35]

Despite their virtues, growth-accounting studies cannot provide a very deep or complete explanation of how information technology helped to boost productivity. Such an understanding, as the McKinsey examples make clear, requires exploring the ways in which it enabled firms to overhaul their operations. Over the last several decades, the mass-production business model pioneered by Henry Ford has been giving way to a more flexible, "build-to-order" ideal associated most closely with Dell Computer. The new business methods, which are considered more fully in Chapter 4, involve gearing production to advance customer orders, coordinating operations closely with suppliers, and introducing less hierarchical working arrangements in which employees are given more responsibility to make decisions and are supported and encouraged by more training and by performance-linked pay, such as profit sharing and stock options. Together with the new technologies, these new ways of working have drastically reduced business inventories, improved the quality of goods and services, shortened production cycles and sped up distribution, and raised productivity and profitability. At the same time, the need to integrate the new technologies with appropriate new business practices in order to realize their joint potential helps to explain why it took so long for productivity growth to take off. It also took time for the new technologies and new business methods to permeate the economy sufficiently to make a difference in its aggregate performance. And measurement problems may have masked some of the improvements, particularly the qualitative ones. These issues are the focus of the next chapter.

Why Did It Take So Long?

SINCE THE END of the 1990s, when productivity growth began to reflect the changes that had been percolating in the economy for twenty-five years, it has seemed surprising that the acceleration did not occur sooner or that anybody doubted it would happen eventually. Before productivity began to revive, however, there was a troubling disparity between everyday experience and the economy's stagnant productivity growth. Not only were ever-more-powerful computers seeming to pop up on every desk; but steel mills appeared to operate without workers, and ATM machines made it possible to get cash, make deposits, or transfer money at almost any time and in almost any place. Similarly, the Internet put all sorts of information at one's fingertips, E-mail vastly expanded our ability to stay in touch, and flocks of new and improved medical procedures radically improved people's lives, including laser surgery, MRIs, organ transplants, and joint replacements. In addition, for most of the 1980s and 1990s the economy seemed immune to serious disruption, and inflation continued to fall even as labor markets tightened and unemployment fell. And, of course, the stock market hardly ever went down.

There always were three plausible explanations for the apparent disconnect between sluggish productivity growth and the wonders of life in the new economy—a conundrum made even more pointed because it arose in an economy that continued expanding for almost two decades and because anecdotal evidence linking greater business efficiency with the growing use of information technology kept cropping up. First, it was possible that the examples of great productivity improvements were isolated and unrepresentative and that the impact of information and communications technology on the economy as a whole was far smaller than they suggested. Second, the paradox might have been the result of inadequate measurement that failed to capture the underlying improvements in economic growth and productivity. Third, it was possible that the expected improvements in productivity would occur but would simply take longer than many people expected. Each of these explanations has been at least partially validated by subsequent events, especially the last two.

Although the wildest hopes for productivity growth may have been disappointed, the evidence discussed in Chapter 1 shows quite clearly that the pessimism reflected in the first possibility was unwarranted. This chapter focuses on the last two explanations for the apparent productivity puzzle. Both help to explain the lag in the revival of productivity growth, and neither is unprecedented. Economic historians who have studied the impact of revolutionary new technologies have found that it frequently took decades before a substantial effect was felt throughout the economy. Since the early 1990s, for example, Paul David has been arguing that the transformation of American industry by new electric power technologies also was "long delayed," not reaching fruition until the 1920s, at least four decades after the first power plant was built. In the meantime, there was a long "productivity pause" as the technologies evolved in ways that made them more useful and companies learned how to deploy them effectively, trained their workers appropriately, and made other necessary investments. Exploiting the new technologies efficiently necessitated changes in the way businesses were organized and managed, and sometimes necessitated political changes as well.

Epoch-making new technologies, such as electric power, the steam engine, which propelled the first industrial revolution, and the microelectronics of today's economy, are sometimes called general-purpose technologies. Unlike innovations with circumscribed applicability, these are far more encompassing and important, playing a broader "enabling" role in "opening up new opportunities rather than offering complete, final solutions" to specific problems. But, by their nature, these general-purpose technologies do not arrive fully formed, accompanied by a grand design or blueprint describing how they should be used. Rather, they tend to evolve in unexpected ways, making them helpful in an increasing variety of applications, while complementary new operating methods are generally discovered through similarly long and tortuous periods of trial and error. The steam engines used to pump water out of mines in the second half of the eighteenth century, for example, differed greatly from those that powered railroads a hundred years later, and the transistor, which was invented in 1947, did not evolve into the microprocessors that run personal computers until the late 1970s. Similarly, electric power did not come into its own until an extensive distribution network was put in place and the cumbersome steam-powered factories of the nineteenth century were supplanted by single-level facilities that could better accommodate new mass-production methods. All of this took time and effort, both for people to understand what was possible and necessary and for enough companies to invest in the new equipment, plants, and working arrangements to affect the economy meaningfully.[1]

Compounding the problem of interpreting productivity's slow response to changes under way in the economy was the likelihood that official statistics had underestimated productivity growth, in part because they have trouble coping with the improved and innovative goods and services that new technologies produce. Even more important, however, may have been the fact that many of the costs of adopting the new technologies were expensed all at once rather than capitalized and depreciated over time, as was true of software expenditures until very recently. Information technology's contribution to the productivity revival became much clearer after October 1999, when software purchases began to be treated as investments and earlier national income accounts were modified accordingly. The impact of similarly treating other intangible investments in new working arrangements, such as the costs of designing and reconfiguring facilities and training workers, may be much greater than for software, perhaps several times as large.

BUILDING A CRITICAL MASS

One of the clearest reasons for information technology's relatively small contribution to economic and productivity growth before the mid-1990s is simply arithmetic: despite growing by about 12 percent a year in the first half of the decade, the sector was too small a share of the economy to make much of a difference. After 1995, however, investments in information and communications equipment accelerated dramatically, growing almost twice as rapidly and boosting their contribution to productivity and economic growth. Technology's contribution increased both because the sector was growing so fast and because the cumulative effect of its rapid growth over a period of years heightened its importance in the economy, and hence the impact of its faster growth. As noted in Chapter 1, after 1995 investment in IT equipment grew by more than 20 percent a year, boosting its average rate of growth for the decade to roughly 16 percent and accounting for approximately 20 percent of the economy's growth in the second half of the 1990s. At the end of 2000, information technology and software constituted more than 35 percent of all investment and almost 7 percent of gross domestic product, or GDP, compared with roughly 15 percent and 2 percent, respectively, in 1990. In part because its share of the economy had increased so much, IT equipment and software had a far bigger impact, accounting for about two-thirds of the acceleration in labor productivity growth after 1995, about a third because it raised capital intensity in other sectors and another third because of rising efficiency in producing the equipment. It also enabled many businesses to make extensive changes in their operating methods, helping other sectors of the economy to become even more efficient. To the extent that these efficiency gains in the rest of the economy are attributable to workplace innovations made possible, or enhanced, by advanced information and communications equipment, the technologies' contributions are greater still.[2]

Although these results now appear inevitable, perhaps even a bit overdue, behind the numbers lies a prolonged, difficult, and often fortuitous process of innovation-induced changes in supply and demand for the new equipment, a progression that flowed ultimately from the inventions of the transistor and the computer in the late 1940s. Figure 3 captures the essence of these forces, showing how technological advances in producing information and communications equipment drove prices dramatically lower and how these lower costs encouraged more and more investment in the technologies. One line in the figure charts prices of computers and peripheral equipment over the last twenty years, while the other three track annual investment in IT equipment by three important components of the economy, wholesale and retail trade, financial services, and manufacturing. The price trajectory falls dramatically from the upper-left-hand corner to the lower right, while demand in each sector explodes from the lower-left-hand corner to the upper right, especially after 1995, when overall IT investment grew roughly twice as fast as in the early 1990s. As the figure also shows, this happened partly because computer prices fell by about 30 percent a year from 1995 to 1999, almost twice as rapidly as they dropped in the first half of the decade. And the accelerated decline of computer prices in the last half of the 1990s occurred in large part because the semiconductor chips that run them were improving so markedly.

Lower prices increased the use of computers and other IT equipment, but they were not the only factor. The high-tech investment surge also occurred because businesses learned to use the equipment more effectively and because of what economists call "network effects." In industries with network effects, such as computers or telecommunications and Internet services, the value of the products

FIGURE 3. *Computer Prices and Investment in*
Information Technology by Major Industries, 1979–2000

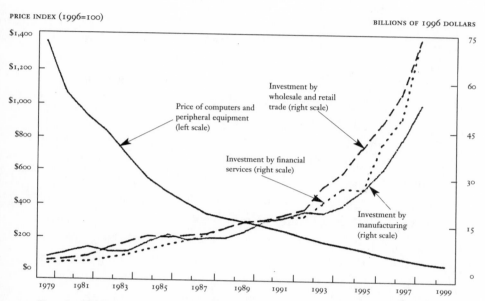

PRICE INDEX (1996=100)

BILLIONS OF 1996 DOLLARS

For the purposes of this figure, information technology consists of computers, pe-
ripheral equipment, software, and communications equipment; investment is
measured in billions of 1996 dollars; and computer prices are measured by an in-
dex that had a value of 100 in 1996. The data are from the Department of Com-
merce (Bureau of Economics Analysis) and Department of Labor (Bureau of
Labor Statistics). This figure appeared in the 2001 Economic Report of the
President, *p. 95.*

and services increases as more people are hooked up to the network, creating a self-reinforcing cycle (or "positive feedback"). As more and more users connect to a network, more and more want to be connected. According to one estimate, the value of a network of computers grows exponentially, rising in proportion to the square of the number of users. Network effects help to explain the rapid spread of the Internet, which acquired 50 million users faster than any other technology. In November 1999, roughly five years after Netscape's Navigator Web browser became available to the public, the Internet reached approximately 120 million Americans, more than 60 percent of whom were using it regularly. Echoing this growing use of the Internet, the number of additional phone lines doubled between 1993 and 1997, rising from 9 million to 18 million.[3]

The advances in our ability to process, store, and transmit information that are reflected in the falling prices and increased use of IT equipment are so great that they are hard to appreciate fully. Over the last thirty years, for example, the cost of processing information has fallen more than seven thousand–fold. Since 1980, this cost of carrying out 1 million processing instructions per second—a megahertz—has fallen from more than $100 to under 20 cents. Similarly, the cost of storing 1 million bits of data on a computer's hard drive, a megabyte of storage, has fallen from more than $5,000 in 1970 to about $600 in 1980 and less than a penny today. Finally, the cost of sending 1 trillion bits of information has fallen over the last thirty years from about $150,000 to about a dime. Much of that improvement is due to the development of fiber-optic cables, fine glass fibers about the size of a human hair through which lasers direct narrow intense beams of highly focused light that have been modulated to allow them to carry conversations and other data and information. (A laser—the term derives from an acronym compiled from an early description of the underlying process, "light amplification by stimulated emission of radiation"—is a device for creating intense beams of coherent light, that is, light that consists of waves whose length and phases are highly correlated, producing a carrier onto which signals containing information can be blended.) Not only is this method of sending information much faster than using electrons moving through copper wires; it also is less susceptible to interference. The first transatlantic fiber-optic telephone cable was installed in 1988 and could carry almost 40,000 conversations simultaneously, compared with fewer than 200 for the best copper wires. By early 2001 a commercial fiber-optic system could carry almost 50 million simultaneous conversations, and experimental systems had reached the equivalent of about 150 million concurrent exchanges, but copper lines still could not carry more than 1,000 conversations at the same time.[4]

The improvements in computer processing power and storage capacity reflect the workings of Moore's law, a conjecture about the future possibilities of the semiconductor chips that run computers and other electronic devices such as televisions, cellular telephones, and kitchen appliances. The law is named for Gordon Moore, a cofounder of Intel Corporation, the leading chip maker and a driving force of the microelectronics revolution. In 1965 Moore observed that the number of electronic circuits that could be etched on chips was doubling every year, and he predicted that the pattern would persist for ten years. The more circuits that can be fitted on a chip, the greater its memory and the faster its processing speed, because there is less space between them to slow things down. Greater density also means that new performance features can be added to the chips. Moore has likened greater chip density to more intense real-estate development, observing that the price of a chip has remained relatively steady at "about a billion dollars an acre," but because more and more "electronic functions" have been packed on each chip, their effective prices, which reflect their enhanced capabilities, have become "cheaper and cheaper." As the pace of compression slowed somewhat, the law was modified so that it now envisions a doubling of computer processing power every eighteen months. Computer scientists think it will continue to hold for several more decades, although it will eventually be limited by the wavelengths of light used to etch the circuits on the chips and by the size of atomic particles.[5]

Moore's law, Intel points out in its advertising, has become "shorthand for the rapid, unprecedented growth of technology." Perhaps the idea is so ubiquitous because it is an element of regularity in a history of invention and technological advance marked more by unexpected discoveries and unusual coincidences than by predictable progression. But the consistent pace of improvement envisioned by the law is deceptive insofar as it masks the many engineering feats and struggles necessary to produce a steady increase in chip density. "In one respect," Moore told an editor of *Scientific American* in 1997, "it has become a self-fulfilling prophecy. People know they have to stay on that curve to remain competitive, so they put in the effort to make it happen." Intel's success in meeting these challenges has improved efficiency for computer users and countless others and has created great wealth for the company's workers and shareholders. Indeed, in late 2000 Moore set up a $5 billion foundation to support research on scientific and environmental issues that most sponsors find too risky. At the time, it was estimated to be the eighth-largest foundation in the United States.[6]

A BRIEF HISTORY OF THE TRANSISTOR

The information revolution is largely a revolution in electronics that began with the invention in 1947 of the transistor, a device made of semiconductors, such as silicon or germanium, whose ability to transmit electrical impulses can be regulated, thus allowing it to process information that is encoded in binary form.* (In a binary system, each bit of information can take on one of only two values, either "zero" or "one.") Transistors are the hearts, or brains, of all electronic devices, ranging from calculators and portable radios, which for a while were called "transistor radios" or simply "transistors," to digital cameras, computers, and the guidance systems of spacecraft and sophisticated missiles and other weapons. They also regulate fuel-injection systems in cars and can adjust steering and braking systems in case of dangers caused by skidding. Transistors work much like gates or switches, allowing current to flow when they are open but not when they are closed; by opening, say, when a "bit" of information is one but not if it is zero, they can convey that information and process it in specified ways.[7] Developed over the next fifty years in ways that often were not anticipated, the transistor spawned at least three closely related new

---

*Silicon and germanium are materials that fall somewhere between good conductors of electricity, such as copper, and insulators, such as rubber. The great achievement of the inventors of the transistor was to create a device made of these materials that could switch from one state to the other, from functioning, say, as an insulator to functioning as a conductor of electricity, in a controllable way. Short as it is, the time it takes to switch from one state to the other is one factor limiting a computer's processing speed.

industries—the chip, or semiconductor, industry and those that produce electronic computers and computer software—and transformed virtually all others. Before transistors, the digital circuits that ran computers were made of vacuum tubes, which are much larger, use more energy, dissipate more heat, and are less reliable than transistors. Modern computers contain more than 10 million transistors, and it is hard to imagine how personal computers would have been possible without them.

John Bardeen, Walter Brattain, and William Shockley invented the transistor while working at Bell Laboratories, the research arm of AT&T located in Murray Hill, New Jersey. A decade later, the three men shared the Nobel Prize in physics for their invention. But the breakthrough was not fully appreciated at first, *The New York Times* reporting in December 1947 only that the transistor might be useful in developing better hearing aids. Its maturation into a revolutionary general-purpose technology owes much to the unintended consequences of U.S. antitrust concerns and Cold War defense policies. When they made their epochal discovery, Bardeen, Brattain, and Shockley were working in Bell Labs' research program in solid-state physics. Solid-state physics is now the largest field within the entire discipline, but the Bell Labs program was unique at the time, having been started in the 1930s in hopes of uncovering a means of easing growing bottlenecks in AT&T's long-distance telephone service, which depended on cumbersome mechanical relays to route calls through its lines. And although the transistor would solve that problem and many more, AT&T could not develop the new device fully. Shortly after the transistor's invention, the Antitrust Division of the U.S. Department of Justice filed a major action against the company, greatly influencing the evolution of electronic technology, the direction of scientific research, and the development of the new economy. Most significant, the antitrust threat helped persuade the company to license the new technology widely rather than attempt to create new businesses based on the transistor. The licensing process began with a six-day seminar held at Bell Laboratories in April 1952, for which participants paid twenty-five thousand dollars each to learn about the new devices and how to manufacture them. Four years later, the company went even further, settling the antitrust case by signing a consent decree in which it agreed to limit itself to providing tele-communications services and equipment, formally conceding to others commercial development of the transistor.[8]

AT&T's decision to license the new technology opened up the field, and major improvements of the transistor followed soon there-after. Many of the people who helped to develop and commercialize transistors were scientists and engineers working at small specialized firms such as Texas Instruments, which made instruments used in oil exploration, and Motorola, which manufactured car radios. Also central was Fairchild Semiconductor, a company set up in Palo Alto in 1957 by Gordon Moore, Robert Noyce, and six other scientists and technologists who had defected from Shockley Semiconductor, the company William Shockley formed when he left Bell Labs two years earlier. Texas Instruments produced the first commercial transistors in 1954, an achievement followed less than five years later by the invention of the integrated circuit, essentially a combination of connected transistors on a single silicon chip. Jack Kilby of Texas Instruments and Noyce independently created, and patented, inte-grated circuits in 1959, but Noyce's version was more efficient and easier to produce and consequently became the industry standard.

Frustrated by their corporate parent, Fairchild Camera and In-strument Corporation of New York, Noyce and Moore left Fairchild Semiconductor in 1968 and formed Intel, using $500,000 of their own money, $2.5 million raised from venture capitalists, and $300,000 from Grinnell College, Noyce's alma mater. The beginning group also included Andrew Grove, the well-known CEO of Intel from 1987 to 1998, who had joined Fairchild in 1963 shortly after earning his Ph.D. from Berkeley. Intel initially specialized in complex computer-memory chips and soon came to dominate that part of the industry. The company raised transistor technology to a new level in

1971, however, when Ted Hoff, one of its engineers, developed the silicon-etching process that made the microprocessor possible. Hoff was thirty-two when he made this discovery, roughly the age Noyce had been when he invented the integrated circuit. Called a "computer on a chip" because it houses all the logical and mathematical functions necessary for running a computer, the microprocessor transformed the industry and perhaps the entire economy. Among the many dramas it set in motion was the development of the personal computer, which resulted in both the rise of Intel and Microsoft to the top ranks of the world's companies and, despite the success of its new machines, a fall in IBM's standing, at least until the company was reorganized in the mid-1990s. Together with the VisiCalc spreadsheet, the personal computer made it much easier and quicker to evaluate investments under alternative assumptions and thus may also have been instrumental in launching the takeover wave of the 1980s, which helped remake the business landscape.[9]

U.S. defense requirements influenced the development of the transistor in two important ways. First, military and space programs provided a large and growing demand for semiconductors, accounting for 40–45 percent of sales of discrete semiconductors from the mid-1950s to the early 1960s, and more than 70 percent of sales of integrated circuits from the early 1960s through the buildup for the Vietnam War in the middle of the decade. Military demand for highly reliable components to be used in applications such as the Minuteman guidance system was significant in its own right, but it also helped to establish the dependability of integrated chips for commercial users. Second, the U.S. Defense Department, unlike its European counterparts, was willing to buy equipment and components from relatively young companies, such as Texas Instruments and Fairchild, that had not supplied the military before. Moreover, to ensure that its supplies would not be interrupted, the Pentagon insisted that its contractors develop a "second source" of supply. Because components produced by all suppliers had to be identical, companies supplying the military had to share their technology and designs with their competitors, intensifying competition and stimulating further creativity and innovation in the emerging industry.[10]

The development of semiconductors was also influenced by a string of serendipitous events and relationships. Although it is impossible to know how information technology would have evolved without them, the author Tom Wolfe has highlighted a number of coincidences that may have shaped the particular path it followed. Many of these chance connections center on Grinnell College in Grinnell, Iowa. In 1948 Robert Noyce, who would turn out to be a key player in the microelectronics revolution, was a senior physics major at Grinnell studying under Grant Gale, a young physics professor who had been John Bardeen's classmate at the University of Wisconsin. In addition, Bardeen had grown up in Madison, Wisconsin, with Gale's wife, while Oliver Buckley, president of Bell Labs from 1940 to 1951, was a Grinnell alumnus. Partly because of these relationships, Gale was unusually interested in the transistor and was able to get hold of two of the early devices. In the fall of 1948, he taught a course about the transistor to Grinnell's eighteen physics majors, including Noyce. The uniqueness of his experience became fully clear to Noyce when he entered graduate school at MIT the following fall and discovered that none of the professors was interested in the transistor and no courses involved the transistor or solid-state physics.

Wolfe thinks there were other sociological aspects to the development of semiconductors beyond the Grinnell connection. He finds it striking that most of the major figures in the electronics revolution were from small towns in the Midwest and West and went to school there. In addition to Noyce, Bardeen, and Buckley, he points out, Brattain came from Washington State and attended college there; Shockley grew up in Palo Alto when it was just a small college town and went to Caltech; and Jack Kilby was from Jefferson City, Missouri, and went to the University of Illinois. (On the other hand, Shockley was born in London and, like Noyce, got his Ph.D. at MIT;

Bardeen, whose father had been dean of the medical school at the University of Wisconsin, earned his doctorate at Princeton; and Brattain was born in China.) Their shared small-town background, with its emphasis on self-reliance and persistence rather than social standing or position, Wolfe believes, helps to explain "the passion and the daring" of the engineers and scientists who drove the semiconductor revolution. It is noteworthy, for example, that Noyce's management philosophy stressed discipline, commitment, and independence and eschewed the hierarchy and social structure of the mature bureaucratic companies of Galbraith's industrial state, such as IBM or Fairchild Camera. According to Wolfe, Noyce and the other employees of Fairchild Semiconductor were appalled when Fairchild's chief executive, John Carter, arrived for a visit in a black Cadillac limousine with a uniformed driver who waited outside all day, "*doing nothing . . . but waiting for a man who was inside.*" At Intel, as at Fairchild, Noyce introduced many of the organizational arrangements that characterize the new economy. Among other things, he gave all the engineers and most office workers stock options, and while he and Moore clearly were in charge, they tried to operate as much as possible without layers of management, relying instead on "councils" of workers from different areas of the company to solve operating problems. It should hardly be surprising that it took so long for older, more established companies to learn to work in this way.[11]

The "serendipitous history" of the transistor, Nathan Rosenberg emphasizes, is not unusual in the history of technology. The laser, another major technological breakthrough that helped to create the new economy, had a similar upbringing. Like the transistor, the laser was invented at AT&T's Bell Labs in the late 1950s, shortly after Bardeen, Brattain, and Shockley won the Nobel Prize for the transistor. Together with fiber optics, it has revolutionized telecommunications and had a profound impact on a wide range of delicate surgeries, including repair of detached retinas and gallbladder surgery. Lasers are also used in making semiconductor chips and computer printers and in fields such as textiles and metallurgy. Yet, according to Charles Townes, who won the 1964 Nobel Prize in physics for his work on the laser, not only was the basic research that led to the invention "universally eschewed in applied laboratories"; even after Bell Labs got interested and the ideas for the laser began to coalesce, he writes, "the new device was so far out of the normal tradition that its value for applied work was not immediately obvious." Indeed, Bell Labs' patent experts initially refused to apply for a patent for the laser "because, it was explained, optical waves had never been of any importance to communications and hence the invention had little bearing on Bell System interests." They soon relented, however, as the device's potential became clearer, but even so, the laser could not be used to transmit telephone signals before there was a way of protecting its intense light waves from interference, which was not possible until fiber-optic cables were developed, also at Bell Labs, in the early 1970s. The first fiber-optic transmission system was tested in Atlanta in 1976, a commercial system was installed in Chicago a year later, and, as noted, the first transatlantic system came on-line in 1988.[12]

Such failures to anticipate future development of new technologies are not confined to the recent past. For example, Alexander Graham Bell's 1876 telephone patent was offered to Western Union for $100,000, equivalent to $2–$3 million today, but was turned down; instead, Western Union agreed to get out of the telephone business if Bell would stay out of the telegraph business. Similarly, J. P. Morgan decided to back Thomas Edison despite the deep skepticism of his father, who seemed to believe, like the British journal *Engineering*, that electric light might be "good enough for our Transatlantic friends" but was "unworthy of the attention of practical or scientific men." Morgan's Wall Street office was the first to be lit by electric power from the Pearl Street generating plant, which began operating in September 1882, and he persisted in trying to light his home electrically in the face of numerous setbacks and delays, including a fire in the library caused by faulty wiring. Even the steam engine, which played a role in the industrial revolution much like that of the transistor or computer today, began life as a device for pumping water out of flooded mines.[13]

LEARNING TO USE NEW TECHNOLOGIES: ELECTRIC POWER

The development of the transistor illustrates the "extended improvement process" that most important new technologies must go through in order to become useful on a large scale. Seeing things in this light, we can better understand why in the late 1940s the IBM patriarch, Thomas J. Watson Sr., badly underestimated the potential market for computers. He based his assessment on the Electronic Numerical Integrator and Computer (ENIAC), the first digital computer, which contained almost twenty thousand vacuum tubes and filled a room more than a hundred feet long. Even so, it was far less powerful and less reliable, and much more expensive, than an average modern personal computer. Watson can hardly be faulted for not foreseeing the remarkable improvements in computers and telecommunications equipment, which, over the next fifty years, transformed these industries, and greatly changed the entire economy; eventually the new technologies established a large enough presence in the economy to boost overall productivity growth significantly, deflating many of the remaining doubts about their ultimate importance.[14]

Not only did we underestimate the time it took for the technologies to establish a critical standing in the economy; we also misjudged the difficulty of learning to use computers and other high-tech equipment effectively, which led to a delay in realizing their benefits. Improving information and communications technologies have enabled companies to streamline their operations and become more entrepreneurial, following the examples of Noyce, Intel, and many others in eliminating wasteful layers of management and giving more responsibility to workers, but such fundamental changes can rarely be effected easily or quickly. Rather, adopting a new operating philosophy and new business practices generally requires more than new machinery and equipment incorporating the latest technologies; companies must also make complementary investments in training workers to function effectively in the new environment, in redesigning plants and other work spaces to make them more compatible with the new ways of working, and, in recent times, in installing, adapting, and debugging needed software, all of which takes time and effort to appreciate and put in place. Perhaps it should not be so surprising that even as late as 1997, two Princeton economists likened waiting for productivity to pick up to "waiting for Godot."[15]

At that time, shortly before the data delivered the fatal blow, the most powerful counters to such views were historical analogies, drawn most prominently by Paul David, comparing the development and delayed impact of information technology with those of other far-reaching new technologies, particularly electric power. "The transformation of industrial processes by the new electric power technologies," he emphasized, had also been "long-delayed and far from automatic." As with information technology, and for many of the same reasons, it took almost half a century before electric power had a significant impact on productivity growth. The first central power plant in this country, the Pearl Street Station in lower Manhattan, was built in 1882, and the underlying technology was older still. Nevertheless, at the turn of the century less than 10 percent of all urban households were using electric power, and electric motors installed in factories accounted for less than 5 percent of mechanical horsepower used in manufacturing. Electrification of American homes and industry did not gather "real momentum" until after World War I, when central generating capacity expanded widely and rates fell substantially, reflecting advances that had been made in producing electric power, extensive construction of new generating plants, and scale economies realized from coordinating distribution over large areas. Creating these regional power networks was neither straightforward nor easy, often necessitating delicate political compromises and new institutional arrangements, which allowed utility companies to operate over wider areas spanning many political jurisdictions. Samuel Insull, who created the Middle West Utilities Company in 1912, was among the first to set up a holding company to integrate local electricity suppliers into an efficient regional network, demonstrating the effectiveness of such a structure to investors, other entrepreneurs, and politicians. State governments also were swayed by a lobbying campaign, waged largely by the National Electric Light Association from 1907 to 1914, to get them to set up public-utility commissions to regulate distribution of electric power rather than continue to allow it to be governed by cities and towns.[16]

In addition to these constraints on supply, industrial electrification was held back by weak demand, the result of most factories' having been built to run on steam or water power and not being well suited to electricity. These plants were designed to accommodate the "group drive" system for operating machinery and equipment, in which elaborate networks of belts and shafts conveyed power from its central source to large groups of machines throughout the plant. This not only wasted energy because the power could not easily be adjusted to the needs of individual machines, but the bulkiness and weight of the transmission system meant that factories had to be heavily reinforced and, in order to avoid losses from transmitting power over long distances, multistory rather than spread out on a single level. But unlike steam power, which could not be delivered in widely varying quantities because steam engines were not efficient below a certain size, electricity could be adjusted to differing needs—it could be "fractionalized"—an advantage with many implications. Most important, factories powered by electricity could utilize the "unit drive" system, a much more efficient modular setup in which separate "secondary" electric motors powered different machines, or groups of machines, according to their individual needs. Because elaborate belting and shafting were no longer necessary, plants could be built less expensively, perhaps on a single level when that better suited the flow of work.

Nevertheless, because it was often uneconomical to scrap older factories that were still serviceable, businesses tended to adopt electric power gradually, as their steam-oriented plants wore out, rather than revamping all at once. The first adopters were rapidly expanding industries that needed new facilities, including tobacco, fabricated metals, and transportation equipment, as well as producers of electrical machinery and equipment themselves. Not only did it take time for the stock of new electrically powered factories to expand sufficiently to affect aggregate productivity growth; productivity may also have been depressed temporarily because many companies that brought electric power into their existing plants did so in a tentative, experimental way. Much like early users of computers who retained paper-based data-processing and record-keeping systems along with their new electronic ones, factories that introduced electric power in the early part of the century generally left in place the group-drive system of belts and shafts, simply adding primary electric motors as additional "drivers" of the existing transmission systems. "Replacing a steam engine with one or more electric motors, leaving the power distribution unchanged," one energy historian wrote, "appears to have been the usual juxtaposition of a new technology upon the framework of an old one." It was done, he continued, largely because "shaft and belt power distribution systems were in place, and manufacturers were familiar with their problems."[17]

Factory electrification and productivity growth took off after World War I, aided, as was the diffusion of information technology more than fifty years later, by a robust economy, buoyant financial markets, and the development of a new manufacturing model that complemented the new technology. Mass production and scientific management, the production techniques and principles that were to govern manufacturing for roughly seventy-five years, were also introduced to the American economy during the early decades of the twentieth century. Henry Ford is known primarily for developing a new way of making automobiles, but his example was far more influential, demonstrating to all manufacturers how to produce efficiently for a mass market. While Ford's mass-production methods, epitomized by the moving assembly line that he introduced at his Highland Park plant in Detroit in 1913, could efficiently turn out large batches of relatively standard products such as the Model T, they also worked better in single-story electrified plants than in the stacked facilities that had been built to house steam-powered production. In addition to saving energy, these plants allowed companies to process materials more quickly and reliably, and because they could be constructed less sturdily, they cost less to erect. However, even Ford's Highland Park plant did not realize all the benefits of the new production system at first, because it, too, mixed electric power with steam-based distribution systems.[18]

Both the difficulties of phasing in an electric-powered industrial system and its force when well established are evident in productivity statistics for the period, particularly those for the manufacturing sector and for total factor productivity, the residual measure of overall efficiency. As shown in the last chapter, productivity growth increased roughly fivefold between 1800 and 1929, more than doubling from the first half of the nineteenth century to the second half, and doubling again between the long period that dates from 1855 to 1890 and the one that runs from 1890 to 1929, when it rose from 1 percent a year to 2 percent. Moreover, the latter acceleration was entirely due to faster growth in total factor productivity, which more than tripled and thus grew in importance compared with investment in machinery and equipment. But productivity growth did not rise uniformly in the early part of the twentieth century; in fact, it fell at first, stagnated, and then accelerated sharply after World War I. Although the pickup was widely diffused throughout the economy, it was particularly strong in manufacturing, where labor productivity growth and growth in total factor productivity each rose by almost five percentage points, from less than 1 percent a year to more than 5 percent, as the proportion of factory power supplied by electricity increased from just under 50 percent to nearly 80 percent and the fraction of power devoted to secondary electric motors rose similarly, from roughly 33 percent to 56 percent. Regardless of whether we think that penetration ratios of 50 percent constitute critical thresholds for general-purpose technologies, above which productivity growth accelerates—among obvious issues raised by such conjectures are which ratios are most important and how they should be measured—there is a clear statistical relationship between the degree to which an industry electrified during the 1920s and its productivity growth over the decade.[19]

The prolonged and difficult birth of the second industrial revolution is a useful guide for evaluating the emergence of the new economy based on digital computers and high-speed telecommunications. As with computer processing power and telecommunications capabilities in current times, advances in generating and distributing electricity produced sharp declines in the price of electric power after 1910, spurring its adoption throughout the economy, thus establishing the foundation for the productivity surge that began about a decade later. And the acceleration of productivity growth in the 1920s, like that in the late 1990s, was concentrated in the manufacturing sector. Moreover, efficiency in producing electric power, the driving technology of this industrial revolution, grew particularly rapidly, exceeding gains in any other sector of the economy for almost fifty years, until it ceased improving toward the expiration of the golden age. The timing of its abrupt drop is tantalizing, suggesting, as noted in the last chapter, that lower growth of total factor productivity in generating electric power may have been an important element in the overall stagnation of productivity growth during the tarnished 1970s and beyond.[20]

In addition to these similarities, at least four other aspects of the economic transformation based on electric power eerily foreshadow features of today's emerging new economy. First, just as the productivity decline of the 1970s may have been exacerbated by an influx into the labor market of inexperienced workers, mainly baby boomers and women who had not previously worked outside their homes, the productivity slowdown of the early years of the twentieth century has been attributed in part to the difficulty of absorbing almost 20 million immigrants from southern Europe in the decades after 1890.

Second, because mass European immigration was cut off during World War I and curtailed severely after the war, electric power and mass production came of age in an environment of rising wages, reinforcing the need to develop a new relationship with labor that encouraged loyalty and diligence, particularly among skilled workers. During this period of "welfare capitalism," many businesses adopted reforms designed to gain their employees' allegiance, including establishing personnel departments to rationalize hiring and firing decisions and establish clear avenues for advancement and promotion. To create a sense of teamwork and belonging, and to reduce worker turnover, they also sponsored employee organizations—company unions—through which workers could express to management their views about working conditions, and set up profit-sharing and stock-ownership plans. While these measures also helped to deflect the threat of militant independent unions, many business leaders of the time probably believed that they were justified, as Elbert Henry "Judge" Gary, the former judge who served as chairman of U.S. Steel, told the shareholders, "because it is the way men ought to be treated, and because it pays to treat men in this way." The resemblance between the more enlightened labor practices of the 1920s and the working arrangements of today's economy is taken up again in Chapter 4.[21]

Third, after 1910 high-school education expanded markedly, and firms increasingly picked their workers from the growing pool of graduates, much as businesses today seek out those with college degrees, whether because it was a useful screening metric or because high-school graduates had actually acquired skills that would help them in their jobs. In addition, the growing availability of electric power in the 1920s stimulated the development of many new products, including the radio, refrigerator, and electric water heater, and revived older ones such as vacuum cleaners, dishwashing machines, and clothes washers. And because the unit-drive system improved machine control, it allowed businesses to produce more uniform products of higher quality. It is doubtful, however, for reasons discussed in the next section in the context of today's economy and new technologies, that the prices of these new and improved goods and services were measured properly, a problem that may have obscured the productivity revivals in both new eras.[22]

MEASURING ECONOMIC CHANGE

One of the most difficult tasks in measuring economic activity is taking proper account of new goods and services or improvements in the quality of those already being produced. If, to take a relatively straightforward example, the price of a new computer is the same as the price of an old one but the new model processes information twice as rapidly and its hard drive has twice as much storage capacity, then the economically meaningful price of the new computer is roughly half the price of the old one. Adjusting prices for quality in this way is essential to measuring economic output and productivity accurately, since for any given value of production—gross domestic product, or GDP—if prices are overestimated, "real" output and productivity will be underestimated. Of course, the opposite is also true: output and productivity will be overstated to the extent that prices are understated, but though this sometimes happens, it is not nearly as big a problem as exaggerating prices.[23]*

In the United States, a procedure much like the one outlined above is used in determining the prices of products such as computers and automobiles, whose performance characteristics can be measured readily. The resulting "hedonic" price indexes essentially allocate a product's price among a set of relevant attributes, thus enabling the price to vary as these characteristics change. The problem is that we have not been able to apply this approach broadly or accurately

---

*One example of an industry in which productivity has been overstated is the brokerage industry—"security and commodity brokers"—whose output is frequently approximated by revenues from commissions, underwriting profits, and so on. Because the markets of the late 1990s were so frenzied, these measures produced implausibly high estimates of productivity growth, which many researchers, including those cited in endnote 23, ignore.

enough, especially to the dynamic service sector, which constitutes such a large and growing part of the economy. It is unfortunate that many other countries, such as Germany and England, do not use hedonic price indexes; but suggesting, as some have done, that quality-adjusted prices thus make our productivity data "very slippery" clearly is not right. Because prices are meaningful only if they control for changes in quality, they are necessarily hard to measure accurately, but this does not mean we should not try, even if others don't.[24]

Measurement problems such as these are hardly new, but they are much more acute in periods of rapid technological change, such as the present one, when more new goods and services are produced and substantial improvements in the quality of older ones are far more common than in less dynamic times. Measurement in today's economy is particularly difficult for three additional reasons. First, the U.S. economy is largely a service economy, and defining the output of many service industries, let alone measuring it, is conceptually difficult. As the late Zvi Griliches, the father of hedonic price indexes, stated in his presidential address to the American Economic Association in January 1994, "After decades of discussion we are not even close to a professional agreement on how to define and measure the output of banking, insurance, or the stock market. Similar difficulties arise in conceptualizing the output of health services, lawyers, and other consultants." And, he continued, "it is not reasonable for us to expect the government to produce statistics in areas where the concepts are mushy."[25]

The second important point about measurement in the new economy is that problems such as these have become more consequential as services have become more important, rising from about 50 percent of nongovernment economic activity in 1947 to roughly 75 percent today. Perhaps it is only coincidental, but even in the 1970s and 1980s productivity growth held up reasonably well in sectors that are relatively easy to measure, such as agriculture, mining, and manufacturing, while stagnating in service industries, such as wholesale and retail trade, or finance, insurance, and real estate, where measuring output is "notoriously difficult." Indeed, the difficulties are so great that for industries such as education, business services, and, until recently, banking, the Commerce Department's Bureau of Economic Analysis (BEA) essentially gives up, assuming that output grows in line with employment, an approximation that rules out the possibility of productivity growth. All told, input-based measures are used to measure output in industries that make up more than 10 percent of the entire business sector. And because these and other hard-to-measure parts of the economy have been growing so rapidly, a fact that casts doubt on their apparent inefficiency, productivity growth in the entire economy reflected their subpar performance, whether it was real, the result of measurement problems, or a bit of each.[26]

Finally, many of the service industries in which economic measurement is particularly difficult tend to be intense users of computers and telecommunications equipment. Banks and other financial institutions, telephone and communications providers, insurance carriers, and companies engaged in wholesale trade and business services are among the biggest users of computers and other high-tech equipment, at times accounting for more than 50 percent of all such investments. And even though new output measures developed by the BEA have helped make clear that productivity growth accelerated throughout the service sector in the second half of the 1990s, many anomalies remain. As measured, productivity growth is still very low in industries such as banking, insurance, and trucking and warehousing and is negative—that is, productivity is falling—in health care.[27]

Intense use of high-tech equipment by firms in industries with low productivity growth is the core of the productivity paradox, but its prominence in vibrant service industries also suggests that the puzzle is at least partly due to poor measurement. Regrettably, the problems are much clearer than the solutions. Few would dispute that measures of output and productivity would be better if many of the "intangible" costs associated with technology investments were capitalized rather than expensed, or if the benefits from new and improved products and services were more accurately reflected in official statistics. It just is very hard to do. Measures of health-care costs, for instance, are much better than they were but still don't account for the vastly improved effectiveness of procedures such as cataract surgery. Patients used to spend a week or more in intensive care following the operation and had to be immobilized for a period after that; now, by contrast, the surgery is performed with lasers in a doctor's office, and recovery is far less prolonged and onerous. The new price indexes for medical care reflect the lower hospital costs associated with the surgery but totally miss its most significant aspects—it is better and far less burdensome and unpleasant.[28]

In the financial sector, to take another obvious example, innovations such as ATMs have made many basic banking services much more accessible and cheaper than they used to be. And sophisticated new products and techniques, which would not be possible without modern information technology, have allowed capital markets to function more efficiently. Banks and other lenders, for instance, now can purchase insurance against the possibility that some of their borrowers will default, enabling them to control their lending risks more effectively and to devote more capital to other loans and investments. The insurance is a type of "derivative," a growing class of securities that are derived from other, underlying ones, in this case from the original bank loans. In 2002 the market for such credit derivatives was thought to be nearly $2 trillion. Nevertheless, even the new measures of banking productivity miss much of what is happening in the industry, including the impact of products such as these. Banking services used to be estimated using employment trends in the industry, a procedure that made it impossible for productivity to grow. The new procedures base output on the number of transactions completed, an approach that admits the possibility of productivity improvements but still makes little economic sense, since not all transactions are equally important. And although banking productivity grew more rapidly under the new measures, its growth is still very slow.[29]

Although the biases in our measures of economic output and productivity growth seem clear, at least with regard to direction, it is much more difficult to estimate the extent of the errors precisely or to gauge their impact on productivity growth. An extremely powerful illustration of how wrong conventional prices can be, even in cases in which the proper measure is "conceptually simple," was presented by William Nordhaus of Yale University, who analyzed the evolution of lighting in a way that underscores the importance of distinguishing between actual products and the services that can be derived from them. Because there is an objective measure of lighting efficiency, the lumen, Nordhaus was able to construct an historical record of its changing cost, a more meaningful measure of the price of lighting than the usual one, which is derived from everyday prices of the products used to provide light. Specifically, he calculated the changing costs of "1,000 lumen-hours" over the last two hundred years and compared them with price indexes of "fuel and light," which measure the costs of an array of fuels and devices, including candles, kerosene lamps, and electric lights. Although they are only suggestive, his results are astounding: from 1800 to 1992, the conventional price of light overestimated the true price by a factor of approximately one thousand, or by about 3.6 percent a year! And because overestimating prices is the flip side of underestimating output, proper estimates of yearly productivity growth in lighting should be 3.6 percentage points higher than conventional measures.[30]

An ideal system of measurement would apply Nordhaus's approach throughout the economy, but that is too much to expect anytime soon. Meanwhile, we must be content with piecing together the results and implications of a group of isolated studies and with estimating their combined impact on productivity growth. One of the most comprehensive assessments of measurement biases was made by the Advisory Commission to Study the Consumer Price Index, a commission appointed by the Senate Finance Committee in June 1995 that included Griliches. The commission's report, issued in December 1996, concluded that the consumer price index (CPI) overestimated prices by about 1.1 percentage points a year, with a plausible range of 0.8–1.6 percentage points. More than half of the bias was attributed to faulty measurement of new products and quality improvements in old ones. The report stirred substantial controversy, but that was due more to the potential political ramifications of its conclusions, particularly the possibility that Social Security benefits would no longer be linked fully to the CPI, than to criticism of its general findings.

According to Robert Gordon, another commission member, the Bureau of Labor Statistics (BLS) has made, or plans to make, changes in the index that will correct almost half of the upward bias identified by the commission, although little progress can be anticipated in accounting for quality improvements or new goods. Nevertheless, BLS economists and others seem much more mindful of the many anomalies it might resolve. In addition to reconciling the differences in productivity growth between the measurable and hard-to-measure sectors of the economy, and doing away with implausible productivity declines in prosperous dynamic industries, taking better account of quality change might further help to explain why inflation continued falling throughout the 1990s even as the economy grew more rapidly, labor markets tightened, and unemployment fell. How much it might help is suggested by the agency's simulations of productivity growth under alternative assumptions. For example, if total factor productivity growth is assumed to be zero in all industries in which it was negative, including insurance, health services, and banking, then total factor productivity in the entire economy would have grown approximately 0.34 percentage points faster from 1977 to 1997, an increase of about 50 percent. Similarly, if these problematic growth rates were assumed to be 1 percent, then total factor productivity in the economy would have been 0.72 percentage points higher, an increase of more than 100 percent.[31]

Other economists have developed comparable estimates of the consequences for the entire economy of correcting obvious measurement errors, showing that while they may have exaggerated the productivity slowdown after the golden age, they cannot explain it fully.

At best, however, these exercises yield very rough approximations of the consequences of poor measurement for recent productivity growth. They, too, do not address the thorniest issues, including questions about how output should be defined in industries such as banking or how capitalizing and depreciating intangible investments in new business methods and worker training might affect productivity growth, problems that are likely to remain intractable.[32] Even so, measurement errors seem less worrisome now that the productivity paradox has been resolved. The next two chapters examine how this happened in more detail, how the new technologies and new business practices changed the economy and boosted productivity growth, enabling those companies that used them effectively to grow and prosper, while those that did not were left behind.

The Changing of the Guard

ALTHOUGH THERE are many reasons to be optimistic, we will not really know how to rate the new economy until it has been around for at least another decade and probably much longer. The impressive productivity improvements of the late 1990s, so critical to all notions of freshness and significant economic change, are relatively short-lived and, in late 2002, were still being tested by the soft economy, depressed stock market, and continuing revelations of corporate fraud and deceit. The stock market started weakening in March 2000, and the economy followed roughly six months later; both were shaken further by the terrorist attacks of September 11, 2001, and by the business scandals that began to surface several months after that. While their timing and exact nature could not be foreseen, economic reversals and deceitful manipulations of company accounts and share prices were almost inevitable, natural consequences of the bubbly financial markets and frenzied investment climate of the last years of the century. But, as noted in the Introduction, even though economic growth slowed markedly and employment and industrial production fell as in other recessions, GDP itself held up unusually well, at least partly because businesses were better able to control their operations and diversify and manage their risks, thus keeping productivity growing at rates high enough to prevent the sustained drop in economic activity typical of most recessions. The effectiveness of new business methods, technologies, and financial innovations in helping to maintain productivity growth during the recession provides further evidence of their depth and force and suggests that they will continue to have a major impact on the economy, one that should be even clearer once the excesses of the boom have been worked off and the economy picks up again.

Another way to gauge the strength of these changes in the economy is to compare today's companies with those of the golden age of the 1950s and 1960s, as memorialized in John Kenneth Galbraith's 1967 best-seller, *The New Industrial State*. In addition to highlighting many of the salient features of the old economy, the book inadvertently demonstrates how perilous it can be to extrapolate existing conditions too aggressively. Galbraith believed that the bureaucratic firms of the postwar economy would continue to expand and prosper and that as they grew more and more powerful, the economy would increasingly resemble a socialist system, predictions that were soon proven dreadfully wrong. These expectations were so far off because they neither recognized the economy's capacity to change nor took sufficient account of the arguments made against strikingly similar hypotheses that were debated in the 1930s and 1940s. Schumpeter was among those older economists who thought that capitalism would evolve into socialism, arguing, much as Galbraith did twenty-five years later, that innovation and entrepreneurship would become increasingly bureaucratized, thus undermining the system's ideological foundation and leaving it open to attack. This is puzzling, both because Schumpeter's musings about capitalist evolution are inconsistent with his core doctrine of creative destruction and because Galbraith adopted this flawed part of Schumpeter's work without crediting his former Harvard colleague or the other participants in the earlier debates.

The unraveling of the bureaucratic industrial economy of the golden age and the fashioning of a new and fresher one makes clear both how the process of innovation and change—creative destruction—occurs and how it tends to frustrate economic forecasts. Overly aggressive extrapolation doomed not only Galbraith's predictions but also those made two decades later, which suggested that the decline of America's economy, and the rise of Japan's, would continue indefinitely. The evolution of the automobile, steel, and computer industries over the last thirty years in the face of rising competition and important technological advances and organizational innovations shows more concretely how changes in the economy take place, how established companies such as U.S. Steel and IBM decline, and how new ones, such as Nucor and Microsoft, spring up to take their places.

GALBRAITH'S NEW INDUSTRIAL STATE

The industrial economy of the golden postwar years was dominated by large, bureaucratic manufacturing companies such as General Motors and U.S. Steel, companies that are now considered industrial dinosaurs. Yet writing about them just a generation and a half ago, Galbraith marveled at how such "technically dynamic, massively capitalized and highly organized corporations" had transformed the economy through the "application of increasingly intricate and sophisticated technology to the production of things." Going further, he argued that the industrial giants had succeeded through effective planning, which, in addition to scheduling capital investments and future production, was geared toward "minimizing or getting rid of market influences." Together with enlightened government economic policy, corporate planning had, he thought, tamed the business cycle and created an economy that was converging with socialism. "We have an economic system," he wrote, "which, whatever its formal ideological billing, is in substantial part a planned economy."[1]

Before the 1960s, the "mature" corporations that made up Galbraith's industrial system faced little competition from foreign firms. World War II had crippled the strongest potential competitors, and, in any case, imports had been limited by tariffs that averaged roughly 40 percent from the Civil War through the mid-1930s. The infamous

Smoot-Hawley tariff, enacted in 1930 to protect American industry, predictably induced retaliation by other countries, thus contributing to the Great Depression. Chastened by this experience, Congress passed the Trade Agreements Act of 1934, which encouraged more open trade with other countries, ending a seventy-five-year span in which the United States is thought to have been "the most protectionist of the major powers" other than Russia.[2] Competition among American companies in the golden postwar years was also limited because most major industries were what Galbraith called "imperfect monopolies," industries controlled by three or four big companies rather than a single monopolist. Economists typically call these industries "oligopolies," a name derived from Greek words meaning "few sellers." By their nature, oligopolistic firms share many understandings about their common interests and operate with a fair degree of "mutual forbearance," tending especially to avoid intense price competition. As a consequence, prices are higher than the competitive ideal, and what competition there is occurs in areas such as product design, advertising, and customer service.

The large firms of this industrial system had cozy relationships with their workers as well as their competitors. Most of the biggest companies were manufacturing enterprises whose employees were members of major unions. In 1967, manufacturing employment accounted for about 30 percent of all nonagricultural private-sector employment, compared with approximately 14 percent today. In addition, more than 30 percent of the private-sector workforce was unionized, roughly three times union incidence now, and workers in virtually all large manufacturing industries, such as steel and automobiles, were represented by strong unions. Because competition was relatively limited, most large companies and unions could operate under a basic understanding that divided up the system's spoils. This "accord" gave workers wage increases linked both to productivity gains and to inflation, as well as generous pensions, health insurance, and other fringe benefits; it also imposed strict rules governing layoffs and job transfers. In return, the companies got relative labor peace and, more important, an agreed-upon set of issues over which they would have to bargain with the unions. By constraining potential areas of contention, managers ensured that they would have a reasonably free hand in running their businesses.[3]

Galbraith was most interested in the huge bureaucracies—the "technostructure"—that had replaced entrepreneurs in running the large corporations of his new industrial state. "With the rise of the modern corporation, . . . the organization required by modern technology and planning," he wrote, "the entrepreneur no longer exists as an individual person in the mature industrial enterprise." Instead, "the guiding intelligence—the brain—of the enterprise" was now a bureaucracy, including "all who bring specialized knowledge, talent or experience to group decision-making." In a sense, the corporate managers and other members of the technostructure ran the large corporations much as socialist apparatchiks ran planned economies. They owned little stock in their companies and had little incentive to raise profits beyond a minimally acceptable level. Provided this loose standard was met, top managers could pursue acquisitions and growth opportunities that frequently did more to enhance their reputations, perquisites, and power than corporate profits.[4]

Managers could operate in this way because stockholders' power had become "increasingly tenuous." As Adolf Berle and Gardiner Means had argued in the early 1930s, with the passing of entrepreneurs such as John D. Rockefeller Sr., who built and ran his own company, and merchant bankers such as J. P. Morgan, who created major business combinations in the railroad, steel, electrical equipment, and farm machinery industries and actively supervised them on his investors' and his own behalf, share ownership had become widely dispersed, producing a "decline of individual decision-making and control" and "a massive dissociation of wealth from active management." The separation of ownership and control was not only due to the fact that share holding had become less concentrated and more widely scattered; it was also owing to legal, regulatory, and cultural or institutional constraints that prevented banks, insurance companies, and other financial intermediaries from exercising much control over the companies whose shares they owned or held on behalf of their clients. For example, General Motors' top managers prohibited the firm's innovative pension plan from holding large positions in the shares of other companies, or from trying to influence their policies and strategies, decisions that may have been motivated by the desire of the automaker's officers and directors to be treated similarly. GM's example was particularly important because its pension plan was the first established by a major corporation that was designed to invest significantly in equities, and quickly became the model for most other large plans. For many of the same reasons, unfriendly acquisitions and takeovers were frowned on by banks, investment banks, and other institutional shareholders and custodians, and thus were hard to finance and carry out.[5]*

THE DANGERS OF
AGGRESSIVE EXTRAPOLATION

Whether Galbraith's description was accurate or not, his predictions were way off base. It turns out that he was describing and analyzing the past rather than the future, the old economy rather than the new one. Almost as soon as the book was published, the new industrial state began to unravel under the pressure of foreign competition, for which it was unprepared and not nimble enough to respond to, and inflation, which the labor accord, particularly its automatic cost-of-living wage adjustments, perpetuated. In the 1980s the system was pressed further by more aggressive shareholders and hostile corpo-

---

*In addition to the likelihood that GM's managers and directors wanted their pension fund to be no more active in the affairs of other companies than they wanted other funds or GM shareholders to be in the governance of General Motors, one scholar has argued that they also may have constrained their fund's shareholdings because they feared it would harm their defense of a threatened antitrust action if they appeared to be influencing other companies through their pension fund. In addition, GM's managers may have been concerned that the UAW, which, like other unions, was barred by the Taft-Hartley Act from unilaterally controlling such pension funds, might eventually gain control of the fund.

rate raiders who saw opportunities to make companies more efficient and more profitable by streamlining and focusing their operations and eliminating wasteful bureaucracy. Unsolicited takeovers became an important disciplinary force in the economy because of the development of the junk-bond market, which financed many of the forays. The growing threat of such raids forced corporate managers to focus more on improving efficiency, which perhaps explains why the "bureaucratic burden" stopped rising in the early 1980s. One measure, the ratio of supervisory workers to total employment in the private nonagricultural sector of the economy, rose 50 percent in the preceding quarter century, from about 12 percent in 1948 to 18 percent by the mid-1970s and 19 percent in 1982, but fell slightly over the next ten years.[6]

By the mid-1990s, the bureaucratic Galbraithian economy grounded in stagnant, highly concentrated, unionized manufacturing industries had been almost totally transformed, replaced by a much more dynamic and competitive one led by the technology, finance, and media industries. Facile predictions of Japanese dominance and American decline, so prevalent just a decade earlier, were also turned on their heads. Among the more prominent examples was the Yale historian Paul Kennedy's hugely successful book of the late 1980s, *The Rise and Fall of the Great Powers*. Although the book probed far beneath the relative fortunes of America and Japan at the end of the twentieth century—it is subtitled *Economic Change and Military Conflict from 1500 to 2000*—its concern with America's economic decline and Japan's rise is almost certainly what made it so popular. Kennedy argued that Japan was in the process of overtaking the United States as the world's leading economic power. "In the largest sense of all," he wrote, "the only answer to the question increasingly debated by the public of whether the United States can preserve its existing position is 'no.'" And to the question of "how powerful, economically, will Japan be in the early twenty-first century," he answered, "*much* more powerful." His conclusions were based both on Japanese economic strength and American weakness over the preceding ten or fifteen years and on a general historical tendency of great powers to get bogged down in military adventures, as the United States had done in Vietnam, straining their economies and precipitating their decline. Like Galbraith's *New Industrial State*, which twenty years earlier celebrated a system about to disintegrate, Kennedy's *Rise and Fall of the Great Powers* pretty much denoted the high-water mark for Japan, while failing to appreciate the ongoing revitalization of the U.S. economy.[7]*

Five years later, the Princeton economist Alan Blinder proposed an interesting variant of Kennedy's theme, asking not whether Japan would continue rising and the United States declining but whether the formerly socialist economies should look east or west for a model. Blinder based his argument primarily on his belief that it would be easier for the former socialist countries to make the transition to "Japanese capitalism," which is closer to the socialist model than the more extreme American version. "In their rush to emulate the West," he concluded, "these countries seem to have all but forgotten a quite appropriate economic model developed in Japan, a model which not only works well but requires a less violent transition from socialism." Nevertheless, the article is doubly curious. First, the characteristics of the Japanese model highlighted for easy emulation closely resemble those of the U.S. economy's abandoned Galbraithian past: firms don't maximize profits; job security is high and labor mobility low; and relationships between labor and management, and business and government, tend to be "enduring" and "non-adversarial," built around tradition and long-established understandings and accommodations rather than market forces. Second, even if Blinder considered the

---

*In accounting for Japan's strength, Kennedy, like many others, credits the Ministry of International Trade and Industry (MITI) for presciently "guiding" Japanese industries, functioning, he writes, "as a sort of economic equivalent to the famous Prussian General Staff." But MITI's reputation has dimmed with the economy's collapse and may have been overstated even in the good times. For example, as discussed further in Chapter 4, Toyota and other Japanese auto companies seem to have prospered because they "*defied* MITI and set out to become full-range car companies" rather than combine into two or three specialized firms as the planners recommended.

Japanese model only a transitional phase for the former socialist economies, its recent strength clearly was one of the things that made it attractive. However, the article was written when the collapse of the Japanese stock market and economy was well under way. Their weakness would prove enduring largely because the system was so inflexible.[8]

Not only academics were uncritically euphoric about the Japanese economy; so too were investors. In January 1990, with the Japanese stock market trading near its all-time high, the Kingdom of Denmark issued three-year "put warrants" linked to the Nikkei Stock Average. Traded on the American Stock Exchange, these dollar-denominated securities allowed their holders to profit significantly from falls in the Japanese market over the next three years. Over the preceding seven years, the Nikkei index had risen more than fivefold, far more rapidly than the earnings of its constituent companies. Some thought—correctly, it turns out—that the entire Japanese economy, particularly its elaborately intertwined stock and real-estate markets, was a vastly inflated bubble that was likely to burst; but that was a minority view. (The kingdom, which issued the warrants to raise money to cover an anticipated balance-of-payments deficit, was not risking a fall in the market, because it planned to hedge its exposure.) Even if this view had been wrong, however, and the odds of a stock market crash were low, the warrants were still very attractive: the potential profit was large; they were good for three years, long enough for things to change substantially; and they were traded in a liquid market, affording investors an opportunity to sell at any time. Yet the securities were issued at a price less than 8 percent above that day's closing value of the index, the value from which its decline would be measured, and the warrants continued to trade at low prices for a while after that. (In option terminology, the warrants had a "strike price" that was "at the money" and were sold initially at a "premium" of less than 8 percent.) In other words, a hugely "exuberant" stock market had to fall only 8 percent over the next three years for a warrant holder to make money! And if it fell further, warrant holders would profit even more. In fact, the Japanese stock and real-estate markets began to collapse within months, ultimately falling by more than two-thirds and carrying the economy with them. They have yet to recover.

Galbraith's error, like those of Kennedy, Blinder, and bullish investors in the Japanese stock market of the late 1980s, was that he extrapolated recent experience far too aggressively—a problem that recurs repeatedly because it is so difficult to foresee changes or discontinuities in past tendencies. Thus economic predictions are tolerably accurate when progress is steady and they are least needed, but badly miss turning points when, for example, a business expansion is soon to become a contraction, or a bear market in stocks is about to begin, and prescient forecasts are most needed. Exacerbating the fundamental uncertainty that plagues economic forecasts as well as economic policy, however, is that even gross errors don't seem to tarnish the makers' reputations. They may even enhance their standing. Among the few disastrously wrong predictions that have become notorious is one that resonates particularly sharply today. Just weeks before the stock market crashed in October 1929, Irving Fisher, a prominent Yale economist, assured the nation, "Stock prices have reached what looks like a permanently high plateau." Until the economy and the stock market began to weaken in early to mid-2000, aggressive extrapolation of this sort infected a lot of thinking about our new economy, particularly among Wall Street stock analysts and talking heads in the financial media. By early 2001, however, after the Nasdaq had fallen back to levels surpassed two years before, disoriented investors had begun to blame their disappointments on these chastened experts, and some filed lawsuits against them. But this was just the prelude to the main event. As Charles Kindleberger observed in *Manias, Panics, and Crashes*, which has been updated and reissued three times since it was first published in 1978, financial bubbles typically leave behind a wide trail of messy scandals and litigation. And, as if on cue, by early 2002 a full-blown crisis of confidence had erupted as former stock market favorites, such as Enron, Tyco, and WorldCom, were found to have manufactured their earnings through accounting tricks, bogus transactions, and misleading financial re-ports.[9]*

THE FALL OF THE NEW INDUSTRIAL STATE

The disintegration of Galbraith's industrial state and the emergence of a new economy can be seen very clearly in corporate histories of the last twenty-five to thirty years, especially in the contrasts between the decline of old-economy behemoths such as U.S. Steel and IBM and the rise of new-economy powerhouses such as Nucor Corpora-tion and Microsoft. The stories are interesting for at least three rea-sons. First, they illustrate concretely the workings of the "perennial gale of creative destruction," which, Schumpeter emphasized, "inces-santly revolutionizes the economic structure *from within*, incessantly

---

*To be clear: two types of scandalous behavior came to light after the stock market bub-ble burst—one involving misleading accounting, financial game playing, and fraud at companies such as Enron and WorldCom, which is discussed in more detail in later chapters; and another involving conflicts of interest at investment banks such as Merrill Lynch, Credit Suisse First Boston, and Salomon Smith Barney, which may have affected their research recommendations and their handling of initial public offerings (IPOs) of technology stocks in the frenzied markets of the late 1990s. (Some of these firms, in-cluding Citigroup, which owns Salomon Smith Barney, and Merrill Lynch and J.P. Morgan Chase, are thought to have helped Enron and other companies in disguising their true financial condition from investors by creating "special-purpose entities" and participating in questionable transactions.) Since at least the beginning of 2001, in-vestors, regulators, and prosecutors have alleged that the banks had allocated shares in hot IPOs to favored clients in exchange for their investment-banking and trading busi-ness, higher fees, and promises to support the newly issued shares in the market. It also was charged that because they were conflicted, stock analysts such as Henry Blodget of Merrill Lynch and Jack Grubman of Salomon Smith Barney made recommendations designed to attract investment-banking business for their firms, or gain other favors, rather than trying to honestly guide investors. New York State Attorney General Eliot Spitzer has pursued these charges particularly aggressively, uncovering incriminating E-mail messages that suggested links between the firms' research and investment-banking departments and, together with other regulators, negotiating various settlements, in-cluding a large-scale agreement with the major securities firms. Under that accord, ten investment firms will pay fines totaling almost $1 billion, reform the ways in which they conduct research and manage IPOs, and spend more than $500 million over five years on investor education and on providing independent stock research for their clients. (Salomon Smith Barney is likely to pay about a third of the fine and 20 percent of the other expenses.) The investment banks also will set up a fund to compensate ill-treated investors.

destroying the old one, incessantly creating a new one." Second, as was evident in the development of the transistor and the emergence of the semiconductor industry, they show that while the research divisions of many of the leading firms of the old economy played major parts in uncovering critical new technologies, the inventions were often exploited commercially by smaller and younger companies. Third, even though U.S. defense and antitrust policies encouraged this shift in the locus of innovation, the growing importance of newer companies in the process of modernization, and the sleepiness of many industrial giants, are at odds with Schumpeter's belief that monopolistic "establishments" would, despite their market dominance, remain fierce competitors in ways that mattered most, in developing "the new commodity, the new technology, the new source of supply, the new type of organization."[10]

In addition to placing the doctrine of creative destruction at the center of his interpretation of history, Schumpeter used it to respond to theories of "imperfect," or "monopolistic," competition, which he considered among "the major contributions of postwar economics." These models were initially articulated by Joan Robinson, a Cambridge colleague of John Maynard Keynes, and Edward Chamberlin of Harvard, both of whom were concerned with oligopolies and other industries that fell somewhere between the classical poles of perfect competition and monopoly, that is, between industries with many firms, none of which is strong enough to influence prices, and industries controlled by a single seller. They worried that in these increasingly prevalent intermediate cases, small numbers of large companies would be able to differentiate their products sufficiently, whether through advertising or new designs and styles, to enable them to raise their prices without losing significant sales to their competitors. As a consequence, the amount produced in these industries would be smaller, and prices and profits higher, than in perfectly competitive markets.[11]

"Does not this bear out what the man in the street (unless a businessman himself) always thought on the subject of private business,"

Schumpeter asked provocatively, "that private enterprise is little more than a device to curtail production in order to extort profits?" His answer, of course, was that the theories were too static, that "every piece of business strategy acquires its true significance only against the background of . . . its role in the perennial gale of creative destruction" and "cannot be understood . . . on the hypothesis that there is a perennial lull." When the problem was thought of in dynamic terms, economists, he hoped, would see "the large scale establishment" as

> the most powerful engine of . . . progress and in particular of the long-run expansion of total output not only in spite of, but to a considerable extent through, this strategy which looks so restrictive when viewed in the individual case and from the individual point of time. In this respect, perfect competition is not only impossible but inferior, and has no title to being set up as a model of ideal efficiency. It is hence a mistake to base the theory of government regulation of industry on the principle that big business should be made to work as the respective industry would work in perfect competition. And socialists should rely for their criticisms on the virtues of a socialist economy rather than on those of the competitive model.[12]

As it turned out, the large monopolistic firms of the golden age were not nearly as dynamic as Schumpeter expected them to be. It seems that for the top managers and members of the technostructure that ran them, the easy life that their companies' market power enabled them to lead won out over any fears they may have had about potential competition from new discoveries, business methods, or firms. The remainder of this chapter illustrates some of the consequences of such corporate lethargy in the steel, automobile, and computer industries.

The Decline of Big Steel and the Big Three. More than almost any others, the steel and automobile industries exemplify the strengths and weaknesses of the U.S. industrial economy of the golden postwar years. At the end of World War II, American businesses accounted for roughly 40 percent of the world's output of goods and services. American steel and car companies dominated their markets even more thoroughly, producing half of the world's steel and three-quarters of all automobiles. And while some diminution of their supremacy was inevitable, the depth of their subsequent declines must also be attributed to their bureaucratic nature, which allowed the rise of unimaginative managers who, together with their union counterparts, overestimated their companies' competitive strength and did not respond effectively to a changing world economy. Because they had not innovated or kept up with effective new practices, U.S. automobile and steel companies of the 1950s and 1960s were extremely vulnerable to imports from the recovering war-torn economies of Germany and Japan, whose reconstruction was aided and encouraged by America's postwar economic policies.

Consistent with its unquestioned standing as the dominant world power, the United States assumed a leading role in establishing a framework for the postwar global economy. The focus, unlike that of the interwar years, was, as Paul Volcker has written, on creating "a liberal trading order" and quickly restoring "devastated economies." Even before the war had ended, the United States and its allies convened the United Nations Monetary and Financial Conference at Bretton Woods, New Hampshire, in July 1944, which created two of the three major international economic institutions: the International Bank for Reconstruction and Development (World Bank) and the International Monetary Fund (IMF). Sometimes called the Bretton Woods institutions, they were designed to fund long-term development projects and more immediate balance-of-payments deficits, respectively. The third key element of the postwar arrangements, the General Agreement on Tariffs and Trade (GATT), was reached in 1947 and provided a structure for successive rounds of negotiations that have significantly reduced tariffs and other obstacles to trade and investment. In addition to leading the effort to shape these organizations, the United States forgave most war debts, including roughly $40 billion of lend-lease obligations, and extended foreign aid broadly and meaningfully. The European Recovery Program—the Marshall Plan—was organized in 1948 and funneled more than $13 billion to eighteen western European countries over the next four years, allowing them to rebuild their economies with the latest equipment, much of it American. Overall, roughly 70 percent of Marshall Plan funds are estimated to have been spent on U.S. goods. Although Japan was not included in this program, it received aid of more than $2 billion between 1946 and 1952, and an additional $3.5 billion flowed into its economy as a consequence of U.S. procurement spending in the five years following the outbreak of the Korean War in 1950. Critically, according to Toyoo Gyohten, who served in the Japanese Ministry of Finance from 1955 to 1989, American attitudes and policy toward Japan fundamentally changed, shifting from trying to punish a former enemy to encouraging the recovery of a new ally.[13]

By the 1960s, it had become clear that the competitive balance in the world's steel and auto industries was shifting markedly. The U.S. share of world steel production fell from almost 50 percent in 1950 to about 25 percent in 1960 and 20 percent in 1970, while the imports share of the U.S. steel market rose from 4 percent in 1960 to 14 percent in 1970 and almost 25 percent in 1986. The slide of the Big Three—General Motors, Ford, and Chrysler—also began during the 1950s. Automobile imports, which had been almost nonexistent, had risen to 4 percent by 1960 and increased threefold during the following decade, reaching 11 percent in 1970. They had grown to 21 percent of the American car market by 1979, and 31 percent by 1986, and would have gained even more ground if foreign companies had not begun to set up factories in the United States—"transplants"—in order to gain more direct access to the market, protect themselves against adverse currency fluctuations, and escape existing or future trade restrictions. On a worldwide basis, the market share of American car companies fell apace, from roughly 75 percent in 1950 to 20 percent in 1980, while Japan, whose market share was negligible in 1950, had become the world's leading car producer by 1985. Had the U.S. government allowed a foreign automaker to acquire Chrysler in 1978 rather than choose to rescue the company, the American share of the world market would have fallen further.[14]

Rapidly escalating gasoline prices in the 1970s helped the imports significantly, shifting demand toward fuel-efficient vehicles, such as the Volkswagen Beetle, that American firms did not produce. But foreign companies also were more innovative than U.S. automakers, making reliable cars that required little maintenance and introducing to the American market features such as radial tires, disc brakes, fuel-injection systems, and more fuel-efficient engines, which soon became standard on all cars. Even more fundamental, Japanese firms, especially the Toyota Motor Company, forced American companies to become more efficient and provided a model they could emulate. Chapter 4 describes in detail how Toyota developed its lean production system in order to efficiently produce a wide variety of highly dependable, defect-free cars. Ironically, the system's focus on eliminating defects and improving product quality was due in part to an American industrial engineer, W. Edwards Deming, who had been ignored in this country, while its emphasis on inventory control was inspired by the practices of American supermarkets. Now these innovations have largely come full circle as companies such as Dell Computer, whose "build-to-order" model exemplifies the business methods of the new economy, have taken Toyota's approach to a new level.

Like the automakers, big American steel companies were slow to adjust to changes in world steel markets that began to emerge after World War II. Their languor also seems attributable to complacency bred from long and rich histories and commanding market positions. The mature corporations at the industry's core, such as U.S. Steel and Bethlehem Steel, had been around since the nineteenth century, even longer than the big car companies. Indeed, in 1901, just three years after he had created Federal Steel by combining two steel producers, an iron-ore supplier, and two railroads into the second-biggest firm in the industry, J. P. Morgan formed U.S. Steel, merging Federal with Carnegie Steel, the industry leader, and a number of smaller companies, with the intention of "rationalizing" American steel markets. Capitalized at $1.4 billion, U.S. Steel instantly became the largest corporation in the world. Bethlehem was one of the companies included in the "rollup" but soon was sold to Charles Schwab, Andrew Carnegie's chief lieutenant and an architect of the U.S. Steel consolidation. Under his leadership Bethlehem quickly became U.S. Steel's main rival, the second-biggest company in the United States.[15]

Less than three-quarters of a century later, U.S. Steel, Bethlehem, which declared bankruptcy in October 2001, and the other integrated American steel companies were wounded giants, done in both by foreign producers and by innovative U.S. companies such as Nucor. The improved competitiveness of foreign steel companies was partly a consequence of growth in world iron supplies, which tended to neutralize America's long-standing edge in access to low-cost iron ore. Foreign steel firms also benefited from sharp declines in shipping costs, which reduced the cost of shipping iron ore from Brazil to Japan by 60 percent between 1957 and 1968. And they were quicker to adopt new technologies, such as the more efficient basic oxygen furnace for melting iron ore, which was developed in Austria in the early 1950s, and generally built new plants of the most efficient size. As a result, productivity in Japanese steel plants rose so rapidly during the 1960s that their labor costs per ton of steel produced fell by about a third even though wages rose by almost 250 percent during the decade.

Established American steel companies, on the other hand, were slow to modernize, continuing to use less efficient open-hearth furnaces long after the basic oxygen furnace became available. In 1970, for example, more than 95 percent of Japanese steel was produced using basic oxygen furnaces, while the U.S. share was less than 65 percent. American steel companies were similarly slow to adopt continuous casting, a process that bypasses a number of intermediate steps in producing semifinished steel. In 1975 less than 10 percent of

American steel was cast continuously, compared with 31 percent in Japan and 16 percent in Europe. Moreover, established American steel companies compounded the problems caused by their limited investment in new technologies by not closing inefficient plants and by agreeing to outsize wage increases for their unionized workforces. From 1968 to 1978, average hourly earnings of steelworkers rose by 9.2 percent a year, compared with 8 percent for autoworkers and 6.4 percent for private-sector workers outside agriculture, even though productivity in the steel industry fell relative to that in manufacturing. In addition, since the late 1940s, labor contracts in the steel industry have provided workers with generous retirement benefits, including health and life insurance as well as pensions. As the pool of retirees has grown—they greatly outnumber active workers—so too have these obligations, which total roughly $10 billion, consume a meaningful chunk of the companies' annual cash flows, and make mergers, acquisitions, and other restructuring measures that might reduce excess capacity in the industry much more difficult.[16]

Though American companies' share of all steel sold in the United States and in the world has fallen significantly, the country's integrated producers are in much worse shape than these figures suggest. This is true both because these once-dominant companies have been able to limit imports by filing complaints under antidumping laws and because they have faced even more intense competition from innovative minimills such as Nucor, whose growth has made up for some of Big Steel's shortcomings and moderated the decline in U.S. companies' market share. Antidumping restrictions are designed to protect local businesses from imports that are priced "unfairly" low, but despite this reasonable-sounding purpose, they constitute one of the most serious obstacles to freer trade and greater efficiency. Antidumping restrictions are permissible under GATT because in 1947 British negotiators could not get their U.S. counterparts to appreciate the severity of the threat they posed to trade liberalization. If anything, these concerns are more pressing today as the definition of "unfair" pricing has been broadened, permitting wider use of antidumping restrictions to achieve political objectives, even if they come at great cost to all but the direct beneficiaries. Until the early 1990s, antidumping laws had been used almost exclusively by advanced countries, including the United States, the nations of the European Community, Canada, New Zealand, and Australia, which filed more than 95 percent of all antidumping actions during the 1980s. Since 1993, however, new users have filed more than half of the growing number of antidumping complaints, and traditional filers are now more likely to be defendants than complainants.[17]

In the late 1970s, the Carter administration led opponents of inefficient regulation in challenging antidumping laws as wasteful and expensive ways of maintaining employment in an industry or region of the country. According to Robert Crandall, a Brookings Institution steel expert and long-standing critic of antidumping tariffs, they raised steelworkers' 1978 earnings roughly $18 million above what they otherwise would have been but cost consumers more than $1 billion. And in order to get the big firms in the industry to invest in new plants employing thirty-five thousand more workers, the subsidy, he estimated, would have to rise to about $5 billion, approximately $140,000 for each new job.[18] Despite the lopsidedness of the cost-benefit ratio, antidumping laws remain in place because they protect clearly defined and highly focused interests, while the opposition tends to be diffuse and less intensely affected. Indeed, in June 2001, President George W. Bush, apparently concerned about winning support in steel-producing states such as Pennsylvania, Ohio, and West Virginia and fearing that the Democrats would usurp the issue, abandoned his supposed free-trade principles to call for an investigation of dumping by foreign steel companies. Tariffs of up to 30 percent were imposed on steel imports the following March, helping to create a spike in steel prices that was borne by consumers of products that contain steel and by the companies that make them, which greatly outnumber steel producers and employ far more workers. Bush urged protected steel companies to use their subsidized prosperity to become more competitive, but experience suggests this is highly unlikely. Except for minimills, which have rarely asked for or needed protection, American steel companies have used antidumping protection to postpone making the hard choices necessary to become more efficient.[19]

Minimills such as Nucor have taken more market share from the giants than have foreign producers but, since they are homegrown, have helped to keep down the imports share of the American steel market and boosted the U.S. share of world markets. Unlike traditional steel mills that produce steel from iron ore using basic oxygen furnaces, minimills use electric arc furnaces to produce steel from scrap. It's a more streamlined and efficient process that relies heavily on sophisticated computer controls. Nucor has been a leader among minimills in the United States, aggressively seizing the opportunity created by Big Steel's inefficiency and failure to improve. It built its first mill in 1969 and a decade later was the tenth-largest steel company in the country. Now Nucor is the most profitable firm in the steel industry, more highly valued by investors than all the other companies combined, and is expected soon to become the largest firm in the industry based on revenues. Taken together, minimills had accounted for about 25 percent of American steel production by 1980, nearly 35 percent by 1985, and almost 40 percent by the early 1990s. Without minimill production, imports would have accounted for about 31 percent of steel sold in the United States in the mid-1980s, significantly more than their 25 percent share of the entire American market.[20]

Nucor and the other new steel companies have prospered because of their technology and their approach to business; because, unlike the old stalwarts, they are lean, flexible, opportunistic, and willing to take risks. In the late 1980s, Nucor's corporate headquarters in Charlotte, North Carolina, was reputed to be the smallest of any Fortune 500 company, consisting of seventeen people working in a rented suite of offices "the size of a group dental plan." Its workers were not unionized but were highly motivated, often selected for their initiative rather than their experience in the steel industry.

Roughly twenty raw recruits manned the first minimill, the company president, Kenneth Iverson, told a writer from *The New Yorker*, including "carpenters and butchers and sharecroppers. We had one guy who was an adding-machine salesman." The workers earned a relatively small fixed wage and relatively large bonuses that were paid weekly based on production. They worked in teams of about thirty that largely ran themselves, including deciding who should be fired. As minimills prospered and grew, traditional steel companies were forced to respond, in part by adopting many of their methods. Under Tom Graham, who became chief operating officer in 1983, for example, U.S. Steel cut bureaucracy and overhauled its operations, boosting productivity markedly by using nonunion contract workers to get around onerous union work rules.

In 1990 Nucor introduced another major innovation to the steel industry: continuous casting of sheet steel. The process, which was based on unproven German technology, eliminated the costly and time-consuming steps of cooling newly produced raw steel and then reheating it in order to pour it into slabs and press them into thin sheets. "We're going to cast a very thin slab of steel, two inches thick and fifty-two inches wide," Iverson said, "and then we're going to roll it down into a sheet, in one continuous process." The plant was built in Crawfordsville, Indiana, a rural town in the middle of the Rust Belt with easy access to huge quantities of scrap steel. Initially controlled by three layers of software, the new mill was expected eventually to run almost automatically, creating essentially a "desktop steel mill," much as Apple had done for computers. Nucor pursued the project with typical commitment and willingness to go for broke, which may have contributed to a fatality during the first cast of steel, thus tarnishing its success.[21]

Computers and Software: IBM and Microsoft. The computer industry sprang up in the wake of World War II and for most of its first twenty-five to thirty years was dominated by IBM, a company whose name became synonymous with technology. All that began to change, however, with the development of powerful small computers, particularly the personal computer in the late 1970s, and the proliferation of sophisticated, easy-to-use software that accompanied and stimulated their growth. These innovations and the dramatic transformations that ensued—in technology, in the fortunes of companies such as IBM and Microsoft, indeed in the entire economy—were made possible by the invention of the microprocessor and the continuing improvements in computer processing power and storage capacity at the pace predicted by Moore's law. Many of the consequences are evident in the stock market. From 1962 through early 1973, for example, IBM shares rose more than threefold, but they stagnated during the next seventeen years, gaining just over 30 percent from June 1973 to March 1990, a period that runs from shortly before one economic peak to near a more distant one and spans two others in between. By comparison, the S&P 500 rose more than threefold over the same period. And despite a major reorganization that began early in the decade, for the 1990s as a whole the company's shares did no better than the S&P 500 stock market index. Microsoft, on the other hand, has been one of the new economy's greatest successes. Since it became a public company in 1986, the value of its shares has multiplied almost three hundred times, an increase of approximately 45 percent a year, compounded. (IBM returned less than 10 percent a year to investors over the same period.) For a while in the late 1990s, Microsoft was the world's most valuable company, and Bill Gates, its cofounder and guiding force, remains the world's wealthiest person. The widely disparate experiences of Microsoft and IBM are rooted in the contrary aspects of creative destruction, but they reflect as well the influence of U.S. antitrust policy, the costs of overgrown bureaucracy, and luck, both good and bad.

As its formal name—International Business Machines—suggests, IBM evolved from the office-machinery industry that grew up around the turn of the century with the rise of "big business" and the development of scientific management. It began life as the Hollerith Company, named for Herman Hollerith, who invented the electrically powered punched-card tabulating machine to process data collected in the 1890 Census. In 1914 Thomas J. Watson Sr. became general manager of the successor company, the Computing-Tabulating-Recording Company, and ten years later changed its name to IBM. Since the modern digital computer blends tabulating technology with electronics, it is hardly surprising that many early computer manufacturers came from these industries and that four of these companies, GE, Honeywell, IBM, and National Cash Register (NCR), were among the first to license the transistor from AT&T in 1952.[22]

Cold War defense spending played an important part in the development of computers, as it did with semiconductors, but in this case much of the research took place in universities rather than in private companies. The Electronic Numerical Integrator and Computer (ENIAC), generally thought to be the first digital computer, was built by a group led by John Eckert and John Mauchly of the Moore School of Electrical Engineering at the University of Pennsylvania. Their research was funded by the Army Ordnance Department, which was seeking a better way to make ballistics calculations. The machine was completed in 1945 and was first used in building the hydrogen bomb. Not only was the ENIAC physically cumbersome, containing almost twenty thousand vacuum tubes and occupying a room more than a hundred feet long; because it was "hard wired" to perform particular tasks, it was limited operationally as well. The insight that a computer could work much more flexibly if its operating instructions were stored in its memory, where they could be changed more readily, was suggested in 1945 by John von Neumann of the Institute for Advanced Study at Princeton, one of the world's leading mathematicians and a consultant to the ENIAC project. Von Neumann's idea of a "stored program" was incorporated in the next machine produced at the University of Pennsylvania, the EDVAC, as well as in one he built at the institute in 1951, the IAS computer, and quickly became the preferred approach throughout the budding industry. Nevertheless, its advantages could not be realized fully until computers were standardized enough to be able to run the same software programs, a milestone that occurred when IBM introduced its S/360 series of computers in the mid-1960s.

Throughout the 1950s and early 1960s, manufacturers of mainframe computers produced an entire system, consisting of the computer, peripheral equipment such as printers and card readers, and software, including operating systems, programming languages, and applications. Mainframe systems were expensive, difficult to maintain, and incompatible, making it hard to switch from one setup to another even if the same company made the components. Their use thus was limited to large corporations, government agencies, universities, and well-funded research centers. By the end of the 1950s, IBM had far outdistanced its competitors, earning revenues double those of all American computer makers combined. The company was quick to recognize computers' great potential and moved aggressively to exploit its insight, increasing its engineering and technical staff from five hundred at the start of the decade to five thousand well before its end. To head its research effort, it hired the chief scientist of the Office of Naval Research, a leading sponsor of computer science research at universities and think tanks. The company's great success in these years was largely due to the IBM 650, a popular, relatively low-priced computer that is sometimes compared to Ford's Model T. In the course of the decade, IBM sold 1,800 units of the 650, far exceeding sales of any other computer as well as its own forecasts—its planners thought the company would sell only 250 computers. Government demand accounted for 20 percent of these anticipated sales and must have figured prominently in IBM's decision to produce the 650.

In 1964, under Thomas J. Watson Jr., who succeeded his father in 1956, IBM introduced the S/360 family of computers, which, for the first time, were designed so that different machines in the series could use the same software and peripherals. Because all S/360 computers could run the same programs and use the same printers and accessories, customers could pick and choose more freely among a broad range of price and performance options, knowing they could easily upgrade from one configuration to another. This "scalable architecture," Bill Gates has written, "completely reshaped the industry," expanding the market for computers and making the S/360 "a runaway success." It also encouraged the growth of independent companies to write software applications for the S/360 series and to make equipment such as storage disks and printers for them, and spurred production of "clones," computers that were "plug-compatible" with IBM 360s. Gene Amdahl, a former IBM engineer, built the first line of clones in the early 1970s and was soon followed by companies such as Control Data and Hitachi.[23]

At the same time, Digital Equipment Corporation (DEC), a company formed in the late 1950s by Ken Olsen, an alumnus of the Navy's Whirlwind computer project at MIT, was pushing forward in another direction, making computers smaller, cheaper, and more accessible, another key stage in the process that would eventually alter the relationship between hardware and software and undermine IBM's dominance. DEC produced minicomputers, which were much smaller and less expensive than IBM's mainframes. Its first machine, the PDP-1, cost a little over $100,000, a tenth or less of the cost of most IBM computers but still far above a price that could attract a mass market. In addition, DEC computers were aimed at scientists and engineers, a specialized segment of the market who could do much of their own programming and required little support. Nevertheless, they were hugely successful, and by the early 1980s, just before personal computers came to the fore, derailing Olsen's career and company, DEC had become the second-leading computer maker, and two other new companies, Hewlett-Packard and Data General, ranked among the top ten.

The personal computer (PC) arrived on the scene in the late 1970s, less than a decade after the invention of the microprocessor that made such small and powerful machines possible, and unlike most other major innovations of the postwar period it was developed almost exclusively by new companies and received little direct government support. IBM did not start making personal computers until the early 1980s, but its entry into the market helped to legitimize them, precipitating the market's explosive growth. Ironically, the explosion of PCs turned them into relatively low-priced commodities, which demanded greater manufacturing efficiency for producers to turn a profit while simultaneously establishing the primacy of clever software that would enable people to use their computers more easily and effectively. These changes were not good for IBM, particularly since it ceded most of the commercial gains from the PC revolution to Microsoft, its main software vendor, and Intel, which made the microprocessors for its personal computers. Thus, while Microsoft and Intel were taking off, Big Blue endured a prolonged and wrenching decline, a reversal that, like DEC's, was hardly unusual in an industry whose history is marked by missed or unappreciated opportunities.

Apple Computer, a company formed by Steve Jobs and Steve Wozniak on April 1, 1976, produced the first popular personal computer, the Apple II, which was introduced in 1977 and that year generated $2 million in revenue on sales of twenty-four thousand machines. Apple has shaped the computer revolution both culturally and practically, as a leading symbol of entrepreneurial energy and creativity, on one hand, and as a developer of innovative and influential products, on the other. But like so many pioneers, it has not garnered a commensurately large share of the rewards. The Apple legend is one of irreverent outsiders struggling against the establishment, an image that the company's advertisements and its founders' backgrounds encouraged. Jobs and Wozniak had been high-school buddies who shared an interest in electronics. Both dropped out of college and worked for a while as engineers in Silicon Valley, gaining fame for the video game Breakout, which they designed for Atari in four days. Three years later, they created the prototype for the Apple II in Jobs's parents' garage in Los Altos, California, and earned great wealth when their company went public in December 1980. More well known than Wozniak, Jobs is a charismatic, free-spirited salesman who made a soul-searching pilgrimage to India in the early 1970s, became a member of the Forbes 400 at age twenty-five, and subsequently dated the singer Joan Baez, an icon of the 1960s and 1970s and a former girlfriend of Bob Dylan.[24]

Jobs and Wozniak not only produced the first significant personal computer; as James Fallows points out, they also helped to launch the takeover wave of the 1980s. The Apple II, together with the VisiCalc spreadsheet that was introduced in 1979, allowed corporate raiders and analysts to make instantaneous what-if calculations showing how different economic assumptions would affect their deals. They thus could adjust terms and conditions in the heat of battle or strike quickly and unexpectedly, decided advantages if the targets and their advisers were unprepared and slow-moving. VisiCalc became the top-selling software program in 1980, only a year after it was unveiled, demonstrating quite vividly how crucial such widely applicable software was likely to be in establishing a mass market for PCs. Benjamin Rosen, the venture capitalist who later would be instrumental in setting up Compaq, the first company to produce commercially successful clones of IBM PCs, and Lotus, whose 1-2-3 spreadsheet soon supplanted VisiCalc, was one of those who saw this right away. In July 1979, while working at Morgan Stanley as an analyst of the semiconductor and personal computer industries, Rosen wrote a research report about VisiCalc in which he noted a troubling similarity between early personal computers, mainframes, and minicomputers: the hardware was much more advanced than the software, making the machines useful primarily to hackers, scientists, and others who could do their own programming. VisiCalc, on the other hand, was easy to use by almost everybody and could be applied to a broad range of problems. "So who knows?" Rosen concluded. "VisiCalc could some day become the software tail that wags (and sells) the personal computer dog."[25]

Easy-to-use operating systems were similarly critical to mass acceptance of PCs. About seven years after launching the Apple II, Apple created the first user-friendly computer, the Macintosh, which was introduced during the telecast of the 1984 Super Bowl and soon became the model for subsequent designs. Called "the computer for the rest of us," it was promoted from the start as enabling the adventuresome and strong-willed to overcome conformity, embodied in this case by IBM. Unlike other personal computers that required esoteric typed commands that were hard to remember—for example, C:\>a: to access the A drive—the Mac could be operated using graphical commands, a set of icons accessed by moving a mouse. Among the many factors constraining commercial development of graphical operating systems were the processing power, memory, and monitor quality they required. Acceptance also was limited because not enough applications software had been written for such systems. These restraints largely disappeared during the second half of the decade, however, particularly after Microsoft released its first graphical operating system in the mid-1980s and encouraged software developers to write programs for the new system.[26]*

Windows and Mac have become household names, but it is far less well known that the now standard graphical user interface (GUI) was developed not by Microsoft or Apple but by Xerox Corporation's Palo Alto Research Center (PARC), a hotbed of innovation that an authoritative chronicle of the personal computer industry calls "the Valhalla of computerdom, an idea factory spawning the industry's present and future Hall of Famers." Xerox established PARC in 1970 to create "the architecture of information" and to help it move beyond copiers, a market it dominated. By almost any standard, the center's research was hugely successful, producing, in addition to the GUI, a host of technologies that have become hallmarks of the new economy, including computer networking, laser printing, and some of the basic protocols of the Internet. Many important software developers and programmers also came from PARC, such as the founders of Adobe Systems, the company that created Acrobat, Pho-

---

*According to at least one source, Microsoft learned about Apple's graphical operating system while working on software applications for the company. Jobs tried to ensure that Microsoft would not be able to adopt its approach for at least a year after release of the Mac, but sloppy drafting of the agreement dated the restriction from January 1, 1983, more than a year before the actual launch of the new computer.

toshop, and other popular programs for graphic design, publishing, and imaging. So too did Charles Simonyi, who developed a word-processing program there. In 1981 he left in frustration to join Microsoft, where, describing himself as "the messenger RNA of the PARC virus," he wanted to create a full range of applications software, including a spreadsheet, word-processing program, and electronic mail. Simonyi profited enormously after Microsoft went public, while PARC remained "the nutty professor who never makes a dime on his inventions." And Xerox, a shell of what it was when PARC was at its peak, has been unable to expand or diversify beyond copiers, having chosen to let Apple use the GUI concept in exchange for the opportunity to buy a small amount of stock at below-market prices.[27]

Although it has maintained its lead in various niches of the computer market, particularly those that support fields such as publishing, design, and photography, Apple has never really recovered from its decision not to allow clones of its computers. Perhaps because they were blinded by their technology, or fooled by IBM's stodginess into underestimating the power of its brand name, Jobs, Wozniak, and other company leaders appear to have believed that software writers would prefer to create programs for Apple computers, thereby preserving or extending its advantages. Apple thus forcefully contested all attempts by other companies to produce computers that were compatible with Macs. IBM, on the other hand, did not resist the clones, a posture that may have been due to its success with relatively cheap, standardized mainframes such as the 650 and the S/360 series, which clearly survived Gene Amdahl's versions, or to the fact that it entered the PC market late and hurriedly, and wanted to establish a meaningful presence quickly. Regardless of what motivated the decision, buyers responded to the clones' lower prices and IBM's reputation more than to Apple's style and virtuosity, and IBM-compatible PCs quickly became the industry standard. Once they became dominant, network effects made them hard to challenge as more software was written for these computers, attracting more buyers, and more software writers, and on and on. IBM-compatible desktop and notebook computers account for well over 90 percent of all personal computers sold worldwide, whereas Apple machines constitute only 2–3 percent of the market. Dell is the market leader, producing roughly 16 percent of all PCs, with Hewlett-Packard, which merged with Compaq in May 2002, a close second at about 15 percent, and IBM third with 6 percent.

Why did IBM essentially give away what Alfred Chandler considers "the most valuable franchise in American industrial history"? There are two related answers, both of which involve the changing relationship between hardware and software in the PC world. First, as VisiCalc showed, and Rosen and others understood early on, development of a mass market for PCs made computer hardware a commodity, placing a great premium on efficient production, an area in which Dell was soon to break new ground. Much as Henry Ford did for the old economy when he established the assembly-line method of mass production three-quarters of a century earlier, Dell, which Michael Dell started when he was a student at the University of Texas in the early 1980s, developed a manufacturing paradigm for the new economy that has made the company the world's leading producer of PCs. This flexible, build-to-order system relies on the Internet (and before that, the telephone) for selling computers and for coordinating supplies from its many vendors with its product assembly and shipping schedules. The Dell system, which is discussed in more depth in the next chapter, not only is a model for the computer industry but has become a template for much of the manufacturing sector, including the automobile industry.[28]

As for why IBM didn't profit more from software and chips, the answer is more speculative and involves the company's bureaucratic nature and entrenched position in the computer industry. It seems likely, for instance, that IBM underestimated the potential of the market for PCs, perhaps because it was focused on its core mainframe business. It may also have been ambivalent about PCs because it feared undercutting its mainframes. Either possibility, or both, may explain why IBM was late to enter the PC market and why it was so myopic and rigid when it decided to move. In addition, throughout most of the 1970s the company was embroiled in a grueling antitrust battle with the federal government, a conflict that undoubtedly made it wary of trying to extend its market power to new segments of the computer industry. Even so, it is hard to understand why IBM refused Gates's 1986 offer, made after his company had gone public, to let IBM buy "up to 30 percent of Microsoft—at a bargain price —so that it would share in our fortune, good or bad." Perhaps it was just IBM's cultural rigidity—it was known for requiring non-production workers to wear dark suits and white shirts, far different from the practice at Microsoft, as photographs from the period show clearly. After all, even the federal government had taken an equity stake in Chrysler when it bailed the company out in the late 1970s. Moreover, in December 1982 IBM had bought 12 percent of Intel's shares for $250 million, with the possibility of raising its stake to 30 percent in the future, an investment that helped Intel finance the switch from making memory chips to producing microprocessors. For IBM the consequences of not accepting Gates's offer have been severe: a 30 percent interest in Microsoft would have been worth nearly $90 billion in July 2002, not much below IBM's total market value of $120 billion, even though Microsoft shares had fallen further than IBM's from their peak.[29]

In any case, in 1980 IBM set up a crash program in Boca Raton, Florida, to develop a PC and bring it to market within a year. The tight schedule meant it would have to rely on existing components for its machines, including chips, software, and peripherals. For its microprocessor IBM chose an Intel chip, and it picked Microsoft to supply the computer's operating system, although how it decided is not fully clear. Gates, whose main business was designing computer languages, was working on a deal to supply languages to the new PCs and suggested that IBM use CP/M, an operating system produced by Digital Research, a small West Coast company run by Gary Kildall and his wife, Dorothy McEwen. Industry lore has Kildall missing the critical meeting with IBM because he chose to go flying, but in fact McEwen handled the negotiations, which stalled because the nondisclosure agreement IBM wanted her to sign made her uneasy. Even so, Digital Research might still have gotten the business had a necessary upgrade of its system not been delayed; in that case, Microsoft would have licensed the system from Digital Research and sublicensed it to IBM. But fearing that its language deal with IBM would be jeopardized by Digital's failure to produce the operating system, Microsoft decided to develop one itself. It bought nonexclusive rights to distribute QDOS (Quick and Dirty Operating System) from Seattle Computer for only twenty-five thousand dollars, hired its chief engineer, and quickly produced DOS, the disk operating system that later evolved into Windows.[30]

That Microsoft's initial rights to QDOS did not exclude others reinforces the impression that Gates underestimated the importance of the operating-system contract at first, but he quickly realized how valuable it could be, acquiring exclusivity for fifty thousand dollars and, a few years later, settling a dispute with Seattle Computer for about $1 million. Perhaps even more important, Microsoft charged IBM very little to use DOS. "We gave IBM a fabulous deal," Gates has written, "a one time fee of about $80,000 that granted the company royalty-free rights to use Microsoft's operating system forever." Recognizing that the standards for the personal computer industry were still up for grabs—that "the architecture was for sale"—Microsoft wanted to establish its system in the market as soon as possible. Low licensing fees were important, but it also worked with software developers to get DOS-based applications to the market fast. "Our goal was not to make money directly from IBM," Gates later pointed out, "but to profit from licensing MS-DOS to computer companies who wanted to offer machines more or less compatible with the IBM PC. IBM could use our software, but it didn't have an exclusive license or control of future enhancements. This put Microsoft in the business of licensing operating system software to the personal computer industry."[31]

There is little question that the government antitrust action colored IBM's decisions in the 1970s and 1980s and thus may help to explain its shortsightedness, particularly since IBM maintained an extremely hard line in the case for thirteen years, unlike AT&T, which also had to defend itself against a federal antitrust lawsuit in the 1970s and early 1980s. The government resolved both cases in the early 1980s, dropping the case against IBM and agreeing with AT&T to a plan under which the company would divest the seven regional operating companies, the "Baby Bells." (At the time, AT&T was a regulated monopoly that, in addition to providing traditional local and long-distance telephone service through its own network of lines, manufactured telecommunications equipment and conducted basic and applied research at its widely acclaimed Bell Labs. In 1996 the long-distance company spun off Bell Labs and Western Electric, the manufacturing company, as Lucent Technologies.) Within a dozen years, the economy had changed so profoundly, and the fates of the two companies had diverged so sharply—by January 1993 the various parts of the broken-up AT&T as a group had more than tripled in value, while IBM's shares had fallen by about 20 percent— that people involved on both sides of the cases thought that IBM would have been better off if it had agreed to a breakup. "We were forced by the divestiture to make changes that probably were good for us," conceded Robert Allen, AT&T's chairman. "We may have been more fortunate than IBM in that change was forced on us."[32]

Although agreeing to a breakup, or even having a different attitude toward the antitrust threat, might not have altered the way in which IBM entered the personal computer market, a more flexible corporate ethos would probably have hastened the reorganization and streamlining that it began more than a decade later. Under Louis Gerstner, who became chief executive in 1993, IBM refashioned itself as a provider of software systems and services, which accounted for 52 percent of revenues and 67 percent of pretax profits in 2000, compared with 30 percent of revenues in 1992, when the company lost money. And it reinforced this change of direction after Gerstner left the company, announcing on July 30, 2002, that it would purchase the consulting practice of PricewaterhouseCoopers (PWC) for $3.5 billion, far below the $18 billion the consultants wanted from Hewlett-Packard just over eighteen months earlier. Four months later, IBM agreed to purchase Rational Software, a leading supplier of tools used by other companies, including both Microsoft and IBM, in developing software and in deploying it. As with IBM's acquisition of PWC's consulting business, the $2 billion price for Rational is a small fraction of what it would have been two years earlier, although it still represented thirty-three times the company's expected earnings.[33]*

Ironically, toward the end of the 1990s stock market analysts and investors misconstrued the lessons of the 1970s antitrust cases in assessing the potential impact of the government's suit against Microsoft. Drawing on the experiences of AT&T and IBM, they suggested, or hoped, that Microsoft would not suffer if the government split it up. But AT&T had been a regulated, highly inefficient monopoly when it divested the local operating companies, and IBM was not much more dynamic. Both companies had immense opportunities to reduce waste and bureaucracy and improve efficiency. Microsoft, on the other hand, is an unregulated, hugely profitable, fierce competitor, and it is hard to imagine that it could become more efficient if forced by the government to split itself into two or more parts. At best, any benefits from the plan were highly uncertain, while the risks of costly disruption were substantial and virtually guaranteed. This is especially true because Microsoft is facing significant challenges in the marketplace, both from the Linux operating system and from Java-based platforms for Web-based services, supposedly the next generation of computing. It is fitting that IBM, now reconfigured as a provider of e-business solutions that would benefit from a

---

*To avoid any confusion with data discussed at the beginning of this section: IBM returns cited in this paragraph refer to a different period, which includes the effects of the 1990–1991 recession and the initially tepid recovery, years when the shares fell sharply. The stock did well between the company's revamping in 1993 and 2001, a period that also coincides with the technology-led boom and stock market bubble.

standard operating system, has become one of the strongest backers of the Linux challenge to Microsoft.[34]

ADDENDUM: GALBRAITH, SCHUMPETER, AND THE CONVERGENCE HYPOTHESIS

Galbraith is far from the only well-known economist to suggest that capitalism would converge with socialism. Not surprisingly, the hypothesis flourished in the 1930s and 1940s, stimulated by the trauma of the Great Depression, which infected the economy until the United States began gearing up for World War II in the late 1930s. There were two distinct strands of speculation about convergence: one centered on the need for more government intervention in capitalist economies to overcome their supposed long-term tendencies toward stagnation, and the other involved the possibility that socialist economies would become more efficient by adopting important features of market systems. In particular, it was thought that better information technology would enable socialist planners to calculate changing arrays of "shadow" market prices that could be used to guide resources to those parts of the economy where they were most needed and wanted.

Schumpeter's doctrine of creative destruction should have been an effective counter to both arguments, at least on the abstract level on which they were contested. Its emphasis on the critical importance to capitalist development of innovation and technological change, and on the inherent unpredictability of the process, contains a clear warning about the hazards of assuming that most technological frontiers have been conquered and that investment opportunities will be few and far between. Similarly, one would think that the entrepreneurial essence of the process of innovation would make it impossible for socialist planners to replicate. As it turns out, however, Schumpeter pursued only the first of these points and, at the same time, proposed a theory of the "inevitable decomposition of capitalist society" in which he contended that capitalism would eventually evolve into socialism for cultural, as opposed to purely economic, reasons. Basically, he believed that entrepreneurship and innovation would become so routinized and bureaucratic that they would undermine the system's ideological foundation. Implicit in this conjecture, however, is the questionable assumption that the forces of creative destruction would not, or could not, reinvigorate stagnant, bureaucratic corporate structures, a possibility that seems inconsistent with the idea itself. As noted at the beginning of this chapter, Schumpeter's flawed theory of "what will kill capitalism" anticipates much of the argument of *The New Industrial State*, and it is therefore curious that Galbraith did not acknowledge the prior contribution of his former colleague.[35]*

The "stagnationists" viewed the Great Depression not simply as a harsh and prolonged phase of the business cycle that was exacerbated by misguided monetary, fiscal, and trade policies but also as a symptom of capitalism's loss of vigor. This gloomy perspective is associated most closely with Alvin Hansen, a Harvard colleague of Galbraith's and Schumpeter's who thought the slump resulted from serious longer-term problems, primarily declining population growth and a drying up of "any really important innovations." Schumpeter demurred strongly to this judgment, writing in a chapter titled "The Vanishing of Investment Opportunity" that "the widely accepted view that the great strides in technological advance had already been made and that but minor achievements remain" exemplified "that error in interpretation that economists are so prone to commit." Consistent with his emphasis on innovation and discovery as capitalism's driving forces, Schumpeter believed that economists such as Hansen

---

*In *The New Industrial State*, there is only one indexed reference to Schumpeter (and none to the other main protagonists), and it falls far short of acknowledging the extent to which Schumpeter anticipated Galbraith's convergence argument. Footnote 6 on page 71 of that book quotes only Schumpeter's brief description in *Capitalism, Socialism and Democracy* of "the entrepreneurial type as well as the entrepreneurial function." But beginning in the very next paragraph, Schumpeter goes on to argue that the function is "being reduced to routine," undermining the "position of the capitalist entrepreneur" and ultimately the system itself.

did not sufficiently appreciate that "technological possibilities are an uncharted sea," which means "there is no reason to expect slackening of the rate of output through exhaustion of technological possibilities."[36]*

The second part of the convergence thesis was the focus of a controversy over whether socialist planners could mimic a capitalist price system in efficiently allocating resources among competing uses in the economy. Called the "socialist calculation debate," it featured the Polish economist Oskar Lange, who had worked under Schumpeter at Harvard in the mid-1930s, on one side, and the Austrians Ludwig von Mises and Friedrich Hayek on the other. Although it was important ideologically, the debate was fundamentally sterile, since it was concerned only with a hypothetical question: If planners had all the necessary information about production possibilities and people's tastes and desires, could they establish a system of incentives—that is, prices—that would encourage economic agents to produce what people wanted at minimum cost? Lange tried to show that they could by postulating a trial-and-error procedure in which socialist planners acted as auctioneers. In his model, planners announce a starting set of "accounting prices," require that producers act as if they are maximizing their "profits," and simply raise the prices of goods and services that are in short supply and lower the prices of those that are oversupplied until everything balances.[37]

The problem with Lange's trial-and-error argument, however, is that at best it merely replicates market outcomes in a stationary econ-

---

*Although Hansen was one of the most prominent "Keynesians" of the early postwar years, the author of *A Guide to Keynes*, which introduced many students of the 1950s and 1960s to Keynes's *General Theory*, did not get his stagnationist hypothesis from Keynes, who was concerned primarily with cyclical problems rather than secular ones. Indeed, as Landes points out, except for the stagnationists and their opponents, most economists of the time were absorbed by the immediate problems of the business cycle and even the stagnation debate took place within the cyclical framework developed by Keynes. Schumpeter was unique in emphasizing the importance of technological change and innovation to long-term growth, but in speculating about the demise of capitalism, he seemed to lose sight of the extent to which creative destruction could frustrate such predictions.

omy. As Mises emphasized in this context, and Schumpeter made famous more generally, the most relevant question for any economy is not how it administers "a given industrial apparatus" but how its structures change, how innovation and technological advance create and destroy them. In this dynamic context, what matters most are those data that are continually being developed through experimentation and innovation, information that is unknowable in advance, even in a capitalist economy in which investors and entrepreneurs have great motivation to invent new and improved ways of doing things. It is hard to imagine how socialist planners could, in theory or practice, approximate or simulate this newly emerging information that is so critical to economic progress.[38]

Schumpeter did not apply his doctrine of creative destruction to the calculation debate because he believed, with Lange, that "there is nothing wrong with the logic of socialism." And, like Karl Marx, he thought that capitalism would eventually undermine itself and evolve into socialism, although he thought it would happen for ideological and cultural reasons. Nathan Rosenberg is one of the few fans of Schumpeter to point out how paradoxical it is that he, "a man of deeply conservative instincts, should have written far more extensively, and far more convincingly, about the essential economic workability of a socialist society than did Marx, the foremost exponent of socialism." It is even more ironic, he writes, "because, for reasons that Schumpeter of all people should have understood, centrally-directed socialist societies were economically unworkable. Moreover, a primary reason they were unworkable is that they could never learn how to exploit technological innovations."[39]

For Schumpeter, as for Galbraith twenty-five years later, the critical element in the progression from capitalism to socialism was bureaucratization rather than economic hardship and class struggle, a process that hardly required a revolution. Amid the wreckage of the 1930s he correctly pointed out that "there are no purely economic reasons why capitalism should not have another successful run." Nevertheless, he believed that it would fall eventually, because "its very success undermines the social institutions which protect it, and 'inevitably' creates conditions in which it will not be able to live and which strongly point to socialism as the heir apparent." In his view, the root problem was that "capitalist enterprise, by its very achievements, tends to automatize progress . . . [and] make itself superfluous." Innovation would be "reduced to routine," and as a result the role and social position of the capitalist entrepreneur would be "undermined," leaving the system exposed and "politically defenseless" against ideological attacks led by intellectuals. Unlike other economic systems, capitalism, Schumpeter wrote, "creates, educates and subsidizes a vested interest in social unrest." Or, as Galbraith said of the new industrial state, "it brings into existence, to serve its intellectual and scientific needs, the community that, hopefully, will reject its monopoly of social purpose." Neither Schumpeter nor Galbraith, however, took sufficient account of the system's capacity to renew itself.[40]

New Ways of Working

THE CAPSULE HISTORIES of the semiconductor, computer, automobile, and steel industries provide a broad sense of how businesses changed in the last few decades of the twentieth century. This chapter analyzes the new working arrangements they have adopted and presents evidence of their effectiveness. That major changes in business methods should be necessary in order to exploit important new technologies is hardly surprising: it would be unusual, and perhaps a bit unsettling, if technology were all that mattered. Moreover, a defining characteristic of far-reaching general-purpose technologies is that they stimulate the refinements, complementary innovations, and organizational changes necessary to make them effective on an extended scale. The symbiotic relationship between technological and institutional innovation is evident in earlier economic transformations, which also were powered by mutually reinforcing sets of new technologies and business practices. The industrial revolution of the late eighteenth and early nineteenth centuries, for example, was propelled by the development of steam power and iron machinery and by the accompanying shift from handicraft to factory production, while the railway age of the last half of the nineteenth century was marked by proliferating rail, telegraph, and telephone services and the rise of "big business"—large, integrated corporations with widely dispersed operations. In the early decades of the twentieth century, the economy was transformed again by electric power, the internal combustion engine, and petrochemicals, and by the adoption of mass production, the manufacturing method developed by Henry Ford and his Ford Motor Company.

The organizational innovations of the new economy can be understood both as a means of better utilizing emerging information and communications technologies and as a reaction against the rigidity and wastefulness of an aging industrial economy based on "Fordist" mass-production principles. By the early 1970s, as Chapter 3 showed, many of the pillars of the American economy had become dreadfully sclerotic, unable to cope with aggressive foreign competition and innovative domestic companies utilizing promising technologies and business practices. Reluctantly, and gropingly, even these laggards were forced to experiment with alternatives to their hierarchical operating methods, particularly leaner, more flexible, and more entrepreneurial arrangements modeled on the example of Japanese firms such as the Toyota Motor Company. The new ideal, associated with companies such as Dell Computer as well as Toyota, involves matching production more closely to customer orders, an objective that generally entails producing a greater variety of products in smaller batches, coordinating operations closely with suppliers and designers, giving workers more responsibility to make decisions, and supporting and encouraging them with more training and with pay linked to their performance, such as profit sharing and stock ownership. These new ways of working have drastically streamlined all phases of business operations and raised productivity and profitability, but they take time and effort to implement. Effecting such deep organizational changes helps explain why it took so long for information technology to boost productivity growth meaningfully, as Chapter 2 emphasized. Here the focus is on how these new business practices work.

FROM FORD TO DELL:
MASS PRODUCTION TO MASS CUSTOMIZATION

Henry Ford developed mass production, the manufacturing model that held sway for most of the twentieth century, but the term "mass production" was apparently coined by an editor of the *Encyclopaedia Britannica* who in 1925 asked Ford to write an article for a three-volume supplement he was preparing. The piece first appeared as a feature story in a Sunday edition of *The New York Times* titled "Henry Ford Expounds Mass Production: Calls It the Focussing of the Principles of Power, Economy, Continuity, and Speed." Although the article was attributed to Ford, it was written by his spokesman, William Cameron, who later said that he "should be very much surprised to learn that [Henry Ford had] read it."[1]

Mass production originated as a new approach to making automobiles, but its influence was far more pervasive, demonstrating to all manufacturers how to produce efficiently for a broad market. As the *Britannica* article suggests, Ford was not shy about publicizing his innovative methods, and they spread rapidly throughout the economy, shifting attention to larger-scale production and spurring growth and productivity. "The Ford Motor Company," the historian David Hounshell writes, "educated the American technical community in the ways of mass production." Unlike other turn-of-the-century automakers who used skilled craftsmen to produce small quantities of expensive cars tailored to their customers' needs, Ford concentrated on producing large quantities of standardized products at low cost, and his success initially elicited caustic responses. In 1912, for example, an English automotive journal commented:

> It is highly to the credit of our English makers that they choose rather to maintain their reputation for high grade work than cheapen that reputation by the use of the inferior material and workmanship they would be obliged to employ to compete with American manufacturers of cheap cars.

A year later, Ford introduced his first moving assembly line at his Highland Park plant in Detroit and by 1914 was probably producing more cars than all English manufacturers combined. By the early 1920s mass-production techniques had spread throughout the U.S. automobile industry, tripling its annual output to more than 3 million cars, with Ford accounting for about two-thirds of the total. These methods also began to be used in producing electrically powered consumer durables such as washing machines, refrigerators, vacuum cleaners, and radios, as well as farm equipment and other products whose potential sales were large enough to justify the necessary investments in new factories and equipment.[2]

The key to mass production, Ford believed, was the "simplicity" of its constituent operations, a consequence of dividing the production process into a finely specified sequence of steps that could be carried out by unskilled or semiskilled workers using specially designed limited-purpose equipment. Beyond repeatedly performing their specific tasks, assembly-line workers had no role in the operation. Thinking about issues such as product design, how the factories should be laid out, what each assembler should do, or scheduling deliveries of materials and shipments of finished products was done by professionals: designers, industrial engineers, production engineers, and so on. Workers were discouraged from offering suggestions for making their own jobs more efficient. Even chores such as cleaning work areas, repairing equipment, or checking product quality were done by specialists, including housekeeping workers, equipment repairmen, and quality inspectors. And because production was geared to meet anticipated demand—that is, goods were "built-to-forecast" rather than to meet firm orders—and equipment could not readily be stopped and started, companies tended to accumulate massive inventories of final goods, materials, and work in progress.[3]

Carrying out the simple individual tasks of Fordist production required standardized parts of uniformly high quality that could be fit together easily without interrupting the assembly process, a need that few others recognized but one that Ford pursued with "near-religious zeal." Aided by improved machine tools that could work with hardened metals that would hold their shape, Ford-produced parts became increasingly homogeneous and easy to assemble, enabling the company to progressively routinize workers' tasks and speed the flow of work. It helped that Ford cars were designed to be easy to manufacture as well as easy to operate and repair, especially the Model T, which was introduced in 1908, the nineteenth model Henry Ford had built since the original Model A in 1903.

Before 1908 Ford cars had been assembled at a single station, frequently by one or two assemblers who worked an average of almost nine hours on each set of tasks, such as attaching the wheels, springs, motor, transmission, and generator to the chassis, before performing the same operations on another car. In this early setup, assemblers had to collect the parts needed for each phase of their work and file and smooth them so that they fit together. However, by the end of 1912, the last year before Ford began using the moving assembly line to carry the car in progress from worker to worker, the assembly process had been streamlined and the individual steps pared down so much that workers were spending less than 2.5 minutes on each set of tasks for which they were responsible. The moving assembly line cut the average "task cycle" in half, to about 1.2 minutes, and the time required to form an almost finished vehicle fell even more, from twelve and a half hours to about an hour and a half.

Ford's development of the moving assembly line to improve productivity in his plants illustrates a critical difference between his approach and that of Frederick Taylor, with whose scientific management it is often linked. Like Taylor, Ford and his engineers constantly sought to establish precise procedures and standards for performing most efficiently the tasks involved in producing automobiles. Indeed, Ford and other Detroit-based companies may have adopted many of the core principles of "Taylorism" before Taylor did. But, more fundamental, "the Ford approach was to eliminate labor by machinery," Hounshell concluded, "not, as the Taylorites customarily did, to take a given production process and improve the efficiency of the workers through time and motion study and a differential piecerate system of payment." In other words, "Ford engineers mechanized work processes and found workers to feed and tend their machines"; as a consequence, "the machine ultimately set the pace of work at Ford, not a piecerate or an established standard for a 'fair day's work.' This was the essence of the assembly line and all the machinery that fed it."[4]

By boosting productivity, assembly-line production allowed Ford to keep prices low, thus increasing sales and, because mass-production techniques were so effective in capturing economies of large-scale production, enabling it to reduce prices further as more cars were produced and unit costs fell. Between 1908, when the first Model Ts were produced, and the early 1920s, when more than 2 million were made, the Model T's price fell by almost 70 percent after inflation. The assembly line was introduced at Ford's Highland Park plant in mid-1913 but was resisted at first by the workers. For the year as a whole, employment averaged 13,623, but only because nearly 65,000 workers were hired, enough to make up for more than 50,000 who left the company in frustration, out of boredom, or because they couldn't keep up with the pace of the line. The turnover rate averaged 370 percent for the year but was much higher in the months after the assembly line was installed. "So great was labor's distaste for the new machine system," a Ford biographer wrote, "that toward the close of 1913 every time the company wanted to add 100 men to its factory personnel, it was necessary to hire 963."[5]

Although Detroit was not yet a union town, the threat of unionization and work stoppages may have concerned Ford more than high turnover. High fixed costs and dedicated machinery made mass-production plants particularly vulnerable to strikes and disruptions, and the Wobblies—the Industrial Workers of the World, or IWW—had been active in Detroit in the spring of 1913, briefly stopping production at Studebaker. Whether reducing turnover or staving off the Wobblies and other unions was the main factor, Ford moved quickly to stabilize relations with his workers, establishing his famous "five-dollar day" in January 1914. Under the plan, workers would continue to earn a base wage of $2.34 per day, which had been set just three months earlier, but they could also qualify for supplements, boosting their daily pay to $5 or more. These bonuses were called "profit-sharing" payments, but they were based on a worker's "character" rather than his effectiveness. To determine who was worthy, the company established its intrusive Sociological Department, whose members visited workers every six months to ensure that they were leading "clean, sober, and industrious" lives, in "well lighted and ventilated" homes, located outside "congested and slum areas of the city," making it unlikely that they would waste the money in "riotous living."

The five-dollar day generated favorable publicity for the company, burnished Henry Ford's image as an industrial statesman, and, by raising workers' incomes, increased their buying power and thus their demand for other goods and services if not for cars. Business leaders initially denounced Ford as a utopian, a socialist, and "a traitor to his class," but by the 1920s many had come to appreciate the benefits of higher wages and profit sharing in raising morale, productivity, and aggregate demand and in gaining labor peace. High wages were an integral part of the philosophy of "welfare capitalism" that many leading companies adopted after World War I, and even though he eschewed general wage increases after 1919 and fought viciously against unionization of his company, Henry Ford continued to celebrate the advantages of greater pay, maintaining, for example, in *Today and Tomorrow*, which was published in 1926, that the "wage motive" was "the fundamental motive of our company." But higher wages only were justified, he believed, if they stimulated workers and managers to boost productivity and lower prices. "It is this thought of enlarging buying power by paying high wages and selling at low prices which is behind the prosperity of this country," he wrote. "If we set ourselves to the payment of wages, then we can find methods of manufacturing which will make high wages the cheapest of wages."[6]

Ford's obsessive quest to control production costs by mechanizing, standardizing, and simplifying the work process extended beyond his search for better ways to manufacture automobiles. He also sought to integrate assembly operations with many of the other steps involved in making and distributing cars, including producing the necessary steel, glass, and tires and transporting the raw materials and finished products to and from the Ford facilities. This vision was embodied in the mammoth Rouge production complex, built shortly after World War I on a two-thousand-acre piece of land along the Rouge River in Dearborn, just outside Detroit. Rouge was the largest industrial complex in the world, an "industrial colossus" that employed almost 100,000 workers at its peak. Extreme and striking, a facility in which raw materials "came in one gate, while finished cars went out the other gate . . . completely eliminating the need for outside assistance," Rouge symbolized the possibilities of "vertical integration" that other companies sought to emulate. Ford even tried to add raw materials to the mix, maintaining a rubber plantation in Brazil and iron mines in Minnesota. He also had fleets of ships, railroad cars, and airplanes for carrying resources, equipment, and finished cars.[7]

Ford was motivated to integrate in this way because he was much more efficient than his suppliers and thus could profit from doing more things internally, but he also distrusted others and seemed to need to control everything himself. Whatever the benefits in the short term, the managerial difficulties of coordinating such large and diverse operations were equally great, especially for somebody who could not bear delegating authority. In addition, Ford's obsession with manufacturing may have caused him to neglect marketing and design. For almost twenty years, the company concentrated almost exclusively on the Model T, leaving it vulnerable to competition from General Motors, which had adopted Ford's production methods but also had created a far broader product line with annual model changes. In 1927 Ford was forced to stop producing the Model T and closed the Rouge complex for almost a year in order to develop new products. Fittingly, because it was so representative of its patriarch's strengths and weaknesses, Rouge was the setting for a bloody labor battle about a decade later in which the United Automobile Workers won the right to represent Ford workers, the last of the Big Three's employees to be organized.[8]

If Ford and Rouge are emblematic of the old business system, Dell Computer, which Michael Dell describes as *virtually* integrated," is representative of the new one. What he means, beyond the clever wordplay, is that Dell has succeeded by "focusing on delivering solutions and systems to customers" and "stitching together a business with partners that are treated *as if* they're inside the company," rather than by following Ford's example and trying to do everything itself. In other words, the company, which sells directly to its customers the computers that they specify, is largely a middleman, coordinating its selling and assembly of computers with the activities of outside suppliers, service technicians, and delivery firms such as Airborne Express and UPS. Virtual integration would not be possible without sophisticated information and communications technology. With it, Dell has been able to expand its direct-to-customer business model and become in less than twenty years the world's leading computer maker, with 2001 sales of approximately $30 billion and a market value, even at its low point on September 21, 2001, of more than $40 billion. It employs fewer than twenty thousand people directly but four or five times as many through the business it commits to its partners. Dell's superior efficiency was especially apparent during the 2000–2002 economic slump, when it slashed prices aggressively and gained market share, a strategy that may have helped drive Compaq and Hewlett-Packard, the second- and fourth-ranking computer manufacturers, to merge.[9]

To better appreciate how the system works, consider Dell's relationships with some of its vendors and big customers. Sony produces monitors for Dell's computers, and they are so reliable that Dell doesn't feel it has to test them or carry any buffer stocks. It doesn't even have to take delivery of the monitors. Instead, Michael Dell recounted, "we went to Sony and said, 'Hey, we're going to buy two or three million of these monitors this year. Why don't we just pick them up every day as we need them?' " What actually happens is that Dell instructs "Airborne Express or UPS to come to Austin and pick up 10,000 computers a day and go over to the Sony factory in Mexico and pick up the corresponding number of monitors. Then while we're all sleeping, they match up the computers and the monitors, and deliver them to the customer." For Sony, the relationship with Dell is a large source of demand, and because Dell builds computers only in response to firm customer orders, its needs are relatively predictable, at least in the short term. Moreover, Dell's advanced data-sharing systems allow it to communicate this information to its suppliers, in some cases reporting its inventory levels, replacement needs, and delivery schedules hourly.

Similarly, because Dell maintains electronic records of customer orders, including the exact specifications of their computers and workstations, its technicians can pinpoint problems much more easily and precisely when complaints arise. And for large customers such as Boeing and Eastman Chemical, it often provides special services. Boeing has more than 100,000 Dell PCs, and to service its needs, Dell stationed roughly thirty people at the company who "look like Boeing's PC department" but are not employed by Boeing and probably are not even employed directly by Dell. Eastman Chemical, on the other hand, has developed unique software packages for its workstations, and Dell maintains in its factory a high-speed network and massive server loaded with the relevant software components, enabling it to equip Eastman's new computers during the assembly process with the particular software mix that each requires, saving the company roughly three hundred dollars per machine.[10]

One of the most obvious advantages of the Dell build-to-order system is that it substantially reduces the need for inventories, and some of the clearest evidence that companies have adopted such new operating methods can be seen in the decline in inventories throughout the economy over the last twenty years. Relative to sales, inventories in the goods-producing sectors of the economy have fallen by about 20 percent since the early 1980s, driven largely by the fall among durable-goods producers such as Dell and Ford, whose inventory-to-sales ratios dropped roughly 30 percent during this period. Curtailing inventories lowers businesses' operating costs, but it also appears to have helped reduce the volatility of economic growth and inflation, reinforcing the benefits of better monetary policy that has aided the economy since Paul Volcker became chairman of the Federal Reserve System in August 1979. Better inventory controls increase profits because less money is tied up in carrying inventories and because firms with lower inventories tend to link them to product lines that are selling well, making it likely that fewer items will become obsolete or have to be discounted or written off. For the U.S. durable-goods sector, the capital freed up by carrying fewer inventories is on the order of $500 billion, saving roughly $25 billion in annual carrying costs if financing rates are around 5 percent and more if they are higher.[11]

Progress in controlling inventories and managing supply chains has encouraged automakers and other businesses to think about capturing the even bigger payoffs that may be possible by further emulating Dell's methods. For example, automobile inventories are now about $100 billion, and McKinsey & Company consultants estimate they would be 60–80 percent lower if cars were built to order rather than in anticipation of future sales. According to Nissan, the resulting savings could be as much as thirty-six hundred dollars per car. The problem for the automakers, however, is that most auto plants do not make money unless they operate at 80 percent of capacity or higher. As a result, the potential advantages of building to order are likely to be eaten away by inefficiently small production runs unless demand can be spread out appropriately or production methods made flexible enough to accommodate lower volumes more effectively.[12]

In fact, Dell not only builds its computers solely in response to firm orders; it also encourages buyers to customize them to fit their own needs. (An ad that ran widely in the fall of 2000, for example, featured a typical teenager dressed in baggy pants and sneakers and slouched before his computer, telling readers, "Everyone at school bought these shoes and got this haircut, but my computer is 100% me.") Even if they don't customize their computers, however, Dell customers pay for them when they place their orders, giving the company free use of the money until it must pay its workers and suppliers for producing the machines. In the first few months of 2000, Dell's average float—prepayments that are temporarily available to the company—was about $1.5 billion, roughly two-thirds of its monthly sales. Assuming Dell earns 5 percent on the money, float of this magnitude contributes close to $100 million to its annual earnings, a further attraction to automakers and others not yet engaged in mass customization or able to get customers to prepay.

Dell is able to produce customized computers for a mass market because they can be built from a limited number of modular components that can be assembled quickly in response to customer specifications. And while automobile suppliers have been working closely with car companies to design and produce complete units for the manufacturers to assemble, including systems for braking, climate control, and car interiors, there may be limits to how far they can go, particularly since the United Automobile Workers remains strongly opposed to modularization because it would reduce even further the work done under their contracts with the Big Three automakers. The attractions are so great, however, that automakers are unlikely to stop trying to become more like Dell, transforming themselves into virtually integrated "brand owners" that simply design, engineer, and market cars, while outsourcing everything else. A Finnish engineering company currently makes Porsche Boxsters, and even once-proud Rouge, which now houses only three thousand workers producing eight hundred Mustangs a day, is heading in that direction, undergoing a $2 billion face-lift designed to turn it into a flexible assembly plant of the future.[13]

NEW TECHNOLOGY AND
NEW BUSINESS PRACTICES

Although Dell's build-to-order business system is broadly representative of the new ways of working in the new economy, and shows how sharply they differ from the mass-production methods of Henry Ford, no single company reflects the full array of arrangements that have sprung up over the last two decades. The new methods encompass a variety of elements, technological as well as organizational, new machinery and equipment as well as new ways of compensating workers, and new relationships between managers and workers and between companies and their customers and suppliers. Moreover, the individual components of these systems have been tailored and combined in different ways to fit the needs and circumstances of different companies, often through prolonged and difficult trials and errors. Regardless of the specific configurations, however, the ingredients of the new arrangements tend to reinforce one another, making them far more effective when they are used in combination than when they are adopted individually.

One way to get a sense of the breadth and scope of these new practices is by distinguishing among the ways in which they utilize new technologies, influence business operations, and vary across firms and industries throughout the economy. In general, technological advances over the last several decades have reduced business costs and altered business practices in at least three important ways. First, powerful small computers linked in high-speed networks have reduced the costs of collecting, processing, and transmitting information, allowing many businesses to integrate more closely with their suppliers and customers. Second, new information and communications technologies have been incorporated in computer-controlled machine tools and other modern equipment, making them more precise and flexible, easy to switch from one task to another. The new equipment has made it possible for manufacturers to produce a wider array of styles and products in smaller batches, with better control over quality. Companies also have discovered they can better operate in this way if they are less rigid and hierarchical and more collaborative; as a consequence, they have broadened the scope of jobs, raised skill requirements for their workers, and provided more training and more incentive pay. Finally, machine-tool makers can produce such sophisticated equipment because of advances in computer-aided design and manufacturing (CAD/CAM), which, as the name implies, uses powerful computers and advanced software to design and make things. CAD/CAM has shortened product-development cycles for many companies, including machine-tool users as well as makers. It has also enabled designers to ensure that their products are easy to manufacture. Thus, by the late 1980s, GM's manufacturing equipment was sufficiently flexible, and its design process efficient enough, to enable it to produce samples of the next year's models in an operating factory without interrupting its regularly scheduled production, the first time such realistic testing was possible.[14]

Closer Links with Suppliers and Customers.   Dell, like Wal-Mart, which was discussed in Chapter 1, is a particularly good example of how the Internet and other new technologies for processing and transmitting information have enabled companies to change the ways in which they interact with their suppliers and customers, reducing costs, raising productivity, and in many cases blurring the traditional boundaries between firms and their suppliers. Many other companies have improved their supply chains similarly, including:

• UPS, a Dell partner that has increasingly used the Internet to service its customers more efficiently and effectively. By the late 1990s, its Web site was fielding close to a million tracking inquiries a day, costing the company about ten cents to provide the necessary information for each package, compared with two dollars over the telephone.

• Eastman Chemical, a large Dell customer that now handles about three-quarters of its own purchases electronically at a cost of forty-five dollars an order, roughly one-third the cost of processing them using paper records and the telephone. Between 1991 and 1999, Eastman's sales rose from roughly $3.5 billion to $4.6 billion, yet by using the Internet to process its orders, the company was able to cut its purchasing staff almost in half, lowering costs and freeing about forty workers for more challenging jobs.

• Baxter International, a large maker of health-care products that in the 1980s created an electronic system to handle orders from hospitals more efficiently, hardly an insignificant improvement, since big hospitals make more than fifty thousand orders a year. Nevertheless, it was soon apparent that this "ASAP" system enabled Baxter to do much more to help hospitals manage their supplies, including designing more efficient storage areas, computerizing their inventory-control systems, and replenishing their inventories automatically as needed. ASAP cost about $30 million to develop and requires $3 million a year to operate, but it reduced Baxter's order-processing costs by $10–$15 million a year, providing a substantial return on its investment even before accounting for the additional business it generated.[15]

The video-rental and trucking industries are less common examples of how advances in information technologies have enabled businesses to streamline and improve their relationships with suppliers and customers. The video-rental industry consists of about twenty thousand stores that rent movies and other videos to the public. About half the stores are owned by independent operators or small chains and half by large chains such as Blockbuster, Inc. These firms can buy or rent their films from the distribution arms of the movie studios that produced them or from independent distributors. Videos are significant for the studios, accounting for more than half of all domestic revenues, even though most rental stores bought their tapes prior to 1998, paying roughly seventy dollars each, a price that appears to have limited their stock and constrained revenues for the studios, rental firms, and other distributors. Revenue-sharing contracts in which the stores pay a small up-front fee of approximately five dollars and share rental revenues with the studios had been around for about a decade but were not widely used because not enough stores could afford the smart cash registers and special networks that would allow the distributors to monitor rental revenues and ensure accurate accounting. By the mid- to late 1990s, however, easier access to the Internet, lower computer prices, and new software that could track rental revenues reduced monitoring costs significantly, making revenue sharing feasible for at least half of all video-rental outlets. Wider use of revenue-sharing contracts in 1998, when retailers chose them for roughly half of all films for which it was an option, raised film inventories by about a third, boosted revenues, and increased the combined profits of the rental firms and distributors by roughly 7 percent.[16]

In trucking the story is even more straightforward. Productivity in trucking depends on filling trucks as close to capacity as possible, which requires matching shippers' demands with trucks that can service their needs efficiently. Better matching has an especially big payoff when partially filled trucks can pick up extra cargo from customers along their routes, but doing so depends on having real-time information about customers' needs and locations. Growing use of electronic tracking systems—onboard computers that use wireless transmission technology to communicate with a central base—has enabled truck dispatchers to keep abreast of customer shipping needs and truck locations and match them with each other; as a result, loads have risen noticeably as these devices have become more prevalent.

Although truckers and trucking companies had been using onboard computers since the late 1980s, their use picked up markedly as prices fell during the 1990s. Between 1992 and 1997, for example, almost 60 percent of all trucks two years old or younger were equipped with electronic monitoring systems, compared with only 15 percent of trucks that were at least seven years old. The more advanced devices record trucks' precise locations and enable the truckers to communicate with their dispatchers in close to real time. They also record information about how the trucks are operated, including when they are turned on and off, how fast they are driven, how often they brake abruptly, and when the engines malfunction. Simpler "trip recorders" perform only the latter functions and are not much use in enabling dispatchers to help keep the trucks full. But according to one study, the advanced systems raised capacity utilization 11 percent in trucks that had them in 1997, and even more for trucks used for longer hauls. For the entire industry, these improvements were worth approximately $15 billion. And because Schneider National of Green Bay, Wisconsin, had its trucks equipped with systems like these, its dispatchers were able to guide to safety the eighteen company drivers who were in Manhattan when terrorists attacked the World Trade Center on September 11, 2001.[17]

CAD/CAM and Flexible Manufacturing. The machine-tool industry, which makes machines and equipment used by the entire manufacturing sector, including machine-tool makers themselves, has been a central conduit through which information technology has helped boost productivity. Computer-aided design and manufacturing have improved productivity in the machine-tool industry itself, in manufacturing industries that use its more powerful and precise machines to produce better products more efficiently, and in the industries that use these improved products to deliver superior services to their customers. Many of the gains are evident at Huffman Corporation, a modestly sized machine-tool maker in Clover, South Carolina. One of the company's machines cuts and shapes metal components for power-steering systems in cars. Because they are better designed and easier to make and are produced using more advanced equipment, these "elevator-sized" machines are now made in approximately eight hundred hours, about a third less time than five years ago. They are also about 20 percent cheaper and much smaller (they used to be "room-sized"), in part because their electronic components are so much more compact. Huffman's rising productivity is reflected in its operating profits, which have grown by about 35 percent a year over the last five years even though its sales rose by only 8 percent annually. Their advanced technology also makes Huffman-produced machines much more precise and easy to operate, able to produce parts that fit together far better. As a consequence, power-steering systems are cheaper to manufacture and less noisy, benefiting automakers, their suppliers, and customers.[18]

Huffman also makes a grinding machine that produces broaches used by surgeons performing hip-replacement operations to shave and shape a patient's bones so that the new hips will adhere properly. Until recently, these instruments were made by hand, but Huffman's computer-controlled machines can produce broaches that are sharper and less expensive and take about one-tenth the time to make, less than twenty minutes today compared with more than three and a half hours in 1994. Paragon Medical, Inc., a broach maker, bought $5 million of Huffman's machines between 1998 and 2002, enabling it to reduce its costs by about 20 percent a year, with further improvements expected. (The machines can run more rapidly than the speeds at which they are used, but the workers are not yet able to keep up with the faster pace.) And the new devices enable surgeons to do a better job in less time. "You can sculpt the bone with more agility because of improvements in the instruments," claims the head of orthopedic surgery at Pascack Valley Hospital in Westwood, New Jersey, reducing the time of hip-replacement surgery by more than 15 percent. These improvements are real and meaningful, as anybody with titanium hip joints knows well, but many of the gains for patients and doctors are very hard to measure precisely and do not show up in any productivity statistics.

Smaller, smarter machine tools that are more flexible and easier to use frequently stimulate comprehensive changes in the way manufacturing is organized. The aircraft-engine maker Pratt & Whitney, for example, is trying to do away with its mass-production-based system in which engine parts are produced in huge batches and then spend days or weeks in inventory, moving long distances within its plants to reach the next stage of processing. Turbine blades produced in the company's 1.3-million-square-foot factory in North Haven, Connecticut, spend ten days traveling to the machines that will carve notches in them so that they can be attached to the other parts of the engine, a procedure that takes less than five minutes. By using smaller grinders and other machine tools that can be operated by a single worker, the company hopes to keep parts flowing from step to step in the production sequence, eliminating waste and generating significant productivity gains. In the new setup, a blade spends about two hours in the entire notching phase, including travel time, and seven days in production, roughly a third of the time it takes to make and finish blades under the old arrangements. They will cover about a third of a mile in completing the process, less than a quarter of their former journey. Pratt & Whitney believes the overhaul will enable it to close the North Haven facility, eliminate seventeen hundred jobs, and move all the work to a newly designed 300,000-square-foot plant in East Hartford, changes that will pay for themselves in about three years.

LEAN PRODUCTION: A NEW MANUFACTURING MODEL FOR THE NEW ECONOMY

The working arrangements that Pratt & Whitney is instituting in East Hartford combine modern machine tools with some of the organizational innovations that were developed by the Toyota Motor Company after World War II, when it became clear that the company could not simply mimic the mass-production methods of the American or European car companies. In 1950 Eiji Toyoda, an engineer and member of the company's founding family, made a pivotal visit to Ford's Rouge plant, the largest and most efficient manufacturing complex in the world. At the time Rouge was producing roughly seven thousand cars a day, while Toyota had produced less than three thousand in its entire lifetime. Perhaps because he knew he would have to do things differently, Toyoda recognized at Rouge "some possibilities to improve the production system" that over the next fifty years would transform not only automobile production but all of manufacturing, and most other businesses as well.

Toyoda developed many of the basic principles and techniques of the new production system in the 1950s and 1960s, in collaboration with Taiichi Ohno, Toyota's chief production engineer. The process came to be called "lean production" because, compared with mass production, "it uses less of everything": less factory space, because its plants are more compact and accumulate fewer inventories; less time to design and develop new products, because lean producers empower relatively small groups of engineers and designers to control the projects from beginning to end, drawing on people from all relevant specialties, including suppliers and sometimes frontline workers, to ensure that the new products and components will be easy to manufacture; and less effort in fixing faulty products, because lean companies seek to be defect-free at every stage of production and try to catch mistakes early, before they are passed on and become more difficult to fix. And since lean techniques are flexible enough to be used efficiently on a relatively small scale, practitioners can offer consumers a much greater variety of higher-quality products. In a sense, lean manufacturers combine some of the best features of both craft and mass production.[19]

Like most important technological innovations, lean production evolved gradually, in ways that were not fully anticipated, motivated from the start by a compelling need to make the reigning manufacturing model fit the capabilities of the small, capital-constrained postwar Japanese economy. Toyota and the other budding Japanese car companies were relatively free to experiment, because they had less invested in the old system and because they were protected from international competition, and from outside control, by high tariffs on imports and a government ban on foreign investment in the industry. None of this would have mattered very much, however, had the twelve carmakers gone along with the Ministry of International Trade and Industry, which wanted them to merge into two or three large firms, each specializing in a particular segment of the automobile market. Instead, they became full-line car companies by turning the prevailing Fordist production model upside down. Mass production mechanizes and standardizes the work process and treats its workers as if they were cogs in the machines they tend. In lean production, on the other hand, workers play a much more active and thoughtful role, one in which they are relied on to analyze and fix problems as they arise, and continually question how the work process might be improved and made more efficient. "The truly lean plant," a book based on the findings of the Massachusetts Institute of Technology International Motor Vehicle Program concluded, "transfers the maximum number of tasks and responsibilities to those workers actually adding value to the car on the line, and it has in place a system for detecting defects that quickly traces every problem, once discovered, to its ultimate cause."[20]

As implemented by Toyota, this seemingly simple change in perspective had enormous, and often surprising, implications. For example, it quickly became clear that for the system to be effective, workers had to be better informed about how the production process was organized, and not constrained by narrow job assignments and classifications. They also were more valuable if they were trained in a wide variety of skills and encouraged to use them freely, perhaps by having part of their pay tied to company productivity or profitability. Finally, the system proved more efficient if the workers were not isolated but were grouped in self-directed teams and production cells in which they collaborated with their fellow workers and managers in designing, organizing, and operating an entire phase of the production process, including controlling quality, maintaining their work area, filling in for absent co-workers, and stopping the entire assembly process to correct serious problems, an option that is rarely used. Fulfilling these responsibilities might also require team members to work closely with designers and suppliers to ensure that components are compatible with one another and easy to assemble and arrive when they are needed.

These insights and organizational changes did not arise all at once but evolved incrementally. One of the first things Ohno did was to experiment with new ways of changing the dies on the big presses that stamp out the roughly three hundred steel panels that are welded together to make a car body. Different automobile models require different dies, and changing these templates had long been a major obstacle to more flexible use of the stamping machines. The big American companies used specialists to change them, a process that generally took a full day; as their production grew, they bought more presses that they could dedicate to making large quantities of specific parts. But Toyota's capital budget was limited and potential demand for its cars relatively small, forcing Ohno to come up with a method for producing its line of automobiles using only a few presses. He decided to try changing the dies more frequently, having regular production workers who would otherwise be idle make the changes, and to use rolling platforms to help them move the dies to and from the stamping machines. By the late 1950s, Toyota workers had become able to change dies in about three minutes, making it feasible to produce parts in small quantities. It also turned out to be cheaper to make them on a smaller scale, because less capital was tied up in carrying large inventories and because it was easier to pick out defective parts from smaller batches, thus catching them before they were incorporated in assembled cars, where the problems would be much harder to fix.[21]

The Toyota production system is rightly famous for its "just-in-time" method of inventory management, since low inventories are both a consequence and a driving force of lean production. With few inventories there is little margin for error, placing a great premium on getting things right at every step in the production sequence and quickly correcting mistakes when they arise. This, in turn, requires a workforce that is versatile, trained in various aspects of production, and able to exercise initiative and anticipate problems before they come up. Ohno appears to have recognized the importance of controlling inventories from observing American supermarkets. "Combining automobiles and supermarkets may seem odd," he has written, "but for a long time, since learning about the setup of supermarkets in America, we made a connection between supermarkets and the just-in-time system." Particularly important was Ohno's image of workers restocking the shelves as soon as they were empty. Just-in-time delivery is the principal means of coordinating the flow of materials, parts, and partially finished automobiles within lean factories, and of controlling when supplies arrive at the plants and when finished cars are shipped to dealers and customers. The method seeks to ensure that suppliers and workers at each stage of the production sequence produce and deliver to the next stage only those parts and cars in progress that can be worked on immediately.

Ohno hit upon a simple signaling mechanism to synchronize the flow of materials through his plants: the kanban, or production-scheduling card, which was placed in the containers used to carry parts and materials throughout the factories. Thus empty containers could immediately be sent back to the areas from which they came with instructions to make more parts. In Ohno's view, the kanban is the "operating method of the Toyota production system." Similar signaling devices convey instructions from Toyota to its suppliers, and between these companies and their subcontractors. Later, the company's dealers also became part of just-in-time production, taking orders for cars to be built to specification over the next few weeks, thus anticipating aspects of Dell Computer's build-to-order methods that are now the envy of most automakers and other manufacturers.[22]

The success of the Japanese carmakers over the last fifty years is probably the clearest confirmation of the advantages of lean production. Starting from near zero in 1950, they were making almost 30 percent of the world's automobiles by the early 1980s. Comparisons made by the MIT international automobile project provide more direct evidence of Japanese firms' superior efficiency: in 1986, for example, a typical Toyota plant could assemble a car in about half the time of a representative General Motors facility—sixteen hours versus thirty-one. Moreover, Toyota factories used only 60 percent as much factory space per car and carried parts inventories that would last approximately two hours, not two weeks. Cars produced in lean plants also had fewer defects, about 45 for every 100 Toyotas produced, compared with 130 for every 100 GM cars, helping to explain why 20 percent of American factories was sometimes set aside for fixing flawed cars. And even though American companies began to adopt lean-production techniques in the 1980s, Japanese firms continued to be more productive while greatly expanding their product lines. By 1990, Japanese carmakers were producing about eighty-four different models annually, up from forty-seven in 1982, and redesigning them every four years; American companies, on the other hand, produced about fifty car models that they kept in service for roughly ten years.[23]

NUMMI—a Toyota-GM Joint Venture. New United Motor Manufacturing Incorporated (NUMMI), a joint venture between General Motors and Toyota that was established in 1984 to produce small cars and trucks in a former GM plant in Fremont, California, is another illustration of how effective the new operating methods can be when implemented thoroughly and purposefully. By the early 1980s, the Fremont plant had become known as one of the worst in the GM system, and thus one of the worst in the U.S. automobile industry. It was plagued by alcoholism and drug use among its workers and exceptionally high levels of absenteeism—on some Fridays and Mondays there were not enough workers to run the assembly line. Productivity at Fremont was notoriously low, and its cars were rife with defects. GM finally closed the plant in 1982, and the joint venture began producing cars at Fremont two years later. Other than setting up a stamping operation near the welding area, so that panels no longer had to be shipped from GM's big stamping plant in the Midwest, NUMMI did not introduce much new technology to the old facility. It also did not try to do away with the United Automobile Workers (UAW). More than 80 percent of the company's workers had worked in the old plant, including the leaders of the union local. Yet productivity at NUMMI was soon almost double the best levels achieved at the old Fremont plant, and about 40 percent higher than the average GM plant, while quality was comparable to that of any other automobile plant in the United States. Workers' satisfaction with their jobs, as measured by independent surveys, was also much improved.[24]

Among the changes made at NUMMI were a number of measures common to most lean producers that altered the way in which work was organized and shifted the relationship between management and workers. First, a new set of senior managers who were experienced in lean-production methods was brought in from Toyota. Second, the union contract was simplified and gave the UAW a formal consulting role in matters ranging from the pace of production to the company's capital investments. The company also agreed that it would cut managers' pay and recall outsourced work before laying off employees. Third, job applicants were screened jointly by management and the union, and all workers received extensive training—250 hours during their first six months (compared with fewer than 50 hours at a typical plant) and continued training after that, all emphasizing teaching a wide range of skills. Fourth, the number of job classifications was cut back to two (compared with fifty or more at a typical plant), wage differentials between them were reduced, and rotation among jobs was increased. Fifth, workers were divided into teams of five to ten people responsible for both organizing their assigned work into specific tasks and determining how frequently to rotate among them. Team leaders were chosen by a union-management committee, earned less than fifty cents an hour more than other workers, and met frequently with the other workers to discuss ways to improve their work. Finally, workers were paid bonuses based on the plant's efficiency and customers' satisfaction with its cars.

These seemingly simple changes turned a miserably inefficient automobile plant, which employed fifty-seven hundred people when it closed in 1982, into one of the most productive in the GM system, with few capital improvements and largely the same workforce. In some respects it was almost as efficient as Toyota's Japanese plants, requiring only three more worker hours to assemble a car (nineteen versus sixteen) and matching their quality achievements of approximately forty-five defects for every one hundred cars. NUMMI used more factory space per car and held larger inventories than Toyota's factories, but these shortfalls were due in part to the bad layout of the old plant and the need to import many parts from Japan. Even so, its parts inventories averaged only two days, compared with two weeks in a representative GM plant. Moreover, in 1991 approximately 90 percent of NUMMI's workers said they were "satisfied with my job and environment," as compared with 65 percent in 1985, the year after production started, while the absentee rate was about 4 percent, less than half the GM average and one-fifth the rate at the old Fremont plant.

Because of its low capital costs and use of the workforce from the old Fremont plant, NUMMI stands in sharp contrast to the Saturn Corporation, a GM subsidiary that was established at the same time. Saturn also was supposed to be a model of how new working methods based on labor-management cooperation could reinvigorate the company. But unlike NUMMI, Saturn was built from scratch and was expensive and self-consciously experimental, making it very unlikely that it could ever be replicated on a large scale. The company was initially set up and run in partnership with the UAW, largely through self-directed work teams, and had a great deal of independence from its corporate parent. Based in a newly constructed $5 billion complex in Spring Hill, Tennessee, Saturn employed a specially recruited workforce, many of whom were sufficiently committed to its philosophy to move there. Nevertheless, its early success was not enough to cover the costs of the large investment, and its performance deteriorated once the novelty wore off and its workers' enthusiasm dimmed. Rather than changing its parent or the national union, Saturn has become more like the rest of General Motors, and its workers and union leaders more like their counterparts in the UAW. "It's no longer a different kind of car company," said Michael Bennett, the head of the UAW local at Saturn from 1986 to 1999. In its early years, Saturn's president ran the company and reported directly to GM's president. Now he runs only its manufacturing operations and reports to a GM vice president, while the design, marketing, and engineering heads report to other GM executives. The workers also have opted out of the experiment, replacing Bennett and his associates with more traditional union leaders and rejecting the flexible work rules and incentive-based pay of the early Saturn contracts in favor of more typical arrangements in which their compensation does not vary with performance.[25]

TECHNOLOGY, WORKER SKILLS, AND NEW WORK PRACTICES

Companies such as Dell, Toyota, and Nucor can operate so flexibly and efficiently because they have developed new approaches to doing business, learned to use new technologies effectively, and forged closer links with their customers and suppliers, but their proficiency depends as well on the new relationships they have established with their workers. Unlike the rigid contractual arrangements of the postwar industrial economy, which limited workers' initiative and imaginations, the new setups encourage them to make decisions and support them with more training and with pay tied to their performance, including profit sharing and stock ownership. These arrangements are not entirely new, however; in fact, American companies have been experimenting with less hierarchical, incentive-based work practices since the early years of the Republic. Albert Gallatin, who later served as Treasury secretary under Thomas Jefferson and James Madison, established the first profit-sharing plan in the United States in 1795, at his glassworks in New Geneva, Pennsylvania. The "democratic principle upon which this nation was founded," he believed, "should not be restricted to the political process, but should be applied to the industrial operation." A century later, during the period of "welfare capitalism," profit-sharing and stock-ownership plans were widely used to stimulate productivity and weaken the attraction of trade unions and radical ideas, and because businessmen such as Judge Gary of U.S. Steel felt they represented "the way men ought to be treated." At the peak of the movement in the 1920s, as many as

6.5 million workers owned stock in their companies worth about $5 billion (equivalent to more than 15 million workers and $250 billion in stock in the 1990s). These workers constituted almost 15 percent of all nongovernment employees, and their share holdings accounted for approximately 3 percent of the net worth of all nonfinancial businesses, similar to workers' ownership today.[26]

Welfare capitalism fell apart during the Great Depression, when the economy's collapse undermined not only corporate profits and the value of company shares but also the optimism of many of the country's financial and political elites. Although American business leaders regained their confidence after World War II, they also may have become complacent, settling into comfortable relationships with their workers and the big industrial unions that represented them. As these cozy arrangements began to break down in the 1970s and 1980s, when companies came under pressure from growing foreign competition, more assertive shareholders, and corporate raiders and buyout firms backed by the burgeoning junk-bond market, businesses responded at first by cutting costs through downsizing and outsourcing—laying off workers or replacing full-time employees with outside contractors or less expensive temporary workers. But these measures proved less successful than anticipated, in part because they depressed morale and caused many other workers to leave, intensifying the demands on those who remained.* Increasingly, therefore, companies tried other approaches, giving employees a greater say in how work got done and encouraging them to use it. Most common were "consultative" arrangements such as "quality circles"—periodic voluntary gatherings in which workers have an opportunity to make suggestions

---

*Surveys of corporate downsizing by the American Management Association found that in the early 1990s, fewer than half the firms raised profits and only a third increased productivity, while roughly 40 percent said they were unhappy with the results from downsizing. There is also evidence that the shares of firms that downsize outperform the stock market in the first six months but tend to do worse after three years. Other research has shown that the rise in manufacturing productivity from 1977 to 1987 was split almost equally between plants that had downsized and those that had "upsized"— plants in which both productivity and employment increased.

to cut costs or improve efficiency. But some companies went further, setting up self-directed work teams and production cells in which small groups of workers have control over their work.[27]

Because they make better use of workers' skills, energies, and experience, as well as new technologies, participatory working arrangements can be very effective, but they are hard to establish. Not only must the workforce be reeducated and union ambivalence or resistance overcome; managers have to be persuaded to accept diminished authority. Instituting lean-production methods has also proved surprisingly difficult because of what two Harvard Business School professors have called the "paradox" of the Toyota production system—the fact that on the surface it seems "rigidly scripted" yet at its core is so "flexible and adaptable." Implementing the system effectively, they argue, can be accomplished only if managers and workers understand that it is not a fixed way of doing things but, rather, a method, or philosophy, of experimentation, of constantly testing existing procedures against proposed changes, of always searching for small ways to improve, of what Toyota and other lean producers call "kaizen."[28]

That the new business practices, working arrangements, and technologies complemented one another was clear almost from the start. In the early 1980s, for example, the Manufacturing Studies Board of the National Research Council, a branch of the National Academy of Sciences, convened a committee of nine managers, union officials, and academics to study the diffusion among U.S. companies of advanced manufacturing technology (AMT), techniques such as computer-aided design, engineering, and manufacturing. "Realizing the full benefits of AMT will require *systematic*—not piecemeal—*change* in the management of *people and machines*," the committee concluded. Particularly promising, they thought, were practices such as defining jobs broadly and giving workers responsibilities for making operating decisions and diagnosing problems; using teams as the basic workplace unit; providing more training so that workers would be more effective in carrying out their expanded duties; and paying them according to their mastery of a wide range of skills and tasks.[29] A large body of research conducted during the 1990s has largely validated the committee's expectations. Whether the studies have focused on individual companies, firms in a single industry, large samples of companies spanning a variety of industries, or changes in the economy over time, they generally agree that the rising use of computers and allied technologies has been accompanied by increases in the skills and education of workers and by shifts in the way that work is organized. The company-based studies also show that productivity is greater in "high-performance workplaces," which combine modern information and communications technologies with flexible, participatory working arrangements.

Information Technology, Worker Skills, and Education. Information technology affects workers in two very different ways, both of which help to produce a correlation between the use of computers and the skills and education of the workforce. These relationships arise both because computers, computer-controlled machinery, and other new equipment can *substitute* for workers performing *routine* tasks, whether manual or cognitive, and because information and communications technologies *increase* the need for workers who are more *analytic* and better able to engage in problem-solving tasks. For example, a study of check processing in a large Massachusetts bank discovered that the use of image-processing technology to record images of deposited checks and optical-recognition software to analyze the information on the checks enabled the bank to eliminate manual check processing, a function that had been performed by high-school graduates. At the same time, the new technology led to an upgrading of the "exceptions processing" department, the group that tries to decipher checks that cannot be processed routinely, roughly sixty-five thousand each day. The more skilled workforce in this department was reduced by about 30 percent, but the downsizing was accomplished largely through attrition and was accompanied by a broadening of responsibilities, expanded training, and higher wages for the remaining employees. Productivity in exceptions processing rose by approximately 30 percent, about two-thirds from the reorganization and one-third from the new technology.[30]

The changes at this bank are typical of those that occurred throughout the economy over the last few decades. An economy-wide analysis by the authors of the bank study shows a pronounced increase since the 1970s in the proportion of nonroutine cognitive tasks that workers in most occupations are required to perform. The data also show that occupations that involve more analytic tasks and fewer routine ones have grown in importance. In addition, greater use of computers appears to account for a big part of these shifts in job content and occupational concentration, and they, in turn, explain about a third of the growth of college-educated workers in the labor force, a notable feature of the new economy that helps explain why income inequality also grew. Between 1979 and 2000, for example, the proportion of the civilian labor force, aged twenty-five to sixty-four, that graduated from college rose from about 21 percent to more than 30 percent, while the share that graduated from high school and did not attend college fell from 40 to 32 percent. (The proportion of the labor force that attended college but did not graduate rose from 17 to 28 percent during the same period.) Yet, because demand for college graduates grew even more rapidly than supply, the "premium" they earned compared with those who had only finished high school almost doubled, rising from 40 percent in 1979 to 70 percent in 1993. Since the mid-1990s, however, earnings for workers with different levels of education have grown more equally, and the college premium has not risen further.[31]

High-Performance Work Practices, Information Technology, and Productivity. Many studies have tried to measure the incidence and effectiveness of innovative work practices and their relationship to information technology, and though their conclusions are remarkably consistent, they rely on data that may not be able to bear some of the demands placed on them. Almost all such research uses subjective assessments of the extent to which high-performance practices have been implemented, generally collected through surveys of human-resource managers whose responses probably are not consistent enough to permit comparisons among different companies. Because these arrangements are very much in vogue, it also is likely that businesses exaggerated their presence, particularly companies that use them superficially and thus ineffectively.

Even so, it seems clear that high-performance work practices have spread considerably over the last few decades and have helped raise productivity once they were firmly established. For example, one study found that between 1992 and 1997 the proportions of firms claiming to rotate workers among jobs, or to have adopted quality circles or work teams, rose from 65 to 85 percent, while companies reporting they had taken up more than one of these practices increased from 31 to 71 percent. Similarly, a 1998 survey of 415 businesses in a variety of manufacturing and service industries found that almost 90 percent had some form of incentive pay in their compensations schemes for employees below the executive level. Moreover, approximately one-quarter of the companies had introduced their plans within the last two years, and almost 40 percent had expanded them during the period. Although stock options were less common than either performance bonuses or profit sharing—34 percent of all firms surveyed offered stock options to nonexecutives, compared with 50 percent that shared profits with their workers and 75 percent that paid bonuses to them—they were growing most rapidly, having been introduced within the last two years by 18 percent of the companies in the sample that offered stock options and broadened by 37 percent of those firms.[32]

Taken together, the many studies of innovative work practices have uncovered enough evidence of their potency to help explain their diffusion over the last few decades. Some also make clear why they work in some companies and not in others. An analysis of productivity in the steel industry, for example, showed that when more flexible, incentive-based employment practices are used in combinations whose elements reinforce one another, as they were at companies such as NUMMI and Nucor, they are extremely effective, but when used in isolation, they are relatively weak. Specifically, the authors studied productivity among a sample of steel-finishing lines in the United States and found that it was about seven percentage points higher, and annual revenue $2.5 million greater, in lines that employed broad and deep "clusters" of complementary new work practices compared with lines that operated in the traditional way. These new work practices included high employee participation in teams, significant rotation of workers among jobs, relatively large amounts of training in production and problem-solving skills, systematic sharing of information between management and workers, and meaningful performance-based pay. Less extensive or less complete use of these new work methods, however, had a much smaller impact on productivity, and the adoption of only one of them had very little effect. The steel industry research is unique both in the clarity of its results and in the quality of its data, which were collected by the authors, who personally visited each of the production lines and conducted on-site interviews lasting up to three days. In addition, the sample was designed to cover only lines engaged in a particular kind of steel finishing, a feature of the study that made the data unusually comparable from line to line.[33]

Another analysis of productivity in the steel industry, in which two of the same people participated, explored the relationships among incentive pay, the use of work teams, and the complexity of a given production process. In this case, the authors compared productivity in thirty-four production lines visited between November 1994 and April 1997. Even though the lines were all operated by U.S. minimills and were engaged in the same general type of production, some produced more sophisticated and refined products and used more advanced machinery and equipment, enabling the researchers to construct a measure of production complexity. As one might expect, they found that teams and incentive pay are more effective in less routine

environments in which ingenuity and effort can make a bigger difference. Specifically, the study showed that (1) incentive-pay plans were
typically based on a work crew's output or on the mill's profits and
were used by more than 90 percent of the lines by the end of the period; (2) performance-based pay alone raised productivity by about
half a percentage point; and (3) problem-solving teams were adopted
only when incentive-pay plans were also used and raised productivity
another 0.4 percentage points in the most complex production lines.
Nevertheless, because the combination of incentive pay and work
teams had no impact on the least complex lines, their average impact
was much smaller, increasing productivity by about 0.2 percentage
points for all the lines in the sample, a rise that boosted production
per line by approximately three thousand tons worth more than
$1.4 million. These findings are consistent with those of earlier stud-
ies of incentive pay, which found that it tended to increase productivity when combined with other high-performance practices. Incentive
pay was most effective in smaller companies with plans that paid a periodic cash bonus based on profits, rather than in businesses that
linked their pension contributions to profits or those with employee
stock ownership plans, whose mixed record is discussed in the addendum to this chapter.[34]

Finally, several studies have evaluated the combined effects on
companies' productivity of new technology, new working arrangements, and the skills and education of the workforce. Their findings
thus complement more directly the results of the growth-accounting
studies discussed in Chapter 1 and the economy-wide analysis of the
relationship between technology, job complexity, and worker skills
considered earlier in this section. The authors collected information
about the workforces and organizational practices of a sample of
three hundred large firms in 1995 and 1996 and matched it with data
on the companies' productivity and investment in information and
communications technology. They found that the use of computers and other information-processing and communications equipment

was strongly correlated with the education and skills of the companies' workers and with the extent to which the companies adopted advanced working arrangements, such as decentralized decision making and self-managed teams. Most important, productivity was higher in companies that had at least two of these modern attributes—information technology, relatively skilled workforces, and more entrepreneurial working arrangements—but not in those that had only one of them. Not surprising, workers in the high-performance companies also were better paid.[35]

ADDENDUM: THE MIXED RECORD OF ESOPs

Employee ownership of shares in the companies that employ them has long been considered a promising means of raising workers' incomes, improving productivity, and easing tensions between managers and workers and between richer and poorer members of society. It was a key element of welfare capitalism, reaching almost one-sixth of the labor force in the 1920s and accounting for approximately 3 percent of the equity of all American businesses. Interest in employee ownership revived during the 1980s and 1990s, particularly when the workers at United Airlines acquired 55 percent of the company's stock in July 1994, marking the transaction as the country's largest employee buyout. Participating workers did not actually purchase shares for cash; instead, they agreed to give up wages and benefits and make other concessions valued at approximately $5 billion in return for the company's promise to distribute the shares to them over the next seven years, grant them three of the twelve seats on the board of directors and veto power over major company decisions, and guarantee that they would have majority voting rights in the company as long as they continued to own at least 20 percent of its stock. Labor secretary Robert Reich hoped that such a highly visible example would make employee ownership a more likely possibility for companies trying to reduce costs and increase productivity and profitability. "From here on in," he said, "it will be impossible for a board of directors to not consider employee ownership as one potential business strategy."*

As it turned out, this prediction was far too optimistic. United made a promising start under employee ownership, quickly gaining a larger share of its market and boosting productivity and profitability more rapidly than its competitors. It benefited from the favorable economic climate and from the initial enthusiasm of its workers and managers, a factor that is particularly important in a service business such as air transportation. Within five years, however, the company succumbed to many of the same pressures that have troubled other large employee buyouts, especially those that were arranged to save companies from going out of business or from being sold. The basic problem at United and companies like it was that, as one reporter put it, although "everybody agreed to call workers 'owners,' they did not act like owners and management did not treat them like owners." As a consequence, the airline's pilots, and subsequently its machinists and ground workers, soon sought to recoup through higher wages the concessions they had made in 1994 to pay for their shares in the company, a turn of events that was particularly debilitating because it coincided with the weakening of the economy and with management blunders, such as the controversial attempt to acquire US Airways for $4.3 billion. The September 11, 2001, terrorist attacks compounded United's difficulties, and by the end of October it again was fighting for its life under a new chief executive, its third since the buyout in 1994. United filed for Chapter 11 bankruptcy protection on December 9, 2002, becoming the largest company in the global airline industry ever to do so.[36]

Although some of the carrier's problems were the result of bad

---

*The concessions by the employees who participated in the buyout—the pilots, machinists and maintenance workers, and salaried employees—amounted to about 15 percent of their wages and benefits. Of the three directorships allotted to the employees, one went to each of the three groups. These arrangements enabled the company to issue bonds and preferred stock to raise the money to buy 55 percent of the stock from the old shareholders and issue it to participating employees.

luck, the growing antagonism between management and workers was more predictable, the result in part of fundamental problems with the buyout's structure: the reduced wages and benefits agreed to by United's pilots, machinists and maintenance workers, and salaried employees—the flight attendants, the company's biggest group of employees, did not participate in the buyout—affected them much more immediately than did the shares they got in return, because the stock was to be distributed to their pension accounts over seven years and could not be withdrawn until they retired. Frederick Dubinsky, head of the pilots' union at the company and the group's representative on United's board of directors, highlighted this issue in explaining why the pilots would not agree to new wage concessions to help revive the company and protect their 25 percent equity stake. "If we were to lose the equity at this point, given the value, who cares?" Dubinsky said. "You still have to feed your family. Stock is long term. The grocery bill is short term."[37]

United's employees acquired their shares in the company through an employee stock ownership plan (ESOP), a pension plan that must invest a majority of its assets in the stock of the sponsoring company and is allowed to borrow money (to use leverage) to do so. Louis Kelso, a San Francisco lawyer, set up the first leveraged ESOP in 1956 to purchase majority control of Peninsula Newspapers in Palo Alto, California. Kelso saw employee ownership as a means of giving workers a "second income" from their share in profits, which would help resolve the "under-consumption" of goods and services by which he felt American capitalism was plagued. The use of ESOPs to broaden the distribution of income and wealth appealed particularly to Russell Long, the populist Louisiana Democrat and influential chairman of the Senate Finance Committee who was instrumental in gaining congressional support for ESOPs in more than fifteen pieces of legislation between 1973 and 1987. Long believed that employee ownership would reduce class conflict and improve productivity, thereby justifying the tax incentives that had been granted by Congress to ESOP companies.[38]

Unfortunately, as the evidence discussed in the last part of this chapter shows, simple ownership of shares, particularly deferred shares that are not controlled by the beneficiaries, is not by itself sufficient to bring about the kind of high-performance workplaces that boost productivity and incomes. What is needed, in addition to share ownership, is a broad array of programs giving workers more responsibilities for improving operations and arming them with the skills to do so effectively. The number of employees owning stock in their companies grew from about 6.5 million in 1983 to approximately 14 million in 1993, more than 10 percent of the civilian labor force, with roughly 8 million of these workers holding their shares through ESOPs. Taken together, worker-owned shares were worth almost $300 billion in 1993, about 5 percent of the net worth of all publicly traded companies, but most of these "employee owners" had no greater influence on their companies' policies or performance than other shareholders—and ESOP participants don't even control their shares directly. Like traditional pension plans, ESOPs tend to be controlled by the sponsoring companies' managers, who can use them to further their own interests. During the 1980s, for example, ESOP participants were sometimes asked to help managers frustrate hostile takeovers by refusing to tender their shares to raiders, thus preventing the outsiders from gaining control of their targets.[39]

From the start of the movement, it was clear to some that deferred share ownership would limit the effectiveness of ESOPs in motivating workers and improving corporate performance. In 1975, for example, New York senator Jacob Javits told the Joint Economic Committee of Congress he was "as yet unable to perceive how workers suddenly can become more productive upon the receipt of stock by an encumbered trust in which they have no voting right and no financial relationship." Profit-sharing plans that pay workers a periodic cash bonus based on company profits, on the other hand, establish a more direct and immediate connection between productivity and compensation. Thus, Gordon Cain, an enormously successful leveraged-buyout entrepreneur, felt he needed to supplement employee stock ownership in his companies with profit-sharing plans in which 10 percent of profits was distributed to employees each quarter. As the president of Cain Chemical, one of Cain's largest and most successful buyouts, explained: "Most companies just give employees a turkey or a ham; we give them checks instead. The quarterly payments let employees know where the money is coming from. Every quarter, I would go to each plant and review its performance with the employees . . . At the end of the meeting, I would hand out the checks."[40]

A second major problem with ESOPs is that they have often been adopted, as at United Airlines, when businesses were troubled and jobs threatened. In 1994, the United Steelworkers of America (USWA) had about seventy thousand members who participated in ESOPs at more than thirty steel companies, but many of these plans were devised to stave off liquidation or plant closures. At Algoma Steel, Canada's third-largest integrated steel company, the union developed a bankruptcy reorganization plan based on employee ownership and participation only after the search for other buyers failed. Like United, Algoma prospered for a while under the newly instituted partnership between workers and management, and its stock outpaced an index of steel company shares during the early to mid-1990s. In 1995 the USWA considered the company a model of worker-management collaboration, "more advanced than anywhere in the world." Even then, however, it was reluctant to use union funds to promote and invest in employee buyouts at companies not yet under financial duress.[41]*

For these and other reasons, America's widespread infatuation

*Ironically, the employee buyout of Weirton Steel in 1984, one of the first to rescue a threatened steel company, took place before the USWA accepted their use even in such extreme situations. However, the workers at Weirton belonged not to the USWA but to the Independent Steelworkers Union, which had been formed in 1950 when the National Labor Relations Board forced Weirton to disband its company union. Although the buyout rescued the company, Weirton, too, could not sustain the initial gains, and its stock was delisted by the New York Stock Exchange in September 2001 because the firm no longer met the exchange's viability requirements.

with the stock market during the 1990s had far less to do with Kelso's vision of "democratic capitalism," or with the expansion of ESOPs, than with the raging bull market, the growth of mutual funds, and the shift in retirement saving from employer-managed defined-benefit pension plans to defined-contribution schemes such as 401(k)s, which are controlled by the beneficiaries. These trends also undermined Peter Drucker's prophecy of "pension fund capitalism"—"capitalism *sans* capitalists"—which he thought would result from the growing influence of large defined-benefit plans such as the prototype he helped establish for General Motors in 1950.[42]

The sponsors of defined-benefit plans, as the name suggests, commit to providing agreed-upon retirement benefits to the beneficiaries and make periodic contributions to the plans that, together with the expected returns from investing the plans' assets, are thought sufficient to support the specified payments. Sponsors of defined-benefit pension plans control their investments and assume all the investment risks. In defined-contribution plans, on the other hand, workers determine their annual contributions, which generally are matched to some degree by their employers, decide how to invest the plan's assets, and bear all the attendant risks. The most popular and fastest-growing of these plans are 401(k)s: by 1997 they accounted for approximately 70 percent of the assets, benefits, and participants in all defined-contribution plans, and almost 80 percent of all contributions to them. In addition to their other attractions, 401(k)s are portable from job to job and allow participants to access some of their funds before they retire.

Employee pension funds have been around since at least the Civil War and covered close to 4 million workers and managers in more than 350 large companies by the end of the 1920s. They expanded markedly during World War II, when they were used to circumvent wage controls, and really took off in the 1950s after General Motors introduced its innovative equity-oriented plan in its bargaining with the UAW. By the end of the 1970s, just over half of all private sector workers between 25 and 64 participated in a pension plan. Participation dropped off during the 1980s but regained the lost ground in the 1990s, largely because defined-contribution plans grew rapidly, making up for the decline in defined-benefit plans. About half of the rise in defined-contribution pension plans is estimated to be due to growth in the service sector where traditional plans were less prevalent, while the rest seems the result of employers' replacing their defined-benefit funds with defined-contribution plans, in part because they feared the poor investment climate of the 1970s would continue, burdening them with large obligations to their defined-benefit plans. As it turned out, the changeover coincided with the emergence of one of the most vibrant investment periods in American history, and the new investor class benefited royally, at least until the stock market got too far ahead of itself. Many of these new investors were taken in by the unsustainable stock market returns of the late 1990s and suffered badly when the bubble burst. They may also have been duped by misleading accounting, disingenuous financial reporting, and fraudulent business practices, which helped create the bubble and—when they became known—the severe correction that followed.[43]

FIVE

The Stock Market and the New Economy

THAT THE ECONOMY was changing significantly during the 1980s and 1990s was abundantly evident in the stock market. No matter what index of stock prices we choose—the Dow Jones Industrial Average (the Dow), the oldest index and the one that most represents the old economy, the technology-laden NASDAQ Composite Index (the Nasdaq), or the Standard & Poor's 500 index (the S&P 500), which is somewhere in between—the performance of the stock market in these decades was extraordinary.[1]* Even when calculated over the twenty-year period from January 1981 through December 2000, a span that includes the first part of the stock market decline that began in 2000, when it fell by more than 9 percent, the compound return on owning stocks, measured by the total return on the S&P 500, including dividends, was almost 16 percent a year, approximately

---

*The thirty companies in the Dow account for only about 20 percent of the market value of all publicly traded shares. By contrast the S&P 500, the most widely used index by market professionals, accounts for about 75 percent of this value. The Dow is also unique in that it basically is a simple average of the share prices of the companies in the index, which means that higher-priced stocks have a greater effect on the index than do lower-priced stocks, regardless of the market values of the companies. The S&P 500 and most other stock market indices, on the other hand, are capitalization-weighted, which means that in computing the index each share price is multiplied by the company's market capitalization divided by the market capitalization of all the companies in the index. As a result, more highly valued companies have a greater impact on the index than less highly valued ones.

40 percent above the return over the entire postwar period and double the return over the last two centuries. The 1981–2000 interval is relatively representative of the ups and downs of the last few decades: it runs from shortly before the business-cycle peak of July 1981 to near the crest attained in March 2001 and includes, in addition to the first part of the 2000–2002 market correction, the severe recession of 1981–1982; the violent but short stock market crash in October 1987, when the Dow lost a record 22.6 percent in a single day; the relatively mild recession of 1990–1991; and the financial crisis of 1998 that grew out of the collapse of the emerging Asian economies, Russia's default on its debt, and the failure of a prominent hedge fund, Long Term Capital Management. By comparison, the period 1980–1999, which begins a year earlier and excludes the 2000–2002 setback, produced compound stock market returns of about 18 percent a year, split almost equally between the 1980s (17.5 percent) and the 1990s (18.2 percent).[2]*

*The returns cited here are compound annual returns, as opposed to average annual returns; they also are nominal returns rather than real returns. The difference between nominal and real returns is relatively simple: nominal returns reflect the effects of inflation, whereas real returns show what would have happened in the absence of inflation. The difference between nominal and real returns was approximately 1.5 percentage points a year from 1802 through 1997, but almost 5 percentage points a year since World War II. From 1981 through 2000, however, inflation was much lower, averaging about 3.2 percent a year.

The difference between compound and average annual returns is more complicated, as explained below:

1. The average annual return is the simple average of the annual returns in the sample period, whereas the compound annual return is the cumulative rate of return over the entire sample period, annualized. For example, if an investment gains 50 percent over two years, growing to 1.5 times its beginning value, the compound annual return is 22.5 percent. In other words, an investment of $100 would, at 22.5 percent, grow to $122.50 after one year, and the new principal would rise similarly, to $150 at the end of the second year (that is, $122.50 × 1.225 = $150). The compound return in this two-period example can be calculated as the square root of 1.5, minus one.

2. The more stock market returns vary from year to year, the higher the average annual return compared with the compound return. Between 1802 and 1997, for example, the average annual return was 9.8 percent, 17 percent higher than the compound annual return, 8.4 percent. (In real terms, these returns were 8.5 and 7 percent, respectively.) The difference between them is roughly half the variance of the annual returns, which was about 3 percent over the period (equivalent to a standard deviation of about 18 percent).

Even more remarkable than its longer-term performance, how-ever, was the market's rise since 1995, when productivity and eco-nomic growth began to accelerate. From 1996 through 1999, the S&P 500 earned more than 25 percent a year, while Nasdaq investors did about 1.5 times as well, and more concentrated technology and Internet investors better still. But the most dramatic explosion of technology stocks, and the greatest divergence among the different market indexes, occurred during just eighteen months, from Octo-ber 1998 through March 2000. The Nasdaq Composite Index dou-bled over this period, gaining about 75 percent annually, while the S&P 500 grew at a rate of "only" 30 percent a year. Technology in-dexes rose even more rapidly than the Nasdaq—one index of Internet stocks rose by more than 200 percent over the period—but most stocks in the S&P 500 fell. The Nasdaq peaked in March 2000 and fell more than 50 percent over the ensuing nine months. It fell an-other 30 percent in the first ten months of 2001, leaving the index 65 percent below its March 2000 peak. At its low point on Septem-ber 21, 2001, ten days after the terrorist attacks, it had fallen more than 70 percent from its high; by comparison, the S&P 500 fell less than 40 percent from the end of March 2000 through its low on Sep-tember 21, 2001. Many Internet stocks, particularly on-line retailers

---

3. To see how the disparity between average and compound annual returns is related to market volatility, consider an example in which an investment of $100 rises to $175 at the end of a year and falls back to $150 at the end of a second year. The cumulative return over the two-year period is 50 percent, and the compound annual return is 22.5 percent (see no. 1 above). The average annual return, however, is 44.6 percent, the average of a 75 percent return in the first year and a 14 percent loss in the second year.

4. As the example shows, the disparity arises because, in computing the average return, each year's return is weighted equally even though the high return was earned on a low base and the small loss was from a much higher base. The compound annual return, on the other hand, is derived from the cumulative return, which automatically accounts for both effects.

As shown later in this chapter, actual stock market returns are similar to those in the ex-ample described in no. 3 in that periods of abnormally high returns tend to be followed by periods of much lower ones (that is, the annual returns are "negatively correlated" or "mean-reverting"). As a result, the average return is a misleading predictor of long-term returns.

such as Amazon.com, did much worse than the Nasdaq, losing more than 90 percent of their value in less than two years. From a top closing price of $106.69 in early December 1999, Amazon shares fell to $8.37 in early April 2001 and, after a brief recovery, shrank to $5.97 at the end of September.

After reaching its post–September 11 lows, the stock market recovered significantly, rising 20 percent over the next three months, before fluctuating and then falling again in the spring and summer of 2002. From mid-March through its low point on July 23, the S&P 500 fell more than 30 percent, undercut by the economy's halting recovery, the possibility of war with Iraq, and the corporate accounting scandals that eroded investors' trust, pushing prices below levels last visited in the fall of 1998.* As the Federal Reserve Board chairman, Alan Greenspan, told Congress, "an infectious greed seemed to grip much of our business community" during the "frenzy of speculation in the late 1990s," driving managers to inflate their companies' earnings through accounting gimmicks and other questionable practices, so that they could profit on their share holdings and stock options. And in the spring and summer of 2002, a continuing parade of malfeasants, including former stars such as Tyco, Global Crossing, WorldCom, and Qwest Communications, showed that the problem extended beyond Enron, whose transgressions had been exposed six months earlier, causing its abrupt collapse into bankruptcy. Like betrayed lovers, investors turned on their ex-favorites, dumping shares

---

*To be clear about the ups and downs of the stock market indexes in 2001–2002, which fluctuated considerably as a result of uncertainties afflicting the economy and financial markets: after September 2001, the Nasdaq rose roughly 45 percent in the next three months, but it fell 45 percent between the start of 2002 and the low point reached that October. Similarly, from its low in September 2001, the S&P 500 rose 20 percent by the end of the year, fluctuated during the first quarter of 2002, and fell 35 percent between the middle of March and early July; it then rose roughly 20 percent before revisiting its July lows in early October. The Dow, on the other hand, hardly fell in 2000, but declined almost 30 percent from its peak in May 2001 to the trough reached that September, rose 30 percent in the next six months, and fell 30 percent between mid-March and early October 2002. Overall, the Nasdaq fell 78 percent from its peak on March 10, 2000, to its trough on October 9, 2002, while the S&P 500 fell roughly 50 percent over the same period, and the Dow, which peaked in January 2000, was 35 percent lower in early October 2002.

precipitously and unthinkingly, much as they had bought them in the late 1990s. And because rates of return are sensitive to the endpoints of periods of even twenty years, the sell-offs in 2001 and 2002 depressed returns over the preceding two decades materially: whereas stocks returned nearly 16 percent a year from the start of 1981 through the end of 2000, they returned 14 percent annually through the end of 2001 and 12 percent a year through July 2002, bringing their returns in the 1980s and 1990s back in line with experience over the entire postwar period.

The market reversals of 2000–2002 are further confirmation that the rise of technology stocks since 1995, particularly the eruption from late 1998 until early 2000, was a classic speculative bubble, an increase in prices that was carried much too far and thus could not be sustained. Like most such binges, it was due more to investors' euphoria about the new economy than to reasonable assessments of economic fundamentals, such as interest rates and economic growth or company earnings and cash flows. The combination of important new technologies, unrealistically heightened expectations about the future, and speculative excesses—and the financial shenanigans and fraud that went with them—was neither unique nor surprising, particularly to experienced investors, students of financial markets, or fans of Schumpeter, and by the mid- to late 1990s many of them were warning that stock prices seemed to be out of control. In December 1996, for example, Greenspan worried famously about investors' "irrational exuberance," and the following May Treasury secretary Robert Rubin suggested that they use more "rigor" in evaluating their investments. But these gentle admonitions tended to be ignored, in part because nobody could say when, or by how much, the market's excesses would be trimmed. Indeed, the market's continued rise in the face of these cautions seemed to fuel the speculative frenzy, showing once again how hard it is to predict short-term movements in stock prices.

Despite the hazards of predicting how stock prices will change over the near term, we know that neither overly inflated share prices nor seriously undervalued ones can persist too long. Even the earliest writings about the stock market recognized this dichotomy between the erratic and unpredictable movements in stock prices over the short term and their much more regular and foreseeable tendencies over longer spans. In the first such commentary, in 1688, Joseph Penso de la Vega, a forty-year-old Portuguese Jew from Amsterdam who was a businessman and investor as well as a writer, warned: "Whoever wishes to win this game must have patience and money since the values are so little constant and the rumors so little founded on truth . . . Owing to the vicissitudes, many people make themselves ridiculous because some speculators are guided by dreams, others by prophecies, these by illusions, those by moods, and innumerable men by chimeras." More than three hundred years later, shortly before the air began to leak out of the late-1990s bubble, the renowned investor Warren Buffett echoed these sentiments, reminding us that "markets behave in ways, sometimes for a very long stretch, that are not linked to value." But "sooner or later," he continued, "value counts." Understanding the implications of these comments and making sense of the connections between the stock market and the development of the new economy are the focus of this chapter.[3]

FIRST PRINCIPLES

Perhaps the most important fact about investing in the stock market is that over the long term, stocks in general have been a vastly superior investment. Nobody develops this theme more convincingly than Jeremy Siegel, a professor at the Wharton School of the University of Pennsylvania. As can be seen in Figure 4, which is reproduced from his book *Stocks for the Long Run*, a dollar invested in a representative group of stocks in 1802 would have grown to $559,000 in 1997, after adjusting for inflation, which reduced the value of the dollar to seven cents over this period. By comparison, a dollar invested in long-term government bonds, short-term bills, or gold in the same period would have grown in real terms to only $803, $275, or $0.84,

FIGURE 4. *Total Real Return Indexes for Stocks, Bonds, Bills, Gold, and the Dollar, 1802–1997*

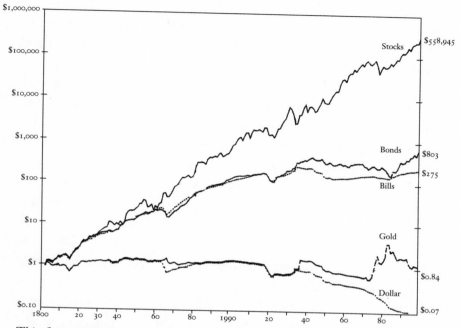

This figure is drawn on a logarithmic scale; thus equal vertical distances show equal percentage changes in the indexes.
Source: Jeremy J. Siegel and Peter L. Bernstein, *Stocks for the Long Run*, 2nd ed. (New York: McGraw-Hill, 1998), p. 11. Reproduced with the permission of The McGraw-Hill Companies.

respectively. In other words, the compound return on stocks over almost two hundred years was about 7 percent a year after inflation, compared with 3.5 percent for bonds and 2.9 percent for bills, while an investment in gold lost money. Many of these relationships are evident in foreign markets as well. In fact, the real returns on British and German stocks from 1926 to 1997 were 6.2 and 6.6 percent a year, respectively, close to the 7.2 percent earned by holding U.S. stocks over these years. Japanese stocks were virtually wiped out during World War II, falling 98 percent in real terms; but the market recovered rapidly after the war, rising at a compound rate of almost 10 percent a year from the late 1940s through the early 1970s, bringing its growth path back in line with the trajectories of the world's other major stock markets. Japanese equities appreciated particularly rapidly in the second half of the 1980s, much as U.S. shares would do a decade later, but they fell dramatically at the end of the decade and stagnated during the 1990s, reducing postwar returns to just 3.5 percent a year after inflation.[4]*

In addition to their unquestioned superiority over very long holding periods, the attractiveness of stocks in shorter time spans grows, and their riskiness falls, the longer they are held. For example, after adjusting for inflation, stocks outperform bonds and bills about 60 percent of the time over any single year but about 70 percent of the time if held for five years, 80 percent over ten years, and more than 90 percent over twenty years. Unlike bonds or bills, stocks as a group have not had losses over any twenty-year period since 1802. It is true that even if we include dividends, it would have taken about fifteen years for stocks bought just before the 1929 crash to recover their value, but since World War II the longest it has taken for an investment in a representative sample of stocks to show a profit has been three and a half years, between December 1972 and June 1976.[5]†

Of course, the long-run superiority of stocks as a group doesn't guarantee results in any particular period or for any particular stock. Especially at times when investing in a representative basket of stocks does not match returns from buying hot stocks or when stocks don't perform as well as investments in other assets, such as bonds, commodities, or real estate, it is tempting to think one can improve on passive stock market returns by timing when to invest in the stock

---

*Because the makeup of stock market indexes such as the S&P 500 is changed periodically to maintain their representativeness, removing companies that have declined in importance and adding others that have risen, index returns are higher than those that could be earned on a passive investment in a fixed group of stocks. Index investors, however, benefit from this "survivor bias" because their portfolios are automatically updated when the indexes change.

†Since there are only ten nonoverlapping twenty-year periods in the last two centuries, the significance of these results for long holding periods is less than it might appear.

market or by focusing on particular shares or stock categories, such as growth or technology stocks. Many devotees of technology stocks in the late 1990s, for example, even those who knew they were seriously overvalued and likely to decline significantly, undoubtedly believed they would get out before their shares fell too much. But it is unlikely that many did, for the second important thing we know about the stock market is that it is very difficult to predict short-term changes in prices or to appreciate when a particular move is likely to persist rather than reverse itself. In other words, market timing doesn't make much sense, especially since the consequences of mistiming or misinterpreting market fluctuations can be very severe. In general, an investor who tried to predict short-term changes in share prices would have to be right about 70 percent of the time to beat the market, and small mistakes can have large consequences. During the 1980s, for example, the average real return on the S&P 500 index was about 12.5 percent a year. But an index investor who missed just the *ten best days* of the decade would have realized only 7.5 percent after inflation, about the same as the return on ten-year government bonds. Similarly, it has been reported that New York University's trustees were so concerned about the high values of shares during the 1980s and 1990s that they shied away from the stock market for most of the period, causing the university's endowment to languish. By the late 1990s, the fund would have been at least one-third larger had they invested an additional $100 million in the stock market in 1982.[6]

Not only is it difficult to time investments in the stock market; active stock picking rarely beats the market averages. One of the easiest ways to see this is to compare the performance of index funds—mutual funds such as the Vanguard 500 that simply buy and hold a representative sample of stocks, like those in the S&P 500—with the results of mutual funds whose managers try to pick stocks that will do well. Over almost any period one chooses, including periods of three years, five years, or ten years, more than 75 percent of all actively managed mutual funds produced lower net returns for investors than did index funds. Between 1984 and 1994, for example, a record

26 percent of all actively managed mutual funds beat the S&P 500, but even then the average actively managed fund returned only 12 percent a year, compared with roughly 14 percent annually for the S&P. Actively managed pension funds and other "institutional" accounts tend to lag behind passive investment strategies by comparable margins. Equally important, active fund managers who do better than index funds in one period rarely outperform them the following year, making a strategy of chasing past performance quite perilous. To illustrate this point in an extreme and fanciful way, *The Economist* calculated what an investor would have earned over the last century had he invested each year in the previous year's best-performing asset, including buying stocks, bonds, real estate, or precious metals in any established market in the world. Starting with $1 on January 1, 1900, this backward-looking investor would have accumulated only $783 by December 31, 1999. An investor with perfect foresight, on the other hand, who each year picked the asset and market that would do best over the next twelve months, would have turned $1 into $9.6 quintillion. Her most frequent choices were U.S. stocks, French stocks, and silver.[7]

CAVEATS AND EXCEPTIONS

Buying and holding a representative basket of stocks is a superior long-term investment strategy because the economy has been so innovative and productive, and has grown so rapidly, over the last two centuries. Stock market returns ultimately reflect the economy's productivity, inventiveness, and growth; since they are much more regular and predictable when measured over longer periods, it makes sense that long-term equity returns have been similarly impressive and that they can be captured effectively by investing in a broad index of stocks, such as the S&P 500, and holding it for a long time. Moreover, buying and holding a representative basket of stocks generally yields better returns than actively picking stocks or trying to time the market, because over long periods markets tend to be "smarter" than most individual participants, making them very hard to beat.*

This means not that the stock market always gets prices right, or that one cannot profit from systematic mispricing, only that it is very difficult, and risky, to try and that few have succeeded in beating the market consistently. Warren Buffett is probably the best-known investor to do so over an appropriately long period of time. Buffett practices value investing, which he describes as a "search for discrepancies between the *value* of a business and the *price* of small pieces of that business in the market." There clearly would not be bargains of that kind if share prices always reflected companies' values. And value investing, at least as he and like-minded investors do it, has produced spectacular results. Ten thousand dollars invested with Buffett in 1956 would have been worth roughly $225 million at the end of 2001, a compound return of about 25 percent a year, more than double the annual return on the shares in the S&P 500 over the same period.[8]

---

*Other financial markets, such as those for bonds, currencies, and commodities, differ from equity markets in important respects, and, as a consequence, investors can earn their fundamental returns only by using investment strategies that take short as well as long positions at appropriate times. (A short position is one designed to profit from a fall in prices. In "shorting" a stock, an investor sells shares he has borrowed, hoping to buy them back later at lower prices and pay off his loan with something to spare. In futures markets, on the other hand, long positions always match short ones, enabling investors to go short directly, without borrowing, a feature of these markets that facilitates hedging.) Capturing the intrinsic returns in such "commercial" markets requires investment strategies that can be short as well as long, because the participants include natural hedgers who use these markets to hedge, or partially offset, risks that arise in the normal course of their business. For example, wheat producers risk the possibility that market prices for wheat will be low when their wheat is harvested, but can use short positions in wheat futures to offset this risk to a greater or lesser extent. Bakers, on the other hand, risk the possibility that flour prices will rise in the future and can offset this risk through long positions in wheat futures.

True hedgers don't care if they make money from these offsetting investments, which are designed to neutralize business risks they must endure. Investors in commercial markets, on the other hand, can profit by bearing the risks that these commercial interests want to lay off, but earning these basic returns requires having long or short positions at different times. Mount Lucas Management Corporation, an investment firm of which I am a principal, has developed several indexes designed to capture the fundamental returns in commercial markets and in combinations of commercial and equity markets.

Buffett attributes his success to the fact that "market prices are frequently nonsensical." Sometimes this is obvious, as in 1973, when he invested $10 million in the Washington Post Company, an investment that was worth about $1 billion at the end of 2000. "The Washington Post Company in 1973 was selling for $80 million in the market," he wrote in an article that is included as an appendix to a 1997 edition of *The Intelligent Investor* by Benjamin Graham, his teacher at Columbia Business School in the early 1950s. "At the time, that day, you could have sold the assets to any one of ten buyers for not less than $400 million, probably appreciably more. The company owned the *Post*, *Newsweek*, plus several television stations in major markets." In most cases, however, the relationship between share prices and values is less clear. In part this is because easily measured assets, such as plants and equipment, have become less important, while less tangible ones, such as brand names, technology, software, and the skills and commitment of the workforce, are now more vital. But it is also because making even general judgments about the intrinsic value of a business is very difficult. Like many other investors, Buffett defines this as the value today of "the cash that can be taken out of the business during its remaining life." Thus he is concerned not simply with a company's growth or even with its reported annual earnings but with how much money will be available for shareholders—over and above the amount the company must invest in the business—over a considerable period of years. Because making even rough estimates of these future cash flows is not easy, Buffett writes, "you do not cut it close. That is what Ben Graham meant by having a margin of safety. You don't try and buy businesses worth $83 million for $80 million."[9]*

*A company's "free" cash flow can be calculated from information contained in its annual or quarterly reports. It consists of essentially three elements: (1) net profit adjusted for any noncash charges, such as depreciation, or nonrecurring ones, such as write-offs of obsolete assets; minus (2) cash needed to finance growth in working capital, which consists of inventories and accounts receivable, less accounts payable; and also minus (3) capital spending. The company's historical results provide a basis for estimating its future cash flows, which then must be "discounted" to the present in calculating intrinsic

Even so, mistakes are likely. Buffett, for example, underestimated the consequences of USAir's relatively high operating costs when he bought shares of the airline in 1989. As a result, its cash flows, and hence its value, were well below the amounts he had expected, and he essentially gave up on the investment, only to see it recover dramatically, which is why he considers his record with USAir "unblemished by success." "I was wrong in originally purchasing the stock," he wrote in his 1997 letter to shareholders of Berkshire Hathaway, the company he runs, "and I was wrong later, in repeatedly trying to unload our holdings at fifty cents on the dollar." Overall, however, he and his investors have prospered because he appreciated the lasting value of strong franchises and good managers in companies such as the Washington Post, Coca-Cola, Gillette, and GEICO and was willing to bet heavily on them when he could buy their shares at prices well below their intrinsic values. Unlike most economists and other investors, Buffett believes that a concentrated portfolio acquired at bargain prices is inherently less risky than a diversified one bought with little margin of safety, that is, with unrealistically high prices relative to earnings or other measures of value that will badly endanger the stock's price if the company does not meet these lofty expectations or if market conditions change.[10]

Economists typically measure a stock's riskiness by the volatility, or standard deviation, of its returns. Thinking of risk in this way makes it relatively easy to measure but may be of limited usefulness when share prices are more likely to rise than fall, as is the case when they are truly undervalued. Buffett thus prefers to focus on the "possibility of loss or injury" rather than on an investment's volatility. By the latter measure, he points out, if the stock of the Washington Post

---

value, a process that accounts for the "time value of money" and thus depends on interest rates. (A further discount may also be necessary to adjust for the uncertainty of the forecast.) For example, if the appropriate interest rate, representing what could be earned in the next-best investment, is 5 percent, then a dollar that will be received in one year is worth about ninety-five cents (since if one had ninety-five cents today and invested it at 5 percent, it would grow to one dollar in one year). In general, the lower the interest rate, the smaller the discount.

Company in 1973 had suddenly fallen even further, the price decline "would make it look riskier," a result he likens to "Alice in Wonderland," since it implies that "it is riskier to buy $400 million worth of properties for $40 million than $80 million." In many respects, Buffett's commonsensical view of risk is not very different from that of J. P. Morgan, who reputedly advised a friend who was losing sleep over his share holdings, "Sell down to the sleeping point."[11]

Since the early 1980s, research in the field of "behavioral finance" has shown that systematic investment strategies consistent with Buffett's more subtle approach can be very effective. These investment rules, whose usefulness has been demonstrated in computer simulations more than in actual trading, are largely of two types: a value-related methodology that looks for undervalued stocks, and a "momentum" strategy that tries to exploit the persistence of short-term trends in stock prices. When investments are made by following rules such as these, they sacrifice subtlety and nuanced judgment for simplicity and uniformity. But tests of such simple trading procedures have shown that even crude measures of value can identify stocks that will yield uncommon returns, at least in certain periods. For example, one important study showed that between 1968 and 1990 portfolios of "value" stocks—defined simply as stocks whose prices are low relative to very rough measures of their worth, such as book value, earnings, or cash flow—that were held for five years outperformed portfolios of "glamour" stocks by about 8 to 10 percent a year and were no more risky.[12]*

---

*Among the financial ratios used to discriminate between value and glamour stocks, the price-earnings ratio (P/E) is the most common. It tells you how much you are paying per dollar of the company's current earnings. The price–cash flow ratio is very similar, since cash flow can be derived from earnings, as described in the footnote on pages 172–173. Book value, on the other hand, is a company's net worth, the value of its assets less its liabilities as shown on its books, and the price–book value ratio tells you how much you are paying per dollar of net worth. But book value has clear drawbacks in measuring a company's economic strength. Not only are intangible assets vastly understated in corporate accounts; but even "hard" assets—property, plant, and equipment—are carried at their original cost less estimated depreciation and not at their current market value or the cost of replacing them.

Glamour stocks, as defined in this study and others like it, are polar opposites of value stocks. They are fashionable, have been bid up, and thus sell at prices that are high relative to variables such as book value, earnings, or cash flow. Thus portfolios of value stocks were constructed by combining the 10 percent of all stocks in the sample with the lowest ratios of price-earnings, price–book value, or price–cash flow, while glamour portfolios were made up of the 10 percent with the highest ratios. These simple measures of relative value are particularly useful in stable environments: if future earnings are likely to be much like past earnings, or even higher, then companies with low P/Es are obvious bargains. However, when circumstances are changing rapidly, or people think they are changing rapidly, past experience may be a poor guide to future stock returns. This may partly explain why value strategies tended to do worse than growth strategies during the 1990s, especially the last part of the decade. But aside from the 1930s, the 1990s are the only decade since the 1920s in which value stocks did worse than growth shares.[13]

Value strategies capture the tendency of share prices to "mean revert," that is, the likelihood that prices that are abnormally low in relation to, say, company earnings will return to more typical levels. Momentum results, on the other hand, show that shares that have done relatively well over the prior six months continue to outperform other stocks over the following six to twelve months but not in the years after that. In other words, it takes about a year for superior performance to dissipate. Specifically, the researchers found that when all stocks traded on the New York Stock Exchange or the American Stock Exchange from 1965 to 1997 were ranked according to their price appreciation over the preceding six months and grouped in ten equally weighted portfolios, the decile of "winners" outperformed that of "losers" by about 1 percent a month over the next six months. The excess returns earned by past winners fell in the second six months after the portfolios were formed, and disappeared after the first year. These findings suggest that it takes some time before investors adjust overly aggressive expectations.[14]

Why do such opportunities for investors exist? John Maynard Keynes hinted at the reasons in 1936 in *The General Theory of Employment, Interest, and Money*. First, he observed, many investors do not look for long-term values but try simply " 'to beat the gun,' . . . to outwit the crowd, and to pass the bad, or depreciating, half-crown to the other fellow," much like "a game of Snap, of Old Maid, of Musical Chairs." As a result, he wrote in a well-known passage, the stock market can be

> likened to those newspaper competitions in which the competitors have to pick out the six prettiest faces from a hundred photographs, the prize being awarded to the competitor whose choice most nearly corresponds to the average preferences of the competitors as a whole; so that each competitor has to pick, not those faces which he himself finds prettiest, but those which he thinks likeliest to catch the fancy of the other competitors, all of whom are looking at the problem from the same point of view.

This way of thinking can create both price momentum in the short term and discrepancies between value and glamour stocks that can be exploited over longer periods. But profiting from such temporary mispricing is not a sure thing, and investors must be able to withstand losses if the momentum of share prices dissipates rapidly or if undervalued shares become even more undervalued before they improve. Buffett's investment in the Washington Post, for example, was acquired at very low prices, yet he sustained unrealized losses on the position that almost caused him to liquidate it in the first few years. And he did not do well during the late 1990s, when technology stocks exploded and other shares suffered. In addition to being able to endure such losses and poor performance, value investors must have confidence and conviction, because this type of investing involves betting against popular opinion rather than simply following the crowd. At the height of technology-stock fever, for example, many investors and pundits taunted Buffett, suggesting that he was washed up, too old-fashioned to appreciate how to invest in the new economy. But such sniping faded quickly with the collapse of tech stocks and the recovery of Berkshire Hathaway, whose shares rose strongly after 1999, gaining more than 50 percent from early 2000 through mid-2002 while the S&P 500 fell by about the same proportion.

If these pressures, financial as well as psychological, meaningfully limit investors' willingness to take advantage of market prices that are sometimes far out of line, they can help to explain the persistence of stock market bargains. "An investor who proposes to ignore near-term market fluctuations," Keynes wrote, "needs greater resources for safety and must not operate on so large a scale, if at all, with borrowed money." Ironically, he continued,

> it is the long-term investor, he who most promotes the public interest, who will in practice come in for most criticism . . . For it is in the essence of his behavior that he should be eccentric, unconventional and rash in the eyes of average opinion . . . Worldy wisdom teaches that it is better for reputation to fail conventionally than to succeed unconventionally.[15]

BUBBLES, MISLEADING ACCOUNTING, AND SHADY DEALING

As is generally the case, the stock market in the 1980s and 1990s both reflected changes in the economy and helped to bring them about, sometimes excessively. It is often claimed that the stock market has very little influence on the economy because most people's share holdings are too small and their value fluctuates too much to affect spending significantly, and because few companies raise funds in the stock market in any year. But share ownership has spread rapidly and extensively over the last two decades and now represents a significant part of many people's financial assets; as a consequence, the stock market may affect total spending more tellingly. The second argument for the stock market's purported lack of influence on the economy, on the other hand, has never been true. Keynes explained why in his *General Theory*: "Daily revaluations of the Stock Market, though they are primarily made to facilitate transfers of old investments between one individual and another, *inevitably* exert a decisive influence on the rate of investment." For, he continued,

> there is no sense in building up a new enterprise at a cost greater than that at which a similar existing enterprise can be purchased; whilst there is an inducement to spend on a new project what may seem an extravagant sum, if it can be floated off on the Stock Exchange at an immediate profit. Thus certain classes of investment are governed by the average expectation of those who deal on the Stock Exchange as revealed in the price of shares, rather than by the genuine expectations of the professional entrepreneur.[16]

If anything, the stock market in the 1980s and 1990s played an even bigger role in the economy than usual, helping to root out bureaucratic waste and pushing companies to become efficient. In concert with the developing junk-bond market, it enabled aggressive firms and investors to acquire stodgy, poorly performing businesses, hoping to improve their operations or sell their assets to other firms that could use them more effectively. And, as the next chapter will show, these hostile takeovers became so pervasive that the threat of being acquired impelled corporate managers to focus more intensely on reducing unnecessary expenses and boosting productivity and profitability. Were it not for the stock market's influence on the economy, Keynes would hardly have been so concerned about the apparent predominance of "game-players" over "long-term investors" in the 1920s and 1930s, and Greenspan, sixty years later, would not have worried so much about investors' "irrational exuberance." Our experience in the late 1990s and early years of the twenty-first century bears out the reasonableness of their fears.

Even in retrospect, however, it is extremely hard to say precisely how much of the stock market's rise in the 1980s and 1990s was due to fundamental improvements in the economy, especially the growing efficiency and profitability of American businesses and the noteworthy declines in inflation and interest rates, and how much was due to investors' extreme expectations about the likely scope of those gains. The exercise is particularly difficult because the frothiness of the stock market stimulated investment in more new technology than could be used productively—witness the many defunct or crippled Internet companies that used cheap capital raised in hyped, and perhaps manipulated, initial public offerings of shares to gear up for business that never materialized. Or consider the telecommunications companies that, much as the railroads had done a century earlier, created far more transmission capacity than was needed, undermining both prices and the companies themselves. This companion bubble in parts of the real economy temporarily boosted investment spending, corporate earnings, and productivity at rates of growth that, like the rising share prices that fed them, could not be sustained.

Misleading Accounting.   Evaluating the stock market in the late 1990s is also very hard because misleading accounting, deceitful financial reporting, and outright fraud greatly inflated corporate earnings, perhaps by 25 percent or even more. While it is unlikely that many companies were as crooked or dishonest as Enron or WorldCom, less fraudulent deceptions were widespread. Even in this realm, however, distinctions are important. First, large numbers of companies "managed" their earnings, producing unrealistically steady results from quarter to quarter because investors and analysts liked them and because the distortions were relatively minor, matters of timing rather than fundamental misrepresentations. Second, and much more significant, many companies took advantage of opportunities to deceive investors that were available under standard accounting rules—generally accepted accounting principles, or GAAP—using them to create financial results that were misleading but did not violate specific regulations. These practices involved, among other things, the ways in which restructuring charges and asset write-downs were presented;

how gains from asset sales, investments, and pension funds were treated; and, most important, how companies accounted for stock options granted to employees.

A corporation's financial statements should present a clear and accurate portrait of its business operations, but, ironically, this larger objective sometimes gets lost in the thicket of individual rules and standards. Even the most precise guidelines require tricky, easily manipulated judgments, such as deciding which expenses can be considered unusual or nonrecurring and how to report them. Overstating these costs, and segregating them from the results for continuing operations, make a firm's ongoing earnings seem higher than they really are. In addition, companies can engineer their earnings through their pension accounting, particularly through the assumptions they make about the returns on the funds' investment portfolios. But option accounting—actually, companies' *failure to account* for the costs of options, which they granted to employees in greater and greater quantities as the stock market exploded—produced the biggest and most egregious distortions of earning in the 1990s. And this loophole was available only because in 1994 Joseph Lieberman and his colleagues in the Senate persuaded the Financial Accounting Standards Board, the industry group that establishes accounting principles, *not* to require businesses to count the fair value of newly granted options as part of their employee compensation costs.[17]*

Because options can produce large future rewards if the issuers

---

*The value of a call option on a company's shares, which gives the holder the right to buy them at a specified price for a given period, reflects the likelihood that the market price of the shares will rise above the option's exercise price before it expires. (Similarly, the value of a put option, which gives the holder the right to sell the shares at the stated price, reflects the likelihood that the stock price will fall below the exercise price before the option expires.) Essentially, the option's value is a weighted average of all possible future values, where the weights are the probabilities that each will occur, variables that depend on the distribution of possible future prices for the shares. For example, if an option's exercise price is $10 and there is a 50 percent chance that the share price will be $15 when the option expires, making it worth $5, and a 50 percent chance that the share price will be $5, making the option worthless, then the option's value is roughly $2.50 ([$5+0]/2). Valuation methods, such as the Black-Scholes model, formalize this idea, using the historical distribution of a company's share prices as a guide to their probable future values and accounting for interest rates and other relevant variables.

are successful, they can be critical in helping young businesses attract talented and energetic employees. Technology firms and other new ventures used options extensively over the last few decades, and they paid off handsomely while the bull market was raging, creating scores of multimillionaires and billionaires, even if some existed only on paper or lasted for just a moment. It is well known, for instance, that numerous Microsoft employees at all levels of the company grew wealthy by exercising the options they were granted, but the company hardly is unique in this regard. One study of employee stock options in the 1990s found that as a group, workers of large Internet companies and other technology firms that went public during the boom earned more from their options than did their bosses. Taken together, the employees of the hundred largest new public companies made close to $80 billion from their options, and although the executives of these firms got far more per person, they earned much less as a group. "No other industry," the authors conclude, "has ever attempted, much less achieved, the depth, breadth and extent of wealth-sharing found among these firms."[18]

Stimulated by such examples, and by those of leveraged-buyout entrepreneurs who used options and share ownership to motivate managers of the companies they acquired, executives of older, more established companies also turned to options more aggressively during the 1990s, often with the support of shareholders who wanted to better align their interests with those of management. But options are far from a perfect instrument for motivating managers and other employees, partly because, as Warren Buffett has long emphasized, they are a one-sided bet: recipients don't lose money if the underlying shares fall, but can achieve great wealth if they rise, even if they grow no faster than the stock market as a whole. At least equally important, a company's top officers and directors generally control the way options are handed out, and in the bubbly 1990s, they granted them on terms and in amounts that bore little relationship to the recipients' performance. Among other questionable features of these grants, the options tended to be struck "at the money," which means their exercise prices, or strike prices, were the market prices at the time of the grants, making them almost guaranteed to pay off. The options also did not require that a company's shares outperform the stock market or the shares of its peers and competitors—that is, they were not "indexed"—another reason they were close to a sure thing. Not surprisingly, given their nature, executive options were granted more plentifully in companies with no strong outside shareholders that might oppose management and, as a consequence, do not appear to have improved the firms' performance. Indeed, one study of executive options over the period 1992–2001 found they were *inversely* related to shareholder returns: shareholders earned lower total returns in companies whose top five executives received more options.[19*]

Large grants of favorably structured ordinary options can also induce managers to manipulate earnings, especially in a frenzied environment where stocks are exploding and everybody is doing it. By not expensing options, including their own, managers inflated their companies' earnings, but the options also boosted stock prices more directly, because many companies aggressively purchased their own shares in the stock market to offset the dilution of existing shareholders, which would occur when the options were exercised, making them even more of a safe bet. In addition, because they were granted so plentifully and on such generous terms, options were a major cause of the huge expansion in executive pay during the last twenty-five years. The compensation of a typical chief executive of a large American corporation rose from about 50 times the pay of an average worker in the mid-1970s to 150 times as much by 1990, and, by the end of the decade, was roughly 500 times as great.[20]

---

*Although they probably were not overly significant in explaining the pattern of option grants, tax and accounting rules governing executive compensation encouraged option-granting and favored ordinary options over index options. In 1993 the IRS ruled that a company could deduct from its taxable income compensation above $1 million per person only if the excess was performance-related. Similarly, the Financial Accounting Standards Board requires that index options be charged against earnings, with the charges changing when market prices change, but does not require that companies expense ordinary options so long as the exercise price is not lower than the market price at the time of the grant.

In the wake of the furor over improper accounting, Standard & Poor's—where were they when people really needed them?—developed a new measure of earnings to help investors assess companies' real performance. Called "core earnings," it is designed to show earnings from a company's principal businesses and can basically be calculated from reported income by deducting employee option costs and excluding gains or losses from asset sales or pension-fund portfolios. (Restructuring charges and asset write-downs already are deducted, while pension-fund gains still boost core earnings indirectly when a fund's investments do well, since sponsors of overfunded plans can reduce their annual contributions.) Standard & Poor's plans to promote the new earnings concept, use it in its own ratings of companies, and report core earnings for firms in its stock market indexes, such as the S&P 500. For the S&P 500, core earnings were approximately 30 percent below reported earnings in 2001 and in the twelve months that ended on June 30, 2002, with unrecognized option expenses and reported gains on company pension funds each accounting for more than half of the discrepancy. (This was possible because other adjustments raised core earnings above reported earnings).

In 2001 and in the year ending the following June, unrecognized option expenses represented about 20 percent of the earnings reported by S&P 500 companies, compared to 8 percent in 2000 and 6 percent in 1999, a result that reflects the companies' lower income and higher option expenses in 2001. Unrecognized option expenses were particularly significant in the technology sector, whose companies grant options more abundantly than other firms, yet their earnings are not comparably large. (By contrast, the financial sector is the second largest grantor of options but also accounts for the largest share of the earnings of S&P 500 companies.). According to tabulations by Bear Stearns, in 2001 the eighty technology companies in the S&P 500 granted 3.1 billion options worth $38 billion, more than 40 percent of all options granted by index members and almost half their total option expense. Had these expenses been recognized, they would have increased the technology sector's loss by 50 percent, to

$116 billion, and, together with option expenses in the other sectors, lowered S&P 500 earnings to $149 billion from $230 billion.

Of the thirteen companies in the S&P 500 that granted options worth more than $1 billion in 2001, Cisco, Nortel, AOL Time Warner, Lucent, Yahoo, and Broadcom had losses from their continuing operations before recognizing the associated option expenses, and four others—Intel, Merrill Lynch, Siebel Systems, and Hewlett-Packard—had unrecognized option expenses that were more than half of their reported income. Cisco's losses, like those of Amazon.com, which is not in the S&P 500, would have been more than 2.5 times as great had its option expenses been recognized in its income statement, while Yahoo's would have been more than 10 times as great as those it reported. Finally, many of these companies received significant tax and cash flow benefits when their employees exercised their options. (When options are exercised, recipients must pay ordinary income taxes on the difference between the market price of the shares and the exercise price of the options, while the issuing companies get a comparable tax deduction, which boosts their cash flow but not their income.) For example, a Merrill Lynch study found that in 2000, sixty prominent technology companies received tax benefits from exercised options that constituted 48 percent of their cash flows, up from 22 percent in 1999 and 9 percent in 1998.[21]

Companies could have expensed newly granted options in calculating their earnings, but, according to Standard & Poor's, only two companies in the S&P 500 did so in 2001. The reason could not have been, as some have argued, that it was unnecessary since option grants do not involve cash outlays, or that their costs are adequately captured in the dilution they impose on existing shareholders. Accountants regularly accrue noncash expenses such as depreciation and amortization, and while options increase the number of shares outstanding when they are exercised, diluting the interests of existing shareholders, they are a compensation expense when they are granted, before it is known whether they will pay off, and both effects should be recognized. It is sometimes claimed that options are too hard to value accurately to include in income statements, but that is not right, either. After all, companies are required to report their option grants, including estimates of their fair market value, in notes to their annual financial reports, and they make these calculations regularly, using the Black-Scholes option-pricing model or other methods.

The real reason option expenses were not recognized in corporate income statements is that temptations to inflate earnings were great and not many investors minded or even paid attention; in fact, they rewarded the deceivers, making honest accounting costly. Now that the environment has changed, some companies are betting that it pays to do the right thing, although for most of them expensing options will not reduce earnings greatly. Coca-Cola and GE were among the first to announce they would expense employee options, with Coke first suggesting it would use competitive bids from investment banks to determine their value but then, like GE, deciding to use the Black-Scholes model. In both cases, however, the effect of expensing options is likely to be relatively slight, since neither company uses them too widely. Coke's income would have fallen by 5 percent in 2001 and 8 percent in 2000 had its option grants been expensed, while for GE, where roughly 12 percent of the workforce owns options, reported income would have been 2 percent lower in both years. By contrast, Amazon, which grants options to almost all employees and will begin expensing them in 2003, would have lost almost $400 million more in 2001, 1.5 times its reported loss, had it expensed option grants. And Intel, which grants options widely and generously enough to have reduced its earnings by 80 percent in 2001 had they been expensed, announced that it will report more information about employee options but won't expense them.[22]

Shady Dealing. The stock market collapse has made everybody more aware of the hazards of inadequate accounting and disingenuous financial disclosures. The disintegration of Enron, and later WorldCom, raised questions about the prevalence of fraud and crookedness, but they appear far less widespread than misleading accounting and excessive grants of executive options. Enron was a gas-pipeline company that became an investor favorite when it turned itself into a trading firm specializing in exotic derivatives and promoted itself as a prototype for the new economy. Initially it concentrated on trading wholesale natural gas and electricity, whose distribution had become much less regulated, but it soon expanded into trading bandwidth, weather contracts, and credit and other financial derivatives. But it is hard to know how successful Enron was, because significant parts of its operations appear to have been made up, constructed with the help of investment bankers, accountants, and lawyers through the use of hidden, "off balance sheet" partnerships, making the company's financial statements even more opaque and misleading than was typical. The partnerships were used to shield company losses and indebtedness from public view and to create phony revenues and earnings. For example, working with Blockbuster, Enron in mid-2001 set up a venture to transmit rented videos to customers over its fiber-optic network. Although the venture never got off the ground—Blockbuster considered it "nothing but a pilot project" and didn't record a gain or loss from its stake in the scheme—Enron booked close to $110 million in profits over the following two quarters. It did so by transferring its interest to a partnership for which it raised money from outside investors, giving them most of the entity's cash flow over the next ten years and guaranteeing that Enron would re-pay their investment if the partnership did not generate enough cash to do so. Now, of course, these investors are claimants in the com-pany's bankruptcy proceedings, while Enron shareholders and em-ployees are pursuing lawsuits and other potential remedies.[23]

In much the same way, the company made itself seem far larger than it was, and appear to be growing much more rapidly, with the help of an accounting loophole that allowed it to count as revenue the gross value of its energy derivative contracts rather than the much smaller and more relevant net value. By using this misleading mea-sure, and executing transactions whose purpose often was just to pump up revenues, Enron in 2000 appeared to be the seventh-largest company in the United States based on sales. It was as if a brokerage firm continually bought and sold the same shares for customers and booked all the purchases and sales as revenue rather than counting only its commissions on genuine transactions. If not for its aggressive use of these techniques, Enron's 2000 revenues would have been less than $6 billion, one-twentieth of the $100 billion it reported, making it the 287th-largest American company rather than the seventh largest. Like so many other hot companies, Enron also issued stock options bounteously, not expensing their value but benefiting materially from the tax deductions that resulted when they were exercised. In 2000, for example, tax deductions on exercised employee options converted a potential tax liability of $112 million into a tax refund of $278 million.[24]

Since at least the late 1970s, the MIT economist Charles Kindleberger has emphasized that scandals such as those that emerged in 2001 and 2002 are common consequences of speculative frenzies, which generally involve infectious greed and shady dealing. "The propensities to swindle and be swindled," he wrote in 1978, when *Manias, Panics, and Crashes* was first published, "run parallel to the propensity to speculate during a boom" and tend to evolve in mutually reinforcing stages. The boom arises because "some event changes the economic outlook," causing stock prices to rise. But as "fortunes are made, individuals wax greedy, and swindlers come forward to exploit that greed," stimulating more speculation. Eventually "the excessive character of the upswing is realized," and a correction occurs. "Crash and panic . . . induce still more to cheat in order to save themselves. And the signal for panic is often the revelation of some swindle, theft, embezzlement, or fraud." Regardless of the precise sequence, rampant speculation and swindling invariably end in collapse and "revulsion," as when Enron's share price fell from near eighty dollars to less than one dollar in the eleven months preceding its bankruptcy filing on December 2, 2001, with half of the decline occurring once questions about its financial reports surfaced at the end of August. Similarly, investors' revulsion and distrust help to explain the 35 percent decline in the S&P 500 between mid-March and early October 2002.[25]

The Extent of the Bubble.   Despite the many ways in which companies exaggerated their earnings in the 1990s, certain factors cut the other way, causing earnings to appear lower than they really are. Most important, profits in the new economy may have been greatly understated because intangible investments have become far more significant, yet, unlike employee options, their costs are deducted fully from revenues when they are incurred rather than capitalized and depreciated over the expenditures' useful lives, as is true of investments in physical assets and even software. In addition, what really matters in historical comparisons such as those used to evaluate the stock market in the 1990s is not whether today's earnings are overstated but whether they are more overstated than in earlier times, and it is well known, for example, that the rampant inflation of the 1970s also distorted earnings significantly.[26]

But even if we accept questionable earnings as real and lasting, it appears that almost half the rise in the S&P 500 in the extraordinary years from 1995 through 1999 cannot easily be justified by economic fundamentals. Earnings of the companies in the index rose by about 9.5 percent a year over this period, roughly 50 percent higher than their rate of growth over the last two decades. Still, the index gained more than 26 percent a year, doubling its value relative to earnings from about 15, the long-term average, to more than 30. Some of this increase in the earnings multiple—the price-earnings ratio, or P/E— can be explained by low interest rates and low rates of inflation. Based on the typical relationship among these variables, several studies suggest that an earnings multiple in the low 20s was appropriate for the S&P 500 at the end of the 1990s. (In the inflation-racked 1970s, on the other hand, it was similarly appropriate for the P/E to be well below average.) P/E ratios of 22 or 23 imply that the S&P 500 was overvalued by about one-third at the end of the 1990s and that roughly 40 percent of its increase between 1994 and 1999 was due to "irrational exuberance." Almost all of these hard-to-justify gains evaporated in the first twenty-one months of the new century. The corrections that followed in the spring and summer of 2002 suggest that stocks were still overpriced, perhaps because earnings were more overstated than previously thought or because future prospects were bleaker than they had seemed. But it is no less probable that investors also overreacted to emerging bad news, much as they had exaggerated good news at the end of the 1990s.[27]

Whatever one thinks of the S&P 500, the Nasdaq Composite Index, which includes all shares traded on the Nasdaq stock market and has a far higher concentration of technology stocks, was much more bubbly. From a short-term low of 104 in May 1999, the earnings multiple for the index had risen to 281 by year-end and peaked at 364 at the end of February 2000. The P/E of the Nasdaq composite is harder to evaluate than that of the S&P 500, however, because many of the fifty-four hundred companies in the index are small and unproven, with little or no current earnings but hopes of very rapid growth if they are successful. And because they issued options more extensively, their earnings were more inflated than those of the S&P 500 companies. More comparable is the Nasdaq 100, an index that consists of the one hundred largest and most active companies in this market, including Cisco Systems, Oracle, Sun Microsystems, Dell, Microsoft, and Intel. These companies are among the sixty members of the Nasdaq 100 that are also part of the S&P 500, while Microsoft and Intel are in the Dow as well. As might be expected, the earnings multiple for the Nasdaq 100 is generally greater than that for the S&P 500 but less than that for the composite. From 1995 through 1999, it too grew much more extreme, rising sixfold, from 23 to 136, and by March 2000 five companies in the index had attained market values of more than $100 billion and earnings multiples above 100:

Cisco, Oracle, Nortel Networks, Sun, and EMC. (The only other company in this category, AOL Time Warner, was not in the Nasdaq 100.) Yet whenever large, established companies such as these have been priced in the stock market at more than fifty times earnings, subsequent returns have been puny.[28]

There are two problems with valuations this generous. First, for both competitive and arithmetic reasons, large companies cannot grow rapidly enough, for long enough, to justify them. Not only does exceptional success elicit more intense competition from both established firms and fresher, more nimble ones, but the larger a business gets, the more its earnings must rise to maintain a given rate of growth. Second, even if large firms were able to grow very rapidly over an extended period, investors would not benefit unless their valuations remained absurdly high. Consider Cisco, a computer networking company whose products and services enable us to transfer information efficiently over the Internet. Everybody seemed to want to own Cisco shares at the turn of the century, and investors' enthusiasm virtually radiated from its stock price and market value: in early March 2000, Cisco was valued by the stock market at approximately $450 billion, largely because its earnings multiple was nearly 150. (By the end of the month, its stock had risen 20 percent more, making it for a short time the market's most highly valued company.) Suppose, however, that Cisco's earnings were to grow by 30 percent a year over the following ten years, a near-record pace for companies that large but one many brokerage analysts anticipated. In order for shareholders to earn a compound return of 15 percent a year over the period, probably far less than they expected, Cisco's P/E in 2010 would still have to be above 30, implying that investors continued to expect record growth. Moreover, its value in the stock market would then be more than 10 percent of the entire gross domestic product, a far-fetched possibility that never had a chance. By mid-2001, the price of Cisco's shares had fallen to around fifteen dollars, and the company's total market value was approximately $100 billion.

REVERSION TO THE MEAN

Although the market's exact moves could not be anticipated, the general course of stock prices over the last twenty years was neither new nor surprising. In fact, the market has gone through very similar gyrations at least three other times in the last hundred years. One of the clearest ways to see this is to look at the multiple of average real earnings for the companies in the S&P Composite Stock Price Index, a measure of the market's costliness that adjusts both for inflation and for short-term fluctuations in earnings. (The S&P composite is a lengthier version of the S&P 500, which was first published in March 1957 and extended backward to earlier years, when it frequently contained fewer than five hundred companies; in 1929, for example, it included ninety.) The economists John Campbell and Robert Shiller are among the strongest advocates of this real, "smoothed" price-earnings ratio, which they define as the inflation-adjusted price of the S&P index divided by the average real earnings of the constituent companies over the prior ten years. Figure 5 on page 192, an updated version of a chart in Shiller's well-timed book of early 2000, *Irrational Exuberance*, shows three clear peaks in the ratio in addition to the one reached in 2000, namely, those attained in 1901, 1929, and 1966. In every case, these local peaks were achieved during periods in which real earnings grew rapidly, causing current earnings to rise relative to their ten-year average. Moreover, the ratio of current to smoothed earnings crested at about the same times that the price-earnings multiple did, suggesting that stock market bubbles have been based on real improvements in the economy that were extrapolated too aggressively. Mounting profits and stock market returns appear to have stimulated investors' imaginations and hopes excessively, making them think that such rapid growth would continue indefinitely or even accelerate and causing them to push share prices and market returns to heights that were hard to justify or maintain. But earnings have never been able to grow at the rates implied by highly inflated

FIGURE 5. *Price-Earnings Ratio, January 1881 Through October 2002*

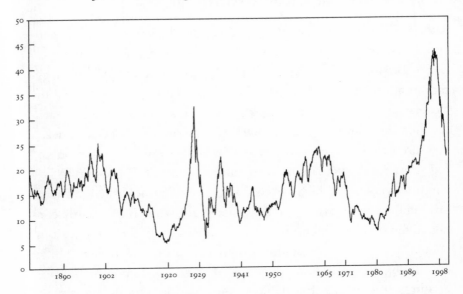

This figure shows monthly values of the real smoothed price-earnings ratio, in which the numerator is the inflation-adjusted price of the S&P Composite Stock Price Index and the denominator is the average of real earnings for the index over the preceding ten years. An earlier version of this chart appeared in Robert Shiller's Irrational Exuberance, *p. 8. This one was constructed from data available on his Web site,* aida.econ.yale.edu/~shiller.

stock market multiples; in fact, even back-to-back decades of robust earnings growth are unlikely.[29]*

For both these reasons—because prices were unrealistically high in relation to earnings that had grown rapidly, and because earnings growth was not maintained—stock market returns were very low in the years following these peaks in the price-earnings ratio, but just how depressed and long-lasting the periods of subpar performance

---

*Because the denominator of the smoothed price-earnings ratio is the trailing ten-year average of earnings rather than current earnings, when earnings are growing the denominator is lower, and the ratio higher, than the usual ones; however, the reverse is true when earnings are falling, as they were in 2001. Thus, as Figure 5 shows, by the end of 2001 the smoothed ratio had fallen from a peak of near 45 to about 27, a decline of roughly 40 percent, but the regular P/E rose from about 30 to near 40, because earnings fell more than share prices.

were, or how differently the corrections evolved, is not appreciated sufficiently. The stock market crash of October 1929 is probably the best known in a long line of financial disasters dating from the collapse of the Dutch market for tulip bulbs in 1637. (Speculators in Amsterdam actually were trading derivatives, futures contracts for rare bulbs.) Following a decade of exceptional returns that was topped off by gains of 37 percent in 1927 and 44 percent in 1928, which Herbert Hoover attributed to an "orgy of speculation," the U.S. stock market reached a peak in August 1929 after rising 30 percent in the first eight months of the year. It fell 5 percent in September but recovered briefly before the collapse began in late October. Panic took hold on Wednesday, October 23, when 6 million shares traded on the New York Stock Exchange and the market lost $4 billion of its value. It intensified the following day, "Black Thursday," when more than 12 million shares changed hands, and culminated on Tuesday, October 29, "Black Tuesday," when investors sold more than 16 million shares, roughly four times the average volume in September. Between October 10 and October 29, the S&P composite index fell from 245 to 162, a decline of almost 35 percent that wiped out more than $15 billion of market value. Prices fell 20 percent for the month and 15 percent more in November, and, despite a small rise in December, finished the year down 12 percent. The market continued rising through the first part of 1930, in what was later called a "sucker's rally," only to resume falling briskly in June, when it lost more than 16 percent.[30]

All told, the S&P composite index fell 12 percent in 1929, 28 percent in 1930, 47 percent in 1931, and 15 percent in 1932. At its nadir in mid-1932, it was down roughly 85 percent, almost double its decline in 2000–2002. (However, the Nasdaq composite fell nearly 80 percent from its peak on March 10, 2000, to the low on October 9, 2002, and since dividend yields were less than the rate of inflation, the real total return on the index was lower still. From 1930 to 1932, on the other hand, consumer prices *fell* by an average of 8.5 percent a year, and dividend yields were near 5 percent, making total real stock market returns substantially higher—that is, less negative—than the rates at which share prices fell.) Even after the market's precipitous fall, however, its recovery from the 1930s lows was slow and drawn out, and the S&P index did not regain its September 1929 peak until September 1954. Part of the problem was the Federal Reserve Bank's failure to prevent the market crash from infecting the banking system and the rest of the economy. (Chapter 7 contrasts these failures with the Fed's much more constructive role in the 1980s and 1990s.) In any case, starting from the end of September 1929 and removing the effects of inflation (and deflation), investors lost 13 percent a year over the next five years, 1.4 percent annually over ten years, and 0.5 percent over fifteen years, but would have earned 0.4 percent a year had they stayed invested in stocks for twenty years. The pattern was different, but the results remarkably similar, following the market's peaks in 1901 and 1966, with real stock prices fluctuating for a while before falling sharply. In the early years of the twentieth century, real returns averaged 3.1 percent a year over the first fifteen years following the peak in the smoothed earnings multiple but fell sharply after that, lowering the twenty-year average real return to a loss of 0.2 percent a year. In the fifteen years after the 1966 peak, on the other hand, real stock returns were slightly negative (-0.5 percent a year) but rose enough after that to boost the twenty-year average return to 1.9 percent, the highest in any of these long post-peak periods.[31]

These earlier episodes of stock market booms and busts, and our experience at the end of the millennium, are just extreme examples of a more general tendency of stock market returns, like the relative returns of value and glamour stocks, to "mean revert." In other words, when market returns have been robust and stock prices are high relative to earnings (or dividends or book value), subsequent returns are likely to be relatively low; and, conversely, when returns have been disappointing and prices are low in relation to these variables, subsequent returns will be relatively high. But it is at least as hard to capitalize on these relationships as it is to profit from the value-growth dichotomy. Consider, for example, what would have happened to investors who believed with Campbell, Shiller, Greenspan, and many others that the market was overvalued in the mid-1990s and thought that it might soon fall. (Campbell and Shiller testified before the Federal Reserve Board in early December 1996, shortly before Greenspan's famous warning about "irrational exuberance," arguing that "despite all the evidence that stock returns are hard to forecast in the short run, this simple theory of mean reversion is basically right and does indeed imply a poor long-run stock market outlook.") Those who bought the S&P 500 at the end of March 1991 and held it through December 1996 would have earned 15.3 percent a year. If they then sold their stock holdings and invested the proceeds more conservatively, they would not have suffered through the corrections of 2000–2002, but they would also have forgone substantial stock returns over the next four years: almost 90 percent, or 17 percent a year, compounded. Assuming they earned 5 percent a year after selling their shares at the end of 1996, these investors would have realized gains of 10.3 percent a year from March 1991 through July 2002, just under what they would have earned by holding the S&P 500 for the entire period, namely, 10.4 percent a year.[32]

As a practical matter, therefore, what mean reversion really shows is how dangerous it is to pile into the market near a peak, and how important it is to think of buying stocks as a long-term investment, albeit one that is likely to do less well when it seems most enticing. In fact, the tendency of stock returns to revert to the mean explains the perverse way in which investors' expectations affect their returns. When, as in the late 1990s, investors expect returns of more than 30 percent a year over the next five or ten years, or think that the risks of owning stocks are low, they buy shares aggressively, thus raising prices and short-run returns but making it far less likely that their longer-term hopes will be realized. On the other hand, investors with a more patient outlook who bought the S&P 500 in 1981 and held on through July 2002, enduring most of its recent sharp declines as well as the milder ones in between, would still have earned returns of almost 12 percent a year, substantially above the two-hundred-year average and roughly 5 percent above the returns earned since World

War II. (One reason these returns were so high is that the period begins near the end of the post-1966 correction, when the P/E was very low.) Similarly, those who bought the S&P composite index at the end of 1925 rather than at the 1929 peak would have had cumulative losses only if they had sold their holdings from late 1931 to early 1933 and would have earned 60 percent, a compound total return of about 3 percent a year, had they held on through 1941, when the long market decline ended. In real terms, these annual returns would have been about one percentage point higher, since prices fell over the period at a compound annual rate of just under 1 percent.[33]

How can mean reversion be reconciled with widely cited evidence showing that even though stocks are riskier than bonds over short holding periods, they become safer compared with these other assets the longer they are held, a finding that seems to suggest that it doesn't matter what price one pays for shares? In fact, when it is measured by the volatility of returns, the risk of holding shares falls more rapidly than the risk of holding bonds as investment horizons lengthen *because* current stock market returns, and price-earnings ratios, are negatively correlated with subsequent returns—that is, outsize returns in one period are generally followed by below-average returns in the next. In other words, the relative risk of holding stocks falls over time because stock returns gravitate back toward the mean, thus dampening their volatility. That is why it is so dangerous to buy stocks when returns have been spectacular and their prices are exploding. While the strategy may work for a few years, over spans of five to ten years or so returns are likely to be lower than they were, causing their variance to fall and making the investment less risky—and less rewarding—than it would have been had it been made when prices were lower.[34]

NEW INVESTORS AND NEW COMPANIES

The stock market of the 1980s and 1990s closely resembles that of the late teens and 1920s. Both were times in which new technologies

helped produce robust economic growth, hopes for new eras of unlimited prosperity, and stock market bubbles that ultimately ended in
collapse and disillusionment. Indeed, the similarities between the
1920s and the 1990s are, as Milton Friedman has pointed out, "un-
canny": the economy grew 3.3 percent a year from 1919 to 1929 and
3.2 percent a year in the 1990s, while stocks rose 333 percent between 1923 and 1929 and 320 percent from 1994 to 2000. (Similarly,
the Japanese economy grew 3.7 percent a year in the 1980s, while its
share prices rose 387 percent in the six years before they crashed at
the end of the decade.) The periods' dynamism was evident as well in
the heightened rates at which companies went public or left the market through mergers or acquisitions. But unlike the crash in 1929 (or
the breakdown in Japan in late 1989), the market collapse in
2000–2002 did not produce a depression or even an overly severe recession. The 1990s were also unique in the extent to which new investors participated in the stock market and helped fuel the boom. In
contrast to the 1920s, when less than 2.5 percent of the American
people owned stock, more than half of all Americans owned shares at
the close of the millennium.[35]

New Investors.   Although it overstates the case to claim, as some have
done, that the stock market bubble of the late 1990s was the first to
"feature small investors as the driving force," there is no question
that they played a more active role than ever before. Many inexperienced investors were drawn to the market by its exceptional performance, by the proliferation of mutual funds, discount brokers, and
on-line trading firms that made access so much cheaper and easier,
and by the popularity of self-directed retirement plans through which
the beneficiaries could invest in stocks. Their deceptively easy early
success, reinforced by high-profile analysts such as Abby Joseph Cohen of Goldman Sachs, Mary Meeker of Morgan Stanley, and Henry
Blodget of Merrill Lynch, as well as by commentary in "internet chat
rooms and nonstop cable television coverage," and perhaps investors'
misunderstanding of the historical relationships between risk and re-

turn, encouraged continued investment in the stock market and contributed to its blowoff, but how much is very difficult to say. It is
clear, however, that many of these new investors got into the market
relatively late and thus had not built up much of a cushion when the
correction came.[36]

Between 1989 and 1998 roughly 30 million more Americans became shareholders, a 60 percent increase that far exceeds the gains in
any decade since World War II. Most of this growth occurred because more people bought equity mutual funds or stocks through
self-directed retirement plans, which grew markedly in the 1980s and
1990s. In 1980, for example, roughly 60 percent of nongovernment
contributions to retirement plans were to employer-controlled
defined-benefit plans. Yet at the end of the 1990s, about 85 percent of
private funding went to retirement plans in which the beneficiaries
made basic decisions about the amount and timing of contributions
and withdrawals and about how the funds were to be invested,
changes that resulted in a big increase in share ownership throughout
the population. Because so many of the participants in these plans
chose to invest in the stock market, the proportion of American families that owned publicly traded shares, whether directly or through
retirement accounts that they controlled, such as IRAs or 401(k)s,
rose from 32 percent in 1989 to 41 percent in 1995. Moreover, by
1995 these stock holdings had accounted for 40 percent of families'
financial assets, up from 26 percent six years earlier.*

For individuals the rise in the number of shareholders was similar,
from 53 million people, or 36 percent of the adult population, in
1989 to 69 million, or 44 percent of all adults, in 1995. By 1998 the
number of shareholders had grown to 84 million, about 52 percent of

---

*As Shiller points out, the development of self-directed retirement plans was encour-
aged by new legislation and regulatory rulings, including the Employee Retirement Income Security Act of 1974, which created individual retirement accounts (IRAs), and
the establishment in 1981 of the first 401 (k) plan, whose tax-deferred aspects were then
accepted by the Internal Revenue Service. Similarly, a 1975 ruling by the Securities and
Exchange Commission did away with fixed brokerage commissions, paving the way for
discount brokers and lower rates.

the adult population. Moreover, the increase in share ownership occurred throughout the income distribution; it rose most rapidly for those with family incomes below twenty-five thousand dollars, and it rose by the largest number of people among those in families earning twenty-five thousand to seventy-five thousand dollars annually. Most of the increase in the number of individuals owning stock was concentrated among people who owned shares or mutual funds in self-directed retirement accounts. For example, the number of people who participated in the market through individual retirement accounts (IRAs) or retirement savings accounts such as 401(k)s rose by almost 40 million, a figure that exceeds the overall growth in shareholders because many people own stock in more than one way. The number of people who owned stock *only* in personal brokerage accounts, on the other hand, fell by more than 5 million during the decade, and those owning stock *only* through direct purchases of mutual funds rose by just 3 million, while the number owning shares or equity mutual funds *only* through an IRA or retirement savings plan rose by 17 million, accounting for approximately 55 percent of the overall increase in shareholders from 1989 to 1998.[37]

How did these new investors do? Some clearly did very well as, on average, the growth of defined-contribution retirement plans more than made up for the decline of defined-benefit plans. Between 1983 and 1998, the fraction of householders aged forty-seven or older holding a defined-contribution plan rose forty percentage points, from 8 percent to 48 percent, while the mean value of these plans increased from $5,000 to $53,000. And although the fraction holding defined-benefit plans fell from 68 percent to 46 percent, and the plans' average value declined from $74,000 to $63,000, average pension wealth—assets in defined-contribution plans *and* defined-benefit plans—rose by about $36,000 and covered slightly more people. Nevertheless, because defined-contribution plans tend to be less generous than the defined-benefit plans they replaced, the median, or typical, level of pension wealth declined for some age-groups, including households headed by a person aged forty-seven to sixty-four, whose median value fell by almost 5 percent between 1983 and 1998.[38]* Moreover, these data do not include the effects of the late-1990s market explosion and its subsequent collapse, which may make these findings substantially worse. And we know that some workers suffered very badly, such as those at Enron, whose 401(k)s had about 60 percent of their assets in company shares, roughly 50 percent above the norm for workers in large publicly traded companies. Many Enron employees thus were hit with a double blow, losing both their jobs and a large chunk of their retirement savings.[39]†

Enron aside, much of the growth in share holding throughout the population took place through ownership of equity mutual funds, thus contributing to their rapid growth and rising importance in the stock market. From 1980 to 1996, the share holdings of mutual funds rose from just over 8 percent of the market's total value to more than 25 percent, accounting for most of the growth in the share of the market controlled by institutional investors, a category that includes banks, insurance companies, brokerage firms, and hedge-fund managers.[40] Because new investors tended to buy stocks through mutual

---

*The median separates a range of values in the middle, so that half are above the median and half below it. Because the average is very sensitive to extreme values, the more dispersed a distribution is, the greater the difference between its mean and median.

†Enron's collapse triggered widespread criticism of defined-contribution plans for allowing workers to maintain such highly concentrated stock portfolios and for permitting their employers to restrict sales of company stock contributed to their accounts. Most of these practices are common among large companies. For plans with more than 5,000 participants, company stock accounts for about 43 percent of plan assets, with more than ten companies above 74 percent, ranging from McDonald's (74.3 percent) to Procter & Gamble (94.7 percent). In addition, roughly 45 percent of firms whose plans allow employees to invest in company shares make matching contributions in those shares. Finally, 85 percent of companies that match employee contributions with company stock place restriction on when it can be sold.
Enron prohibited employees who were not yet fifty from selling Enron shares that the company had contributed to their 401(k)s, but the workers had bought additional Enron shares on their own—perhaps as much as half their total holdings of company stock—which they could have sold but didn't. Enron employees were also prohibited from making any changes in their accounts during a "lockdown" period for administrative changes, which took place from October 26 to November 13, 2001. Lockdowns are not unusual, but this one occurred after the company's problems became clear and its stock was in free fall. The shares fell by about a third during the period, from $15.40 to $9.98.

funds, how they fared during the 1990s can be approximated by analyzing the growth in mutual-fund assets and fund returns in these years. Investors in "aggressive growth" funds, for example, did very badly. More than half of the almost $300 billion that flowed into these funds after 1994 arrived from the middle of 1998 on, at rates that reached $5–$10 billion a month in late 1999 and rose to more than $20 billion a month in early 2000. These post-1997 investments were particularly exposed to the Nasdaq correction, which began in March 2000 and was so severe that it wiped out their accumulated profits by the end of the year. For equity mutual funds as a group, the pattern is similar but less extreme. When monthly mutual-fund returns are weighted by the money under management in each period, the results show that cumulative investor profits rose from about $200 billion at the end of 1995 to almost $800 billion by the end of the decade, but fell rapidly after that and were back to $200 billion by September 2001. In short, it appears that many investors discovered the virtues of stock market investing at a very dangerous time, unless they are truly committed for the long haul.[41]

New Companies.   The stock market of the 1980s and 1990s, like that of the 1920s, was unusually dynamic in that many more firms than usual entered and left it. The decades preceding the stock market crash of 1929 were times of great innovation in which new electric power technologies and mass-production techniques spread widely throughout the economy and began to boost productivity and economic growth significantly. In part because they grew up with these new technologies and could exploit them effectively, many of the companies that went public in the 1920s survived the great crash and maintained their presence in the stock market much longer than usual. Public offerings and mergers also picked up markedly in the 1980s and 1990s, when new information and communications technologies and lean business practices began to take hold. Moreover, as software, Internet, and other technology companies went public, the market share of the 1920s entrants began to decline much more rapidly than it had in earlier decades, which suggests (even though it is hazardous to generalize on the basis of such a limited and crude comparison) that the new technologies and businesses of the last few decades may be unusually important to the economy, possibly comparable to those associated with electric power and mass production.[42]

Since the late 1880s, roughly 5 percent of all publicly traded companies have left the stock market each year, whether through merger or business failure or because they preferred to be private, while new firms have gone public at about twice that rate (although entry rates are even more variable than exit rates). This continuing process of exhaustion and renewal explains why over time older cohorts of entrants constitute a smaller and smaller fraction of the market's total value. Few companies remain from those that went public around the turn of the last century, for example, and those that are still around are among the most successful, such as General Electric, which first sold shares to the public in 1892 and is still going strong. Others, such as AT&T and U.S. Steel, which went public in 1901, are past their prime but are still hanging on. (Not surprising, in light of his influence at the turn of the century, J. P. Morgan was a major backer of all three companies.) Companies that went public at the turn of the century generally lost market share rapidly in the years 1915–1930 and 1985–2000, when so many new businesses emerged and rates of stock market entry and exit doubled. In some respects, the spike in initial public offerings in the 1990s was even more exceptional than in the 1920s because market entry had been so slow since the great crash and depression, whereas it had been very rapid in the early years of the twentieth century.

The large number of firms that entered the stock market in the second and third decades of the twentieth century maintained their standing in the market longer than usual, accounting for $1.5 trillion of stock market value in 1998, not much below the shares of the cohorts that went public in any of the five decades between the 1920s and the 1980s. Although many fell precipitously when the market crashed in 1929, including Procter & Gamble, Caterpillar, and IBM, whose shares fell roughly 80 percent, they were sound enough to recover strongly, generating long-run stock returns in line with the market averages.[43]* Despite their uncommon endurance, however, these 1920s companies lost market share at a rate that rose sharply in the early 1980s, when companies better able to exploit new information and communications technologies proliferated and grew rapidly. This may be because these innovations also are unusually powerful, likely, perhaps, to have an impact on the economy comparable to that of electric power. Even so, the market's history, particularly the experience of the 1920s cohort and the more general tendency for stock returns to revert to the mean, implies that future returns on shares of new-economy companies are not likely to approach those achieved during the stock market bubble of the late 1990s. But less fantastic prices, and more competitive returns, will not diminish the importance of these innovative and rapidly growing businesses. For it is the development of extraordinary new firms and the above-average rates of productivity and economic growth they help to generate—not outlandish stock market returns—that make economies new, more than compensating for periods of subpar advances to produce the seemingly steady long-term progress we have come to expect.

*Like the favorites of the 1920s, the beloved "nifty fifty" of the late 1960s and early 1970s, which include General Electric, Procter & Gamble, IBM, Coke, Merck, and Philip Morris, also earned market-like returns in the period following their steep fall in the 1973–1974 bear market.

SIX

Junk Bonds and Takeovers

As DESCRIBED in the last chapter, the stock market in the 1980s and 1990s was unusually dynamic, comparable in many respects to what it was like in the years between World War I and the Great Depression, when electric power, mass production, and automobiles began to take hold and so many of today's major companies came of age. Both were times in which corporate earnings grew rapidly and stock prices grew even faster, eventually reaching heights that were neither warranted nor likely to last. In both periods, the rates at which companies entered and left the stock market were about twice as high as normal, in part because mergers and acquisitions surged. Mergers, it turns out, like technological progress, economic growth, and stock market booms, tend to come in waves. There were four great merger movements in the last century—one that began in the late 1880s and peaked shortly after the turn of the century, a second that began after World War I and crested in 1929, a third that started after World War II and matured in the late 1960s, and a fourth that took place during the 1980s and 1990s—and each occurred during one of the century's major stock market runs. These also were times of rapid economic growth, unusual innovation, and recovery from wars, recessions, and depressions.[1]

That mergers and acquisitions should be more prevalent in periods of profound economic change and robust stock markets should not be surprising. Mergers are a way for companies to grow or re-make themselves, a means of effecting new business strategies or transforming old ones, and the opportunities and pressures for such experiments tend to be greater when the economy is in flux. For many of the same reasons, it is understandable that economists have not been able to explain the historical pattern of merger activity in precise statistical models, or to predict when mergers will slow down or accelerate, and that mergers have differed in character from period to period. The merger wave at the turn of the last century, for example, is generally thought to have been a movement to create monopolies or near monopolies, which could dominate their industries, "a reaction of epic proportions to the vast changes in transportation, communications, manufacturing technology, competition, and legal institutions" in which large groups of firms in the same industry were combined to create industrial behemoths such as Standard Oil, General Electric, and U.S. Steel. Overall, it has been estimated that more than seventy important industries became near monopolies through mergers completed between 1890 and 1904.[2]

Standard Oil was formed in 1870 and by the early 1890s had acquired more than one hundred oil refiners and controlled about 90 percent of the industry's capacity. Similarly, General Electric was fashioned through an 1892 merger of two large electrical equipment manufacturers, which themselves had been active acquirers of other companies; together with Westinghouse, it then controlled many of the markets in which it operated. J. P. Morgan, the country's greatest consolidator and a backer of Thomas Edison since the late 1870s, opposed the merger between Edison General Electric and the Thomson-Houston Electric Company when it was first proposed in 1891, thinking that the benefits to his company would be small. But he changed his mind within a year, convinced by Thomson-Houston's greater success in the market "that it is desirable to bring about closer management between the two companies." Morgan harbored no such doubts when he organized U.S. Steel in 1901, combining twelve of the twenty firms in the steel industry, including the two biggest, into a company that instantly became the largest in the world, accounting for approximately 65 percent of U.S. capacity to produce steel. Moreover, the twenty steel companies that Morgan had to choose from were the survivors of a process of consolidation, which he helped to engineer, that reduced more than two hundred independent companies to one-tenth that number in roughly ten years.[3]

The ground staked out in the first merger wave, and the refinement of antitrust policy that followed in its wake, helped to make the second wave one of "mergers for oligopoly," as the Nobel Prize–winning economist George Stigler termed them, in contrast to "mergers for monopoly," which dominated the first upsurge. By the early twentieth century, many industries had already been monopolized, and the Supreme Court's decision in the *Northern Securities* case in 1904 made it clear that mergers would now be judged more stringently. The Court essentially closed a loophole in the 1890 Sherman Act, holding that creating monopolies through mergers was no less illegal than establishing them de facto, through collusion, which was always understood to be banned by the statute. And in breaking up Standard Oil seven years later, the courts showed how forceful they could be in dealing with monopolistic companies.* As a consequence, the mergers of the 1920s rarely produced firms controlling near 50 percent of their markets. Instead of turning out industry leaders, many of the second-wave mergers sought to create strong rivals for already dominant companies, as in the steel industry, where Bethlehem

---

*Richard Posner, who later became a judge of the U.S. Court of Appeals for the Seventh Circuit while continuing to teach at the University of Chicago Law School and to write articles and books, has argued that the *Northern Securities* Court was correct in holding that monopoly pricing by firms that have been combined into a single company or trust should not be treated differently from collusive pricing by firms in a cartel. But he thinks the Court erred in focusing on how cartels and holding companies reduce competition between their constituent companies, a perspective that ignores the possibility that they might nevertheless affect the economy very differently. This could happen, for example, if a merger or holding-company amalgamation enables the combined businesses to lower their unit operating costs and thus their prices, an outcome that would not be possible in a cartel. "It was accordingly a relief," he wrote in 1976, that the Court in the *Standard Oil* case decided to apply a "Rule of Reason" in evaluating the economic effects and legality of the trust.

Steel built itself up through acquisitions, buying four steel producers during the 1920s in order to compete more effectively with U.S. Steel. In addition to effecting smaller "horizontal" combinations, the mergers of the 1920s were more likely to join companies with their suppliers or customers ("vertical" mergers) or with firms in unrelated industries ("conglomerate" or diversifying mergers). Large utility holding companies were also put together after World War I, to integrate groups of local gas and electric utilities into more efficient units, but they often were constructed shakily, using debt liberally at each layer of the edifice, and suffered mightily when the stock market crashed and the economy followed. This practice of "pyramiding" is generally associated with the holding-company magnate Samuel Insull, who, several decades earlier, had helped to centralize the operations of Edison General Electric.[4]

The merger wave of the 1950s and 1960s accelerated the drift toward conglomeration, partly because mergers between firms that controlled significant shares of their markets were being judged even more strictly. By then, additional antitrust legislation had been enacted, including the Clayton Act in 1914 and the Celler-Kefauver Act in 1950, and under prevailing interpretations of the various merger statutes, combinations that noticeably raised an industry's "concentration"—generally measured by the combined market share of its three or four leading firms—were likely to be challenged and disallowed. Thus, one study of forty-two large firms that were active acquirers of other companies between 1950 and 1963 found that more than 80 percent of their targets operated in industries in which the buyers were not one of the four largest firms. Sometimes these acquisitions of loosely related companies produced conglomerates with bizarre combinations of businesses, such as Litton Industries, an electronics company that sought to acquire fifty companies each year, quickly branching out into packaged foods, teaching aids, and ships, or International Telephone and Telegraph (ITT), which made more than one hundred acquisitions during the 1960s and owned Hartford Insurance, Sheraton hotels, Avis rental cars, Wonder Bread, and Hostess Twinkies. (ITT also controlled the Chilean telephone company and was accused of aiding the overthrow of the Socialist president Salvador Allende in 1973.[5])

Not only did antitrust policy make acquisitions in the same line of business difficult; it was thought that highly professional, centralized management by technocrats, such as Litton's Charles "Tex" Thornton and ITT's Harold Geneen, could effectively control such widely diverse operations, perhaps even boosting overall efficiency. As it turned out, however, many of these acquisitions were ill conceived, motivated less by economic fundamentals than by blind pursuit of growth, even if it harmed shareholders—managers in those days owned little stock in their companies, and little of their pay was linked to how well they did. Mergers during the go-go years were propelled as well by opportunities for financial alchemy created by the highfliers' rich earnings multiples: by buying companies with much lower multiples, they could ensure that their per-share earnings would rise so long as the underlying businesses did not deteriorate too rapidly. (Something like this also happened in the 1990s, when companies such as WorldCom, Qwest, Tyco, and AOL used their richly priced shares to acquire companies with lesser earnings multiples but more substantial businesses.) But tricks such as these could not forever obscure conglomerates' basic problems, particularly when foreign competition was growing, markets were being freed from overly restrictive regulations, and new technologies and business practices were starting to alter the business landscape significantly. The combination of bloated bureaucracies, unfocused operations, and foolish acquisitions made it very hard for many conglomerates to respond effectively, a failing that helps to explain the slower productivity growth and stagflation that plagued the U.S. economy in the 1970s. The conglomerates' failures also helped to create inviting opportunities for the raids and takeovers of the 1980s.[6]*

---

*To see how differing earnings multiples affect mergers, consider an example in which a buyer's shares are trading at forty times earnings, while its target's shares are valued at only ten times earnings. Since each dollar of the buyer's shares is backed by 2.5 cents of earnings but each dollar of the target's is supported by 10 cents of earnings, as long as the buyer exchanges shares worth less than four times the value of the target's shares, the combination's per-share earnings will rise without any improvements in its businesses.

MERGERS AND ACQUISITIONS
IN THE 1980s AND 1990s

Mergers, acquisitions, and takeovers revived again in the 1980s and 1990s, accounting in some years for about 10 percent of the stock market's total value and for more than 5 percent of GDP in the 1980s and roughly twice as much in the late 1990s—far above the norm in both cases and comparable in the 1990s to the levels reached in the merger wave at the turn of the century. Although they were similar in scale, the mergers of the 1980s and 1990s differed significantly in character. The acquisitions of the 1990s were generally amicable arrangements, negotiated between firms in the same lines of business and typically paid for in shares that never were cheap and sometimes were seriously overvalued. The takeovers of the 1980s, on the other hand, were often hostile, acquisitions that were opposed by the targets' managers and directors, at least at first. They also differed from past or subsequent mergers and acquisitions in the extent to which they were paid for in cash rather than shares of the acquiring company. This was partly owing to the fact that price-earnings multiples in the early 1980s were very low and the shares of many companies truly undervalued, which created a plentiful pool of attractive acquisition candidates but also made buyers' shares a costly acquisition currency. Cash was also used because many of the acquirers were corporate raiders or buyout firms whose shares were not traded in public markets and thus could not be used to acquire other companies.[7]*

Corporate raiders and buyout firms were vital in establishing the aggressive tone of takeover activity in the 1980s, and their forcefulness helps to explain why these acquisitions were so effective in shaking up the established order and moving it in a new direction. Because they operated outside the corporate mainstream, raiders were relatively free to ignore its unspoken ban on unsolicited, or un-

---

*The terms "merger," "acquisition," and "takeover" are roughly synonymous but connote different degrees of aggressiveness, unfriendliness, or hostility. They are listed here, and used throughout, in ascending order of hostility.

friendly, takeovers to pursue acquisitions of companies that were wasteful and badly managed, firms whose assets could be exploited more profitably by focused and highly motivated owners. Raiders and buyout firms were particularly important in helping to break up ill-conceived and inefficient conglomerates, frequently selling their divisions and subsidiaries to firms in the same lines of business. Reallocating assets in this way was possible in part because antitrust policy had become far more flexible, less likely to challenge horizontal mergers *just* because they raised industry concentration ratios. Instead, enforcement focused on mergers' likely economic effects, especially their impact on prices and innovation, a more nuanced perspective that has largely endured.

In addition to reallocating resources, the hostile acquisitions of the 1980s were effective because they posed a threat to inefficient companies, pressuring managers to reduce waste and boost productivity and profitability or risk being taken over. Roughly 50 percent of the more than one thousand large firms included in the Value Line Investment Survey at the end of 1981 were estimated to have received a takeover bid over the following eight years, almost half of which were hostile. In addition, more than 7 percent of the firms in this sample restructured their operations to escape incipient takeover activity, such as that implied by rapid accumulation of large blocks of its stock. Another study, which analyzed sixty-two firms that were taken over in the mid-1980s in transactions valued at more than $50 million, found that more than 70 percent of the acquired assets ended up in firms that were in the same lines of business and that almost half of the initial buyers were private companies owned by raiders or foreign companies controlled by them, such as Hanson PLC, the vehicle of Lords James Hanson and Gordon White. The nontraditional acquirers of the 1980s also instituted new compensation schemes in the companies they bought, emphasizing elements such as profit sharing, stock options, and share ownership, which now are common.[8]

In short, the takeovers and acquisitions of the 1980s were an effective response to the problems, paralysis, and opportunities created by a new industrial state that had grown old in a hurry and could not cope well with large-scale changes in the world economy, a movement that helped to dismantle many bureaucratic companies of the golden postwar years and aided development of the leaner, more flexible, and more vibrant firms of an emerging new economy. And because the 1980s takeovers stimulated so much restructuring throughout the economy, the mergers of the 1990s could proceed somewhat differently, generally seeking to build up companies or expand their scope rather than break them up or try to run them more efficiently.* Even those who don't recognize this link between the mergers and acquisitions of the last two decades, or think the takeovers of the 1980s were bad for the economy, agree that they became such a powerful force only because corporate raiders and buyout firms were able to finance their acquisitions by borrowing extensively, often up to 80 or 90 percent of the purchase price. And the critical element in funding these highly leveraged transactions was so-called junk, money raised through the sale of high-yield bonds, which were marketed mainly by Michael Milken and Drexel Burnham Lambert, the investment-banking firm he came to dominate and stand for.[9]

The story of the gathering boom in the junk-bond market, and the hostile takeovers and buyouts it supported, helps to make clear what a great break from the past junk-bond-financed takeovers represented and why they had such a large impact on the economy. The development of these two markets—the high-yield market and what came to be called the "market for corporate control"—also shows, again, how great investment success tends to raise unrealistic expectations, creating frenzied pursuit of ever-worsening opportunities. As

---

*Because many of the 1990s mergers, like those of the 1960s, were ill conceived, sales and spin-offs of business segments acquired during the decade have risen sharply, accounting for about 35 percent of all merger activity in 2001, compared with roughly 20 percent in the prior two years. This partly reflects the fall in merger activity since the stock market bubble burst, but it also resembles the dismantling of the 1960s mergers that occurred during the 1980s.

in the explosion of technology stocks at the end of the 1990s, the pressure of increased competition in the junk-bond and takeover markets of the 1980s not only drove prices far beyond reasonable levels, inevitably producing collapse, hardship, and distress, but also elicited the swindling and fraud that, as Kindleberger observed, seem to go with the territory.

THE REVIVAL OF THE JUNK-BOND MARKET

Although they were not always called junk bonds, low-rated high-yield bonds have been around since at least the beginning of the twentieth century. Strictly speaking, they are publicly traded corporate bonds that receive a below-investment-grade rating from Moody's Investors Service or Standard & Poor's, the two major rating agencies.* The term "junk bonds" reportedly originated in a conversation between Milken and one of his early clients, Meshulam Riklis, when Milken, after studying Riklis's bond portfolio, remarked, "Rik, this is " 'junk.' "[10] Also called "speculative-grade bonds" because of their low ratings, they are issued by companies whose assets and cash flows provide less assurance that the interest and principal will be paid on time than do the assets and cash flows of companies whose bonds are more highly rated. Because the risk of default or nonpayment on junk bonds is thought to be higher than on investment-grade securities, and because they trade in less liquid markets, they must offer investors higher yields. But if the companies that issue them are more successful than their ratings and yields suggest, investors will be well compensated for bearing the additional risks. That this was likely to be the case in the 1980s was the central observation behind the Milken-led revival of the dormant junk-bond market.

*This generally means they are rated "Ba1" or lower by Moody's, or "BB+" or lower by Standard & Poor's, but ambiguities arise when the agencies are split, one rating them below investment grade and the other above it. Opinions also differ over whether or not to count low-rated convertible bonds—essentially bonds combined with options that give holders the right to buy stock at a specified price—as high-yield bonds.

Junk bonds were not very significant between World War II and the early 1980s, although they had been much used in the 1920s and 1930s, when they accounted for approximately 17 percent of newly issued corporate debt. Because many investment-grade bonds were downgraded during the Great Depression, by 1940 more than 40 percent of all corporate bonds outstanding had received junk-bond ratings. But since few new high-yield bonds were sold after that, their presence eroded as the older ones were extinguished, and in the early 1970s junk bonds accounted for less than 5 percent of all corporate bonds. Although some were newly issued for companies such as Braniff Airways and Metro-Goldwyn-Mayer, most were "fallen angels," downgraded bonds such as those of Penn Central Corporation, which was forced to declare bankruptcy in 1970, when it could not refinance its commercial paper. The large investment banks and brokerage firms were not particularly interested in these securities, and markets for them did not exist. It was in this "obscure backwater of Wall Street," as James B. Stewart characterized it in his 1991 bestseller, *Den of Thieves*, that Michael Milken pursued his obsessions.[11]*

The story of Milken's early life is now well known and differs little in the many accounts that have appeared. He was raised in a middle-class Jewish family in the San Fernando Valley and was a good high-school student, active in student government, a cheerleader who was elected prom king. While still in his teens, he resolved to become a millionaire by the time he was thirty, and he spent the mid-1960s as a business major at Berkeley, aloof from the political and social currents of the time. An active member of his fraternity, he invested money for friends and fraternity brothers, absorbing all losses and keeping 50 percent of the profits. By 1970, two years after graduating from Berkeley, Milken had already decided what he wanted to do. In an op-ed piece submitted to (and rejected by) *The New York Times*, he wrote: "Unlike other crusaders from Berkeley, I have chosen

*Between 1970 and 1976, there were fewer than thirty new offerings of high-yield bonds. Most were underwritten by investment-banking firms that no longer exist, and their entire principal amount was less than $1 billion.

Wall Street as my battleground for improving society. It is here that the government's institutions and industries are financed."[12]

Milken became fascinated with low-grade bonds while still an undergraduate at Berkeley, after reading *Corporate Bond Quality and Investor Experience*, a study conducted by W. Braddock Hickman under the auspices of the National Bureau of Economic Research that evaluated the returns on corporate bonds sold in the United States from 1900 to 1943. The question of whether lower-rated bonds produced higher returns for investors than higher-rated securities had been debated during the 1920s and 1930s by Arthur Stone Dewing of Harvard Business School, who thought they did, and Harold Fraine, later a professor at the University of Wisconsin, who was more skeptical. Fraine's Ph.D. dissertation at the University of Minnesota may have piqued the bureau's interest in high-yield bonds, but Hickman's study reached more optimistic conclusions, finding that a portfolio of high-risk bonds usually outperformed higher-rated, "safer" securities. Nevertheless, Hickman and his associates cautioned that this was the case only "if the list is large and held over a long period" and warned that investors' returns were "subject to extreme aberrations over time."[13]

After Berkeley, Milken attended the Wharton School while working part-time at Drexel Firestone, a declining Philadelphia investment-banking firm descended from J. P. Morgan's Drexel, Morgan and Company. When the company merged with Burnham & Company, a New York brokerage firm, in 1971, Milken was working full-time and commuting from outside Philadelphia to New York every day by bus. According to one writer, he spent his time on the bus reading bond prospectuses by the light of a miner's helmet.* Shortly after the merger, I. W. "Tubby" Burnham, the firm's founder, established for Milken a semiautonomous sales and trading unit with about $2 million in capital. As part of the deal, Burnham agreed that

---

*Apocryphal or not, the miner's-helmet story illustrates how Wall Street storytellers like to create myths about the obsessive drive of people such as Milken. According to one writer who had "unique access" to him, the story is a gross exaggeration that "annoys Milken no end." "I may have used it *once*," Milken said. "Buses *do* have lights."

the department would keep 35 percent of the profits from high-yield bonds as well as up to 30 percent of profits earned in any other business that it brought to the firm. Milken was in charge of allocating and distributing the bonuses within his department, which reputedly had reached the seven-figure range by the mid-1970s. This arrangement was still in effect in 1986, when Milken earned a record $550 million. "The only figure comparable to Milken who comes to mind," the Harvard Business School professor Samuel L. Hayes III told *Business Week* that July, "is J. P. Morgan, Sr."[14]

DEVELOPING A NETWORK
OF INVESTORS

Milken's rise, and the revival of the junk-bond market, were part of a general expansion of debt during the 1980s, which was important to the economy's recovery from recession in the early part of the decade and to its growth in the remaining years. "Credit (actual and anticipated)," concluded a history of borrowing and lending since the Civil War, "played a vital if unsung role in the Reagan prosperity."[15] Federal government debt increased from about $640 billion at the end of the 1970s to nearly $2.2 trillion a decade later, while bonds issued by nonfinancial corporations grew at about the same pace, from roughly $337 billion to just over $1 trillion. Growth in the junk-bond market accounted for much of the explosion of corporate debt. New issues of junk bonds rose in value from less than $2 billion a year between 1980 and 1982 to approximately $13 billion a year in the next three years and about $31 billion annually between 1986 and 1989; as a share of newly issued corporate debt, they increased fivefold, from less than 4 percent to slightly more than 20 percent. In their heyday from 1983 to 1989, newly issued junk bonds accounted for 21 percent of all newly issued corporate debt, compared with between 3 and 7 percent during the previous six years. As a consequence, high-yield bonds outstanding rose from well under 5 percent of all corporate bonds in the 1970s to 8.5 percent in 1984 and 17 percent in 1987.

And while many junk bonds were issued so that enterprising companies such as MCI and Turner Broadcasting could finance growth, by 1985 more than one-third of all newly issued junk bonds were intended to finance mergers and acquisitions. During the peak years of the decade, from 1986 to 1989, almost two-thirds were used for these purposes. (Because debt-financed acquisitions basically substituted debt for equity, their prevalence helps to explain the sharp rise in the debt/equity ratio in the mid- to late 1980s.) Drexel Burnham's share of this highly profitable business averaged almost 50 percent between 1980 and 1989.*

These favorable trends hardly diminish Milken's pivotal role in revitalizing the moribund market for junk bonds. The keys to his success appear to have been indefatigable energy and considerable skills as a salesman. The big Wall Street firms were not very interested in making markets for the few issues of high-yield securities still outstanding in the 1970s, and their research departments did not keep track of the companies that had issued them or know who owned them. Milken, on the other hand, accumulated a wealth of information about junk-bond issuers and holders and used this unique knowledge in his own trading and in cultivating clients who traded through Drexel. His network expanded quickly as he showed that he could make profitable investments in undervalued securities such as Penn Central bonds (the company's assets would eventually benefit those who bought its depressed bonds at twenty cents or less on the dollar). And as he attracted loyal clients, trading volume rose, giving the market more liquidity, thus making it even easier to trade.[16]†

---

*After falling sharply in the early 1990s, the ratio of corporate debt to equity rose again as companies borrowed hungrily to buy back their shares, partly to offset dilution that would occur when employees exercised their options, and to fund investments in the latest technology.

†Investors who bought Penn Central bonds when it declared bankruptcy in 1970 and held them until they made their final distributions in 1981 earned compound returns of 16–20 percent a year, depending on the particular issues they owned. But because the bonds' prices continued falling after 1970, those who bought them in the middle of the decade earned much higher returns.

Milken, James B. Stewart writes, essentially "became the market for high-yield bonds." As with any near monopoly, it was a market that he controlled and could maneuver. There were no published prices, and Milken's "spreads"—the difference between what he paid for securities and what he sold them for—were three or four percentage points, more than ten times as large as the eighth and quarter of a point spreads typical for Treasury and investment-grade corporate bonds. His clients did not seem to care, however, as long as they also made money. Most of them, including Saul Steinberg, Laurence Tisch, Carl Lindner, and the aforementioned Meshulam Riklis, were not part of the Wall Street establishment. An Israeli immigrant and active acquirer of worn-out companies such as Schenley Distributors, or now defunct department stores such as S. Klein and Best & Company, Riklis was best known as the husband of Pia Zadora, a second-tier movie actress and singer. Riklis and other clients issued junk bonds themselves and clearly stood to benefit from greater investor interest in them. Many, having recognized the potential of capital-rich insurance companies as a source of investment funds, acquired or ran such firms and made them the center of their operations. (So did Warren Buffett, an outspoken opponent of the way junk bonds were sold and used in the 1980s.) All were mavericks, and several had run-ins with the Securities and Exchange Commission.[17]*

Milken completed Drexel's first underwriting of a new issue of junk bonds in 1977. The $30 million offering for the oil and gas wildcatter Texas International—now part of Apache Corporation, a much

*Steinberg, whose latest company, Reliance Insurance, declared bankruptcy in 2001, is well known for his audacious attempt to take over Chemical Bank in the late 1960s. After announcing his offer for the bank, however, the stock of his vehicle, Leasco Data Processing, mysteriously dropped more than 25 percent, causing Steinberg to give up the acquisition, which was to be paid for in Leasco shares. His principal investment-banking firm also withdrew, others were pressured not to help him, and regulators in Albany, New York, and Washington, D.C., introduced measures to shield banks from hostile takeovers. "I always knew there was an establishment," Steinberg said, "I just used to think I was part of it." Almost twenty years later, Milken recalled this incident as an example of what the banks might try to do to him for cutting into their corporate lending or funding acquisitions of their clients.

larger oil and gas company that acquired it in 1996—earned the firm an underwriting fee of 3 percent, more than triple the typical fee for underwriting investment-grade bonds.[18]* But Drexel's business really took off when it began financing leveraged buyouts (LBOs) in 1981. By this time, Milken had moved the high-yield-bond operation to Los Angeles, where he consolidated its power and independence and established an identity for the unit that far eclipsed its parent's. He often put in sixteen-hour days that began at 4:30 a.m., and everybody had to conform to his frantic pace. According to some observers, however, the Drexel corporate finance department first came up with the idea of using junk bonds to finance LBO transactions, in which buyers' acquisition vehicles would issue the bonds and raise the other money necessary to complete the purchases of the target firms. Milken was said to have feared at first that the "incremental risk" of high-yield bonds issued to fund LBOs would sour investors on junk bonds generally, but he can't have protested too much, and the firm's business flourished. In 1983 its revenues were almost $1 billion, and Milken's own take was more than $100 million.

The second defining boost to Milken's fortunes was the decision, arrived at late in 1983 and unveiled with great fanfare at Drexel's annual high-yield-bond conference the following spring, to provide junk-bond financing for hostile takeovers—essentially leveraged acquisitions of publicly traded companies carried out against their managers' wishes. This was a natural sequel to the decision to use junk bonds to finance buyouts approved by the people in control of the company, and it followed a similar brainstorming session, about which accounts differ. According to some sources, Milken once again expressed reservations, in this case because he was concerned

---

*Other firms also increased their underwriting of junk bonds in the late 1970s. Overall issuance averaged just over $1 billion a year in 1977 and 1978, compared with roughly $151 million a year earlier in the decade. The surge seems to have been stimulated by faster growth of high-yield mutual funds, which were hungry for investments, since the volume of high-yield bonds outstanding fell by $5 billion from 1974 through 1976.

about the probable backlash from managers and directors of companies that felt threatened and from their political allies. Others remember Milken giving enthusiastic support to financing hostile takeovers. If he had misgivings, they were quickly swept aside by the enormous profits he could envision and by his overriding desire to dominate the market. As Drexel's chairman Robert E. Linton said of him, "Michael wants to win the game. Michael wants to have it all. Michael wants to do every piece of business and every deal and make every dollar."[19]

THE HUGELY PROFITABLE DEALS
OF THE EARLY AND MID-1980s

The early to mid-1980s were a particularly inviting time for acquisitions. The economy was beginning to emerge from the most severe recession of the postwar period, yet valuations of companies in the stock market were historically low in relation to the value of their assets or their potential earning power. In this setting, acquisitions mainly financed by debt—"highly leveraged"—were potentially very profitable, whether they were made with the ostensible cooperation of existing management or against its will. In either case, borrowing large parts of the purchase price significantly increases the rate of return on investment if the acquisitions are successful.* And in order to complete their financing, raiders and sponsors of large leveraged buyouts typically resorted to junk bonds, whose market was largely controlled by Milken. In the financial structure of corporations whose

---

*Suppose a company is purchased for $100 million and sold a year later for $200 million. The profit is approximately $100 million regardless of how much was borrowed to buy the company, but the rate of return on investment varies markedly with the degree of leverage. If nothing was borrowed, the rate of return is 100 percent (the profit divided by the amount invested). But if $90 million, or 90 percent of the purchase price, was borrowed at an interest rate of 10 percent (and interest cost of $9 million), then the equity investment is $10 million, the profit is $91 million, and the rate of return on investment is 910 percent.

capital is mostly borrowed, junk bonds generally fall somewhere between the most "senior" debt (which is often provided by banks) and equity. Senior creditors have a higher claim on company assets and cash flows than the more junior bondholders, who in turn outrank equity shareholders. For much of the 1980s, corporations that were formed to make acquisitions or leveraged buyouts raised about half of their capital from bank loans, some of which were secured by assets of the companies being acquired, and 10–20 percent from equity investments, leaving a critical gap of 30–40 percent, which was filled by selling publicly traded junk bonds or by borrowing from insurance companies and other lenders who specialized in this "mezzanine" level of financing.

Because they were done on such favorable terms and were so highly leveraged, many of the early takeovers and buyouts were enormously profitable, and their spectacular returns probably did more than anything else to excite investors about aggressive acquisitions and junk bonds. One of the most prominent examples of the powers of leverage in an economy emerging from recession, when companies were not valued very highly even though their businesses were poised to improve, was not a Milken deal. In January 1982 former Treasury secretary William Simon and his partners bought Gibson Greeting Cards from RCA for $80 million, $79 million of which was borrowed. Less than two years later the company was taken public in an offering that valued the equity at almost $300 million. The Gibson transaction was extremely well timed, but it also was so profitable because the company was purchased from a very willing seller, one of the large bureaucratic conglomerates that generated many of the opportunities exploited by raiders and LBO firms. Gibson and three other manufacturing companies had been acquired by the CIT Financial Corporation in the conglomerate merger wave of the 1960s. RCA acquired CIT in January 1980 and didn't really know what to do with the manufacturing companies, which were not very large and seemed remote from its main businesses, consumer electronics and entertainment. The CIT companies had not done well during the troubled 1970s, and top management seemed driven to "get them off the books" at what turned out to be the worst possible time.*

Among Milken's noteworthy transactions in these formative years were the November 1984 sale of $1.3 billion of junk bonds for Metromedia Broadcasting to refinance temporary bank loans that the company had taken down in June to go private in the biggest LBO up to that time and the $6.4 billion acquisition of the Beatrice companies by the leveraged-buyout firm Kohlberg, Kravis, Roberts & Company (KKR) about a year later. Drexel earned more than $100 million in fees for financing these deals, apart from the equity interests that Milken took in the newly capitalized companies. These stakes would prove far more valuable than the other fees, because both transactions were hugely successful. Within a year Metromedia had sold its television stations to Rupert Murdoch, another Milken client, for more than the purchase price for the entire company. "Going in," wrote James Grant, publisher of the financial newsletter *Grant's Interest Rate Observer*, "Metromedia had seemed a shot in the dark. Going out—that is, within a few months—it looked like a bull's eye. Its success changed corporate finance."

Beatrice was similarly successful, but it was particularly significant because it was KKR's first unsolicited buyout, "such a sharp departure," Stewart writes, "that KKR's senior partner, Jerome Kohlberg, soon withdrew from the partnership that bears his name, citing 'philosophical differences' with his partners." There were also a number of high-profile raids on large oil companies in this period, including successive attacks on Phillips Petroleum by T. Boone Pickens and Carl Icahn. Icahn's tender offer for Phillips—a public announcement offering to buy out shareholders at higher than market prices—was

---

*I was part of a group that purchased one of the other companies from RCA in mid-1983. By this time, RCA's board had been embarrassed by the success of the Gibson transaction and insisted on retaining a small ownership interest in the company in case it happened again.

notable because it was backed by Drexel's assertion that it was "highly confident" it could raise the financing. This was a change from the conventional (and more costly) "commitment" to do so.[20]

The takeover of Storer Communications, acquired by KKR shortly before it bought Beatrice, highlights many of Milken's operating strategies. Storer owned several television stations as well as the fourth-largest cable system in the country, and Drexel sold almost $2 billion of highly speculative junk bonds and preferred stock to enable the company formed by KKR to buy it. Milken, as was his custom, told the LBO firm that in order to get his clients to buy the securities, it had to give the junk-bond investors an "equity sweetener" in the form of warrants, that is, guarantees that they will be able to buy stock at a fixed price in the newly formed company. Most of the warrants, however, ended up not in his clients' portfolios but in McPherson Partners, a partnership created expressly to hold such equity interests that was owned mostly by Milken, his brother, and their families. The partners at McPherson also included key Drexel employees, as well as mutual-fund managers whose funds were big buyers of Storer securities and other issues sold by Milken, and the chance to participate in McPherson was an incentive for them to continue to be good customers and employees. When KKR sold Storer's television stations and cable systems a few years later, the warrants yielded a profit of almost $200 million, with some of the properties going to other Milken clients whom he also financed.*

These maneuvers, in which valuable warrants and other "gratuities" were granted to important buyers of junk bonds, and securities and properties were traded within Milken's network, were critical to his continued control of about half of the larger, and riskier, junk-bond market that emerged in the second half of the decade. They are also the types of machinations that eventually produced indictments of Drexel, Milken, and various associates; ultimately they led to

---

*Trading securities and properties within his network of clients was facilitated by Milken's practice of overfunding their junk-bond issues—that is, raising more money than they needed, which was often invested in other junk-bond issues that Milken sold.

Milken's guilty plea and the demise of the firm. It mattered little to the junk-bond issuers whether Milken, his favorite employees and fund managers, or the funds themselves got the warrants so long as the deals were consummated. But from the perspective of the ultimate owners of the bonds, such as pension-fund beneficiaries and mutual-fund shareholders, it made a large difference. Not only did Milken's practice of diverting warrants to his own companies deprive bondholders of returns that were appropriate for the risks they were bearing, it also meant that these investors could not rely on their fund managers, or other agents responsible for representing their interests, to make an unbiased appraisal of an investment's risks and rewards. But none of the principals complained: the junk-bond issuers because they didn't care and the ultimate junk-bond owners because they didn't know.*

MANIA, PROSECUTIONS, AND COLLAPSE

By the mid-1980s, the success of highly publicized buyouts and takeovers had made the case for junk bonds far more persuasively than did Drexel's promotional pamphlet "The Case for High Yield Bonds" or any of the academic studies showing that default rates for high-yield securities were low.[21]† These exceptionally profitable deals

---

*One example of how Milken used warrants to lubricate his network involves Patricia Ostrander, a manager of junk-bond investments for several Fidelity mutual funds who got a share of the Storer warrants. She was found guilty of accepting them instead of passing them on to the funds. In sentencing her, the federal judge Richard Owen said:

> It is perfectly obvious from what [Milken] said that he was giving [the interest in McPherson] to Mrs. Ostrander because he wanted to have a nice relationship with her . . . The underlying problem is that this fund officer was entrusted with billions and billions of dollars of the public's money to invest, and . . . [the warrants] put her in a position of obligation to Milken. She had to know that . . . and that's a subversion of the duty of trust that had been imposed on her.

†Because the junk-bond market was growing so rapidly in the 1980s, there was a controversy about how to measure default rates most accurately. If, as was typically done, the default rate in any year was measured by the value of defaults in that year divided by the value of all outstanding bonds, rapid growth of new issues might make it appear misleadingly low, generally about 1.5 percent a year for the period 1978–1986. On the

precipitated a virtual frenzy in the high-yield, takeover, and stock markets. The notion of "private market value"—that is, what a highly leveraged, optimistic buyer might hypothetically pay for an entire company—increasingly influenced stock market valuations and impelled takeover groups to accumulate shares in potential targets, sometimes analyzing deals on the run using the latest personal computers and spreadsheets such as VisiCalc, Lotus 1-2-3, and Excel. Their purchases were followed closely by risk arbitrageurs—professional investors who speculate that takeovers will be consummated— often aided by computer programs that picked out stocks with unusual trading volume. Ultimately, even retail customers were drawn into the action. And LBO firms such as KKR and Forstmann Little & Company proliferated, supported by insurance companies, pension funds, "high net-worth individuals," and others who wanted to share in the abnormally high returns.

Corporate managers responded to the threat of takeovers and buyouts both by fighting them and by adopting their methods. They attacked corporate raiders and their junk-bond financiers in the press, in Washington, and in state legislatures and regulatory agencies. But they also arranged leveraged buyouts of their own companies, thereby taking these companies out of play, preserving their positions, and perhaps even earning returns comparable to those of the big LBO firms. Even if they didn't help to take their companies private, top managers began to serve themselves large option grants, which, they had seen, could be extremely lucrative. At the same time, Drexel's and Milken's extraordinary earnings and influence motivated many of the more established investment banks, including First Boston, Goldman Sachs, Merrill Lynch, and Salomon Brothers, to compete aggressively in the takeover and junk-bond markets. In an effort to capture some of Drexel's large market shares, they sug-

---

other hand, if the default rate was measured separately for each age cohort of bonds (that is, all bonds that were issued in a given year), as a 1989 paper suggested it should be, default rates were more than twice as high.

gested acquisition targets and offered attractive financing to potential buyers.

Once they were more highly contested, however, deals became more reckless. Nineteen eighty-six stands out as a turning point in the takeover and junk-bond markets. Not only did issuance of junk bonds soar between 1984 and 1986, but the average size of each new issue rose sharply, with more than half of all proceeds earmarked for buyouts and takeovers. Not surprisingly, the quality of newly issued junk bonds deteriorated sharply as volume surged after 1985—as Hickman and his colleagues had discovered in their study covering the years 1900–1943. Many companies issuing junk bonds in the overheated markets of 1986–1989 could make the required interest payments only if their cash flow grew rapidly or if they could sell assets at favorable prices, possibilities that depended on their becoming more efficient and on continued growth in the economy and continued strength in the junk-bond and acquisition markets.[22]*

It was at just this time, however, that prosecutions for insider trading and related violations of securities laws, which would eventually undermine Milken, began to emerge, starting in May 1986, when charges were brought against Dennis Levine, a relatively obscure investment banker at Drexel Burnham. Within a year, Ivan Boesky, a risk arbitrageur, and Martin Siegel, an investment banker who had earned his reputation defending clients from unsolicited takeovers, had also pleaded guilty to trading inside information about forthcoming company takeovers. Boesky paid fines and penalties of $100 mil-

---

*Barrie Wigmore, a limited partner at Goldman Sachs, showed that "coverage ratios" for companies that issued junk bonds—the cash that these companies generated, divided by the interest payments they were required to make—fell from an average of 1.2 for companies that issued junk bonds in 1983–1985 to 0.72 for those that issued them in 1986–1988. In addition to the higher risk of default, there was a risk, under such pressure, that future growth and productivity would be compromised by cutbacks in employment, capital spending, or research and development in order to increase current cash flow. Similarly, Steven Kaplan and Jeremy Stein found that among their sample of forty-one large buyouts that had been completed before 1985, only one defaulted on its debt. Of the eighty-three completed from 1985 to 1989, on the other hand, twenty-six defaulted despite the significant operating improvements many made.

lion and promised to cooperate with the accelerating investigation. Drexel and Milken were charged with insider trading, stock manipulations, fraud, and other transgressions in September 1988, and by the end of the year the firm had agreed to plead guilty to six felonies, including racketeering and securities fraud, settle charges with the SEC, and pay a $650 million fine. As part of the settlement, Milken was forced to resign from the company he built.

Boesky was the largest and most widely known risk arbitrageur, in part because of his close ties to Milken, who sold almost $1 billion of high-yield bonds for Boesky's investment firms from 1983 to 1986. Risk arbitrageurs are highly dependent on information about mergers and acquisitions and routinely talk to investment bankers and lawyers involved in deals. They can also be very useful to the bankers and lawyers, since they often control large blocks of stock in target companies and thus can determine the outcome of a takeover struggle. A fine and poorly defined line divides appropriate from inside information—information not generally available that is obtained from people with some involvement with the firms, a category that has expanded over the years to include lawyers and investment bankers who are not employed by a company but are entrusted with confidential information. Boesky clearly overstepped legal boundaries by paying Siegel and Levine for privileged information about companies' takeover plans, perhaps because his investment results had not been matching his reputation and the pressure to meet the interest payments on his own junk bonds was high.

Boesky may also have obtained inside information from Milken or his associates. Milken was indicted for insider trading, for example, for tipping off Boesky that Occidental Petroleum, for which Drexel acted as an adviser, was about to merge with another company.[23] But Milken did not admit this when he pleaded guilty in 1990 and paid a $600 million fine, roughly half of the $1.1 billion he ultimately paid to settle all government claims against him, civil lawsuits as well as criminal charges. Nevertheless, Milken's relationship to Boesky was central to his downfall. Of the six technical felonies to which he pleaded guilty after much bargaining with the government, four involved Boesky. In one, Milken admitted to secretly guaranteeing Boesky against losses in buying the stock of Fischbach Corporation, which another Milken client, Victor Posner, wanted to take over. Posner had been maneuvered into signing an agreement with Fischbach that prevented him from buying any more stock unless another potential bidder acquired at least 10 percent of Fischbach's shares. Encouraged by Milken's guarantees against losses, Boesky acquired 10 percent of the company's shares, thus freeing Posner to acquire control of Fischbach and giving Milken the opportunity to finance Posner's efforts. Boesky did not disclose the guarantees, as required by law, and Milken pleaded guilty to aiding and abetting him in filing false statements.[24]*

In addition to the legal problems engulfing the junk-bond market at the end of the 1980s, the economy began to weaken, further threatening risky acquisitions and junk-bond issues that depended on improved profitability and favorable asset sales. In the middle of 1989, the market was shaken by a series of defaults, including those of Integrated Resources and Southmark Corporation, Drexel-sponsored real-estate syndicators, as well as Resorts International, Seaman Furniture, Western Union, and Campeau Corporation (which had acquired both Allied and Federated Department Stores, owners of Brooks Brothers and Bloomingdale's). The rate at which junk bonds were issued fell drastically in 1990—from approximately $30 billion a year during the previous four years to under $2 billion. Investments in buyouts, which had grown from less than $1 billion in 1980 to a peak of more than $60 billion in 1988, declined to less than $4 billion in 1990. In 1989, junk-bond defaults exceeded $8 billion, more than

---

*Milken pleaded guilty to the criminal charges in 1990. In 1992 he and former colleagues at Drexel agreed to settle civil suits brought by the Federal Deposit Insurance Corporation (FDIC) for about $900 million; Milken's share was $500 million, which he paid in addition to his criminal fine of $600 million. Cravath, Swaine & Moore represented the FDIC, arguing that Milken and his associates had illegally controlled Columbia Savings and Loan and other S&L clients by buying and selling junk bonds on their behalf, thereby costing taxpayers billions of dollars.

the amount of junk bonds issued in any year before 1984 and more than double the amount that had defaulted in any year since at least 1970. The year 1990 was even worse. The deteriorating economy, combined with a scandal-racked junk-bond market that had absorbed so many risky issues since 1985, pushed defaults to almost $20 billion. Instead of making money, investors in junk bonds lost 8.6 percent in 1990.[25]*

July 1990 was later judged to be the beginning of the recession, and junk bonds, takeovers, and shortsighted trading were increasingly blamed for most of the country's problems, including the slowdown in economic growth, the savings and loan (S&L) crisis, and the longer-term declines in competitiveness and productivity growth. There was little truth to any of these charges. Most S&Ls, for example, did not hold enough junk bonds to harm them seriously. Only 5 percent of the 3,025 federally insured savings and loan banks held any junk bonds, only twenty of them held more than 10 percent of their capital in high-yield bonds, and just ten of these accounted for 76 percent of the total holdings. However, many of the S&Ls with significant holdings of junk bonds (among them Columbia Savings and Loan, CenTrust Savings of Miami, and Lincoln Savings and Loan) were important players in Milken's network, and some of their controlling shareholders were eventually convicted of misusing funds with which they were entrusted.[26]† Similarly, the surge in junk-bond defaults occurred despite improvements in the day-to-day operations of many of the companies that issued them. Consider Southland Cor-

---

*To better appreciate the abruptness and forcefulness of the collapse in the junk-bond market, consider the following: from 1977 through 1989, junk bonds produced higher annual returns than either government bonds or investment-grade corporate bonds—10.2 percent compared with 9.3 percent and 9.7 percent, respectively—but for the period 1977–1990, despite their high required interest payments, junk-bond returns trailed both governments and corporates, 8.7 percent versus 9.1 percent and 9.4 percent.

†It is also clear that poor government policy contributed to the S&Ls' problems: poorly conceived deregulation of S&Ls in 1982 encouraged excessive risk taking, while a 1989 law that prohibited junk-bond purchases by S&Ls and required them to liquidate their existing portfolios by 1994 exacerbated the market's fall as well as the losses suffered by S&Ls that held junk bonds.

poration (the owner of 7-Eleven stores), which was acquired in a leveraged buyout financed by Goldman Sachs in 1987. Its pretax earnings increased by more than 11 percent over the next two years, but the company still defaulted in March 1990. Southland's better performance, like that of many other excessively leveraged companies, was simply not sufficient to overcome the burdens posed by the riskier financial structures that were commonplace in the frenzied markets of the late 1980s.[27]*

WAS IT WORTH IT?

Overheated financial markets, speculative breakouts, and the shady dealings that seem to accompany them are nothing new. As in the junk-bond and takeover markets of the late 1980s, and in the market for technology stocks a decade later, they generally originate in real improvements in the economy, in innovations, breakthroughs, or "some event" that, as Kindleberger explained, "changes the economic outlook," creating "new opportunities for profits [that] are seized and overdone, in ways so closely resembling irrationality as to constitute a mania." In the takeover and technology-stock frenzies, investors were encouraged to act in this "overdone" way by analysts, media talking heads, and brokers and promoters who stood to benefit from a buying frenzy even if their clients did not do well. In the late 1980s, buyout firms, deal finders, and investment bankers all were charging hefty up-front fees to arrange transactions and issue junk bonds, which gave them strong incentives to keep the deals and bonds flowing despite their deteriorating fundamentals. "As usual," Warren Buffett wrote in his 1990 letter to the shareholders of Berkshire Hathaway, "the Street's enthusiasm for an idea was proportional not to its merit, but

---

*A number of factors made the post-1985 transactions riskier, including, as Kaplan and Stein show, higher acquisition prices, which necessitated the use of more and more debt, particularly junk bonds; more onerous terms on the smaller amounts of bank debt that helped finance these transactions; a higher incidence of buyouts in more volatile industries; and the fact that deal promoters, investment bankers, and managers took more money out of the companies in up-front fees.

rather to the revenue it would produce. Mountains of junk bonds were sold by those who didn't care to those who didn't think—and there was no shortage of either."28*

Many of the fees were earned just for completing a transaction, regardless of its ultimate success. In addition to the fees of junk-bond underwriters, typically 3 to 4 percent of the size of the issues, which produced payments of approximately $5 billion from 1986 through 1989, there were advisory fees for investment bankers, commitment fees for the lenders, and various legal and accounting fees. (These were several times larger than one might think because each participant typically hired his own experts and counsel.) Firms specializing in buyouts often earned three sets of fees, one for closing transactions, another for monitoring the companies they acquired, and an annual fee of between 1 and 2 percent on the money they managed for investors. Typically, they also took 20 percent of profits on successful deals, without sharing the losses. In total, it has been estimated that buyout fees rose from less than 2.5 percent of the deals' total costs in the first four years of the decade to 5 percent by 1986 and 6 percent in 1988 and 1989.[29]

Fees based on the size of transactions clearly encourage the wrong tendencies, a rush to transact more and bigger deals and to discount the importance of longer-term profitability. Even profit-sharing provisions did not adequately deter rabid deal making, since the fees were often based on the results of individual transactions and did not require profits to be balanced by other losses before gains were split. In addition, most of the detailed work on deals was done by junior employees whose compensation and bonuses were related to their success in completing transactions. These arrangements contributed to the overheating of the junk-bond and takeover markets, to the un-

---

*The worlds of Buffett, Milken, and Wall Street intersected in late 1987, when Buffett rescued Salomon Brothers from a takeover threat by Ronald Perelman, a major client of Milken who is best known for his acquisition of Revlon in 1985. Seven years later, Buffett had to assume control of Salomon to limit the damage from its manipulations of the auctions for government bonds.

derhanded dealing that accompanied it, and to the bankruptcies and distress that followed in its wake. Business failures and unemployment caused by unproductive uses of junk bonds wasted resources and disrupted lives and communities. And these foolish investment decisions were encouraged by the gifts of warrants and other favorable investment opportunities that Milken handed out to important clients and managers of large pools of capital, as well as by the transaction-based fees and bonuses that were paid to deal makers and money managers. The pattern was self-perpetuating: large fees and profits elicited strong competitive responses from others who wanted to get in on the action, such as the investment banks that challenged Milken's hold on the market, inevitably lowering standards and increasing the pressure on Milken to respond in kind in order to hold on to his share of the market.

Even so, the hostile takeovers and junk bonds of the 1980s appear on balance to have aided the economy considerably, helping to make it more competitive and dynamic and thus more efficient. One reason to think so is that the junk-bond market survived both Milken's demise and the 1990 crash, growing into a relatively mature asset class that now is valued at nearly $1 trillion. Junk bonds also have spread to Europe, giving Continental investors and businesses more options in meeting their needs. Junk-bond returns combine features of the returns from stocks, especially smaller stocks, and from more highly rated corporate bonds, making them attractive to a variety of institutional investors, including mutual and pension funds, which together own about 60 percent of all high-yield bonds. And just as Milken's bonds financed dynamic young companies in industries such as broadcasting, cable television, and communications, today's high-yield market continues to make debt financing available to companies that otherwise might not be able to qualify. But even though six big investment banks now underwrite most new issues and provide research for investors interested in junk bonds, the market still is not immune from bouts of overheating—and never will be. In the technology frenzy of the late 1990s, for example, many junk bonds were issued by fledgling telecommunications companies, and this ready financing, combined with that provided by the ebullient stock market, helped fuel the glut of telecom equipment and fiber-optic capacity, the collapse of many of the companies, and the economic slowdown that inevitably followed. And later, "fallen angels" such as WorldCom and Qwest Communications contributed to the junk-bond market's swoon in the spring and summer of 2002.[30]

In addition to the maturation of the market for junk bonds, which reflects their usefulness to the economy, there is much evidence showing that the takeovers and buyouts of the 1980s were important in reducing waste and boosting efficiency. As discussed in the first part of this chapter, the decade's raids and buyouts helped in disassembling unsuccessful conglomerates and other inefficient companies, frequently selling off their assets and operating divisions to companies in the same lines of business that could use them more effectively. And although layoffs contributed to the productivity improvements in companies that were taken over, they were not a dominant factor and involved a high proportion of white-collar employees, who were better able to withstand the blows than blue-collar workers. However, raiders and buyout firms may have influenced the economy most profoundly by rattling the business establishment, serving notice to managers of companies that were not taken over that they risked a similar fate if they did not raise their firms' profitability. They also showed these executives that profitability could be improved by streamlining and focusing their operations, by outsourcing functions that could be performed more efficiently by specialized firms, and by making managers and employees more accountable for their performance, in part by linking more of their pay to their productivity or to their contributions to profitability.[31]

Despite their substantial net benefits, however, the takeovers and junk bonds of the 1980s had so many unfortunate aspects that it is difficult to accept assessments that lionize Milken and his exploits. The claims of Milken and some of his supporters that he was a naive genius, a "social scientist" who just couldn't say no to those who wanted to push leveraged deals beyond the bounds of reason, seem particularly hollow. In one interview Milken even maintained that he had come to oppose the expansion of junk-bond credit as it got too risky. "After 1986," he said, "I felt like a skilled surgeon who's been locked out of the operating room and watches through the glass in horror as some first-year medical students go to work on a patient." Yet he maintained a commanding share of an extremely profitable market for at least a decade, a position that had to be actively created and defended, and he showed no inclination to set stricter standards for the junk bonds he floated.[32]

Since his release from prison in 1993, Milken has been involved in a range of charitable endeavors, particularly programs he established to fund prostate-cancer research, provide college scholarships for needy students, and reward exceptional primary- and secondary-school teachers and administrators. However, in the late 1990s he was investigated by the Securities and Exchange Commission to determine whether he had violated his lifetime ban from the securities business by acting as an investment adviser or broker for former clients such as Ted Turner and Rupert Murdoch. Over a two-year period in the middle of the decade, Milken helped to arrange MCI's purchase of a $2 billion interest in Murdoch's News Corporation—Milken was an early backer of MCI, which was eventually acquired by the higher-flying WorldCom—and facilitated News Corporation's purchase of a 20 percent interest in New World, an entertainment company controlled by Ronald Perelman, yet another old client, and the sale of Turner Broadcasting to Time Warner. For his work, Milken received fees of $32 million from Murdoch, $50 million from Turner, and $10 million from New World. Although the investigation was dropped in 1999, both the SEC and the United States Attorney's Office in Manhattan sent strong letters to President Clinton, urging him not to pardon Milken as he was leaving office. These letters are thought to have dissuaded the president from doing so.[33]

Even if one were to concede all the allegations that have been made against Milken and add them to his admitted crimes and excesses, it is still very hard to take seriously the notion held by many people that Milken's junk-bond operations were a vast conspiracy, a giant Ponzi scheme designed to bilk the public. The changes that junk bonds made possible, both by financing young and innovative companies and by funding corporate raiders and buyout firms, were real and significant and would, as the maturation of the high-yield market and the vibrant new economy make clear, almost certainly have been financed by others, albeit at a different pace and perhaps with a different patina.[34]

Better Monetary Policy

For most of his fifteen-year tenure as chairman of the Board of Governors of the Federal Reserve System—the Fed—Alan Greenspan has been a highly visible and celebrated symbol of the economic boom and exuberant stock market, his reputation and mystique soaring with the fortunes of investors and, at least by implication, the strength of the new economy. His fame was particularly great at the end of 1998, when his monetary policies helped prevent a growing world financial crisis from crippling U.S. markets and derailing the expansion. The Fed cut interest rates three times between the end of September and mid-November and indicated that it was willing to do more if that was necessary to calm financial markets and maintain spending and economic growth. It also helped to organize an orderly liquidation by the private sector of a large, highly leveraged hedge fund, Long Term Capital Management, whose abrupt collapse would have further undermined the shaky markets. In fact, these actions may almost have been too successful, creating a false sense of security for investors—what economists call "moral hazard"—that contributed to the climactic run-up in technology stocks, an eighteen-month explosion that pushed the Nasdaq Composite Index above 5,000 by the time it peaked in March 2000. But this unfortunate consequence of the relief effort was not apparent immediately and, in any case, was probably unavoidable. By the end of 1998 the

Financial Times had christened Greenspan "guardian angel of the financial markets," and on its front cover for February 15, 1999, *Time* magazine announced that he was head of "the committee to save the world."[1]

By 2000 Greenspan was so highly revered that none of the presidential candidates could even contemplate another Federal Reserve chairman. During his campaign for the Republican nomination, for example, Senator John McCain not only pledged to reappoint him but also joked that if Greenspan were to die, "I would prop him up and put a pair of dark glasses on him." Bob Woodward's best-seller *Maestro: Greenspan's Fed and the American Boom*, which appeared that November, may have capped the era of runaway euphoria and Greenspan adulation. By the end of the year, the Nasdaq composite had fallen roughly 50 percent from its peak in March, economic growth had slowed, and Greenspan's critics had seemed to multiply and gather force. Some were former boosters who felt let down, disappointed that he had raised interest rates too much over the prior two years and kept them high too long, weakening both the expansion and stock prices. Others believed that he had been too accommodating, letting the stock market and economic boom get out of hand, thus setting the stage for a more severe collapse. Obviously, both these views could not be correct, suggesting, perhaps, that the Fed had done pretty well. Even if the central bank had erred, however, Greenspan's detractors, despite their contradictory conclusions, shared a faulty premise that also plagued many of his gushing admirers: they all seemed to assume that he was omniscient, that he always knew what had to be done to keep the economy humming and how best to do it. This posture not only trivializes the difficulties and uncertainties involved in making monetary policy but also undermines the credit that Greenspan and his predecessor, Paul Volcker, truly deserve.

Although it did not create the new economy, the bull market in shares, or the long expansion that ran for most of the 1980s and 1990s, unusually good monetary policy played an important supporting role, enabling the record-setting boom to develop and grow. The measures taken by the Volcker- and Greenspan-led Feds stand in sharp contrast to the dreadful policies enacted during the 1970s, which exacerbated the economy's problems, helping to produce stagflation, the unusual mixture of high inflation and high unemployment for which the decade is best known. Volcker, who served as chairman of the Federal Reserve Board from August 6, 1979, to August 11, 1987, inherited an economy in which prices were rising faster than 12 percent a year yet roughly 6 percent of the labor force was unemployed, a combination from which there was no easy way out. Facing up to the problem required that he raise interest rates dramatically, and endure one of the most severe recessions since the Great Depression, in order to root out the self-perpetuating inflationary cycle and establish a sound basis for the subsequent recovery. The Greenspan Fed then could focus on keeping the expansion going, both by limiting the impact of crises that might have impeded its development, including the October 1987 stock market crash and the 1998 financial panic, and, most impressive, by not restraining growth unnecessarily, thus giving the economy room to breathe and grow.

The length and strength of the long boom are ample testimony to the success of the Volcker and Greenspan regimes in establishing an environment in which innovation and investment could flourish and businesses could grow more rapidly and become more productive. Like everybody else, the Fed and other economic policy makers benefited from trends long under way, particularly continuing growth in international competition, in technological and organizational sophistication, and in the depth and vigor of capital markets, as well as the erosion of union power, all of which made the economy more competitive and productive and less susceptible to inflationary pressures. But this favorable backdrop hardly makes the Fed's accomplishments less substantial. The workings of a modern economy are so complex and difficult to decipher and interpret, and its short-term movements so hard to predict, particularly when conditions are changing markedly, that even knowing when *not* to act, when "less is more," is far from simple or straightforward.[2]*

THE FEDERAL RESERVE SYSTEM

The Federal Reserve System is the central bank of the United States, essentially a bank both for other banks and for the federal government, with responsibilities to maintain the smooth functioning of the financial system and, through its monetary policies, to promote price stability and economic growth. The financial panic of 1907, in which J. P. Morgan performed many of these functions, made clear the need for such an institution.[3] The Fed was established in 1913, nine months after his death, and has hardly changed in ninety years. The system consists of the Board of Governors in Washington, D.C., twelve regional Federal Reserve Banks located in major cities around the country, and just over three thousand commercial banks that are members of the Federal Reserve System. (These member banks constitute just under 40 percent of all commercial banks in the United States but tend to be the larger, more important ones.)† The seven governors are chosen by the president, and must be confirmed by the Senate, to serve staggered fourteen-year terms, with only one governor appointed from any of the twelve Federal Reserve districts. The chairman and vice chairman of the board are designated by the presi-

---

*The term "long boom" comes from John Taylor, a Stanford economist and undersecretary of the Treasury for International Affairs, who in April 1998, two years before it started to give out, defined it as the preceding "15-year period of unprecedented stability and virtually uninterrupted growth."

†By law, all federally chartered banks are members of the Federal Reserve System, while state-chartered banks can become members if they meet the system's standards. At the end of 2000, approximately thirty-one hundred of the country's eighty-two hundred banks (38 percent of the total) were members of the Federal Reserve System, twenty-one hundred national banks and almost one thousand state banks. Federally chartered banks are supervised by the Comptroller of the Currency, while state-chartered banks that aren't members of the Federal Reserve System are overseen by the Federal Deposit Insurance Corporation (FDIC), and the Fed looks after state-chartered member banks.

dent from among the governors, and confirmed by the Senate, for terms of four years. Of all these, only the chairman has become a nationally known figure.[4]

The system resembles a corporation in which the regional Reserve Banks are the operating subsidiaries and the Fed chairman, like the chairman of a company's board of directors, is the leader of the Board of Governors, which sets broad policy objectives and oversees the operations of the entire system. The regional banks carry out the system's day-to-day activities, such as clearing checks and wiring funds among commercial banks and other depository institutions; supervising bank holding companies, foreign banks operating in the United States, and state-chartered banks that are members of the Federal Reserve System; and acting as banker for the federal government. When the government wants to raise money to finance its spending, the Reserve Banks hold auctions of Treasury bonds and other government securities and credit the Treasury's account with the money taken in. Almost all of our currency consists of Federal Reserve notes—see the caption above the picture on any bill—which are issued by the Reserve Banks but must be backed by Treasury and other federal government securities. The Fed earns more than $20 billion a year from the interest it receives on its portfolio of government securities and the fees it charges for its services, and after covering its expenses, it remits the surplus to the Treasury.

In addition to performing these routine tasks, the Federal Reserve is responsible for conducting monetary policy, that is, for adjusting the supply of money and credit in order to keep the economy growing rapidly but without inflation. The goals of monetary policy, "maximum employment" and "stable prices," were enumerated most specifically in the Federal Reserve Act of 1977 but remain sufficiently vague that the Fed has considerable leeway in interpreting them. And because governors are appointed for very long terms—fourteen years—and the Fed finances itself and does not depend on congressional appropriations, it is one of the few relatively independent government institutions, free to operate without much interference from elected officials and politicians. Nevertheless, the Fed's independence is far from absolute: there is a need, for example, to coordinate its monetary policies with fiscal policies, taxing and spending measures set by Congress and the president. Moreover, the Fed's chairman and vice chairman are appointed for only four years, and even though their terms do not coincide with the president's, they can be influenced by political considerations and by their desire to be reappointed. Some chairmen, such as Richard Nixon's appointee Arthur Burns, clearly seemed motivated in these ways.[5]*

The central problem in setting monetary policy is determining how to balance the competing goals of price stability and high employment, how, in other words, to prevent inflation from getting out of hand without unduly restraining employment and economic growth. The dilemma arises because acting to lower inflation generally increases unemployment, at least in the short term, and because the maximum attainable rates of noninflationary growth and employment change over time, typically in ways that are not well understood until much later. Sensing changes that are under way before they show up in economic data can be critical to policy makers, since stimulating the economy by lowering interest rates, or not restraining it when growth accelerates, tends to raise inflation unless the economy is operating below its capacity to produce. At the same time, the need to anticipate what is happening before it becomes fully clear makes setting monetary policy an art as well as a science, virtually guaranteeing a plethora of broadly differing opinions about how it should be—or should have been—done.

Populist critics of the Fed such as William Greider, or new-era naïfs who think that we no longer have to worry about rising prices, limits to economic growth, or the business cycle, would have the Fed

---

*Alan Blinder, a Princeton economist and former vice chairman of the Fed, points out that the rationale for Federal Reserve independence—the fact that making monetary policy requires specific skills and experience and that the costs of fighting inflation are felt before the benefits, and thus would be unpalatable to most politicians—applies as well to other government functions such as setting tax policy.

concentrate on reducing unemployment and stimulating growth and pay very little attention to inflation. Most economists, on the other hand, accept the fact that there is a near-term trade-off between inflation and unemployment, and appreciate the damaging consequences of rapidly accelerating inflation, but they are far less united on where to draw the line against a buildup of inflation, mainly because one can never know whether it will grow into a dangerous spiral. (The issue is complicated further by problems in measuring inflation accurately, particularly since the degree of mismeasurement may vary over time.) Many, including the 2001 Nobel laureate George Akerlof and the former Treasury secretary Lawrence Summers, also believe that low or moderate inflation—price increases of 2–3 percent a year or even higher—is better than no inflation because it may make labor markets work better. (Since it is very difficult for businesses to cut actual wages, even in a recession, companies can lower real wages, and thus limit layoffs, only if they contain wage increases and prices rise more rapidly than wages.) Others, particularly Paul Krugman, a Princeton professor and *New York Times* columnist, stress the usefulness of moderate inflation in giving central banks leeway to stimulate a depressed or crisis-threatened economy. The stagnation of the Japanese economy over most of the 1990s highlighted this problem, showing that even interest rates that have been pushed near zero may be ineffective in stimulating a recovery when prices are falling, thus raising the inflation-adjusted cost of borrowing. In other words, when there is deflation, real interest rates tend to be higher than nominal rates and may limit borrowing and spending even though nominal rates are low or falling. Such a possibility became a concern to some in the United States in the spring and summer of 2002, when the economic recovery appeared to be sputtering even though the Fed had kept short-term interest rates below 2 percent.[6]

Even within this widely accepted conceptual framework, which recognizes that growth cannot run wild without jeopardizing price stability and accepts the usefulness of moderate inflation, many difficult questions remain, including, most prominently, how the Fed should decide when to act to restrain inflation and how forcefully to do so. There are basically two ways to set monetary policy, either through preestablished "rules" or by relying on the judgments and "discretion" of the decision makers. With the exception of a system proposed by the Nobel laureate Milton Friedman more than forty years ago, which would have the Fed increase the money supply at a constant rate, most so-called rules are guidelines or objectives that make a central bank's goals explicit and indicate how it should react in different economic environments. If, for example, there were relatively fixed and well-established limits to how low unemployment could fall, or how fast the economy could grow, without triggering accelerating inflation, then the Fed could gear its policies to preset targets: rates of inflation, unemployment, or economic growth that would oblige it to start raising interest rates to cool the economy.

A more specific procedure, proposed by John Taylor long before he was appointed undersecretary of the Treasury for International Affairs in 2001, suggests that the Fed would do well to raise interest rates in proportion to the gap between actual inflation and the target rate, and to lower them in proportion to the degree of slack in the economy, which can be approximated by the unemployment rate or by the shortfall between actual GDP and estimates of its potential. Depending on its assessment of the reliability of its guidelines and the dangers of violating them, the Fed might use its targets to act preemptively, raising interest rates in anticipation of a future pickup in inflation in the hope that by moving early it can cool the economy less wrenchingly, engineering what is known as a "soft landing." Some economists, such as Laurence Meyer, a former Fed governor appointed by President Clinton, favor setting strict inflation targets because it would discipline the central bank, make its actions more transparent, and increase the bankers' accountability. Others in this camp believe that inflation targeting would also enhance the central bank's inflation-fighting credibility, thus lowering people's expectations of future inflation and making the bank's job easier, but there is little evidence that this is true.[7]

The case for discretion and nuanced judgment, on the other hand, for evaluating each new situation afresh using the best information available at the time, has been argued most forcefully by Robert Solow, another Nobel laureate. Solow believes that although there are limits to how fast the economy can grow before setting off worrisome inflation, the danger points change too much, and rarely are known with enough precision, to justify using them as rigid guides to monetary policy. Moreover, because failing to act against inflation as it starts to pick up appears not to be an irreversible error, or one with lasting consequences, and because the harm to the economy caused by restricting growth prematurely is much greater than the damage resulting from a short-term rise in inflation, which may never accelerate significantly, Solow thinks the Fed should not act to restrain inflation until it becomes a visible problem. Fortunately, both Greenspan and Volcker largely followed a flexible and pragmatic course much like the one he recommends.[8]

Despite their many differences, Greenspan and Volcker, unlike many academic economists, seem to share a deep practical sense of how the economy functions and of how economic policy should be made. Both eschew strict inflation targets. Volcker, for example, has written that the Fed should aim for "reasonable price stability," which he defines as "a situation in which ordinary people do not feel they have to take expectations of price increases into account in making their investment plans or running their lives." Similarly, Greenspan acknowledges that the Fed can be "quite explicit" about seeking "price stability and the maximum sustainable growth in output that is fostered when prices are stable," but he also maintains that "price stability is best thought of as *an environment in which inflation is so low and stable* over time that it does not materially enter in the decisions of households and firms." This is especially true in today's economy, in which measuring inflation is so difficult. Even "the simple notion of price," he emphasized in another speech, "has turned decidedly complex." For both reasons, "a specific numerical inflation target would represent an *unhelpful and false precision*" in making monetary policy.[9]

No matter how the Fed sets its objectives, or determines its strategy, it almost always conducts monetary policy through "open market operations," that is, by buying or selling U.S. government securities such as short-term Treasury bills, intermediate-term notes, or long-term bonds in the open market. When it sells these securities, as it did between June 1999 and May 2000, money flows out of circulation and into the Fed's coffers, and interest rates rise. Over this period, the Fed raised the "federal funds" rate, the interest rate on overnight loans between banks, from 4.75 percent to 6.5 percent because it feared the economy was overheating. As it always does, it acted by issuing orders to its trading desk at the Federal Reserve Bank of New York to sell just enough government securities to nudge the funds rate up to the interim targets established by the Federal Open Market Committee (FOMC), the Fed's main body for making monetary policy, which consists of the seven governors, the president of the Federal Reserve Bank of New York, and the presidents of four other Reserve Banks, who serve for one year on a rotating basis.*

When the Fed buys government securities in the open market, as it did in the fall of 1998 and has been doing since early 2001, when it began cutting interest rates to stimulate the economy, money flows into the banking system and interest rates fall. Between January 3, 2001, and December 11, 2001, the Fed cut the federal-funds rate from 6.5 percent to 1.75 percent in eleven steps, most of which pushed it down by fifty "basis points," or half a percentage point. (A basis point is 0.01 percentage point.) The federal-funds rate is the shortest-term interest rate and the only one the Fed can control directly. But while changes in the funds rate generally affect other in-

---

*In addition to open-market operations, the Fed has two other tools of monetary policy, but they are far less important. It rarely changes "reserve requirements," the fraction of their deposits that banks, savings and loans, and credit unions must hold in reserve against potential withdrawals, because it is such a blunt instrument. On the other hand, changes in the "discount rate," the interest rate that banks pay when they borrow reserves from a regional Reserve Bank, do not have much impact and are used only to complement open-market operations. The discount rate is largely symbolic, because most banks borrow reserves from other banks in the federal funds market.

terest rates, such as those for mortgages and consumer or business loans, which influence spending, the links between short- and longer-term interest rates are neither as clear nor as predictable as the Fed would wish. In the 2001 cycle of rate cuts, long- and intermediate-term interest rates did not fall much in the first half of the year, perhaps because they had fallen significantly before the Fed began to ease; but they all fell considerably in the second half of the year, including mortgage rates, which are geared to intermediate-term interest rates, thus helping to keep home values up, counteracting some of the effects of the stock market collapse and keeping the recession from becoming more severe.

Further complicating the Fed's job is that nobody really knows how much a given fall in interest rates will affect spending, or how long it may take to do so, or how strongly inflation and unemployment are likely to change when spending changes. Moreover, since monetary policy affects the economy over long periods of time, it is possible that before the policy begins to work, conditions may change in a way that makes the policy obsolete or counterproductive. In fact, since he thought the judgments required were so difficult (largely because the "lags" involved are both long and "rather variable," and liable to be influenced by political pressure), Friedman, whose work was so influential in establishing a greater appreciation of monetary policy over the last forty years, concluded that discretionary policy was more likely to be harmful than helpful. He thus suggested that in practice we would be better off if monetary policy was set instead by a rule mandating that the money supply grow each year at a modest and stable rate, perhaps the average rate of economic growth. And in light of the Fed's generally mixed record, even an opponent of rule-based policy making such as Alan Blinder concedes, "There is at least an outside chance that Friedman could be right."[10]*

---

*Friedman proposed that the money supply should increase each year at a rate that on average would produce price stability, a rate that he put at 3–5 percent a year, roughly 3 percent to accommodate economic growth and about 1 percent to offset the decline in the velocity at which money circulates.

THE VOLCKER YEARS

The Fed is highly respected now because the economy has done so well for almost two decades, particularly when compared with the 1970s, and because monetary policy was instrumental in getting it back on track. As shown in Figure 6, particularly difficult problems with inflation began to develop in the mid-1960s, when spending for the Vietnam War increased markedly but few measures were taken to slow down the rest of the economy. Fearful of the political repercussions of higher interest rates or tax increases, Lyndon Johnson stubbornly maintained that we could have more military spending without sacrificing civilian production, that the economy could produce more "guns" and "butter" without a pickup in inflation, while the Federal Reserve under William McChesney Martin did not do

FIGURE 6. *Unemployment and Inflation,*
January 1948 Through November 2002

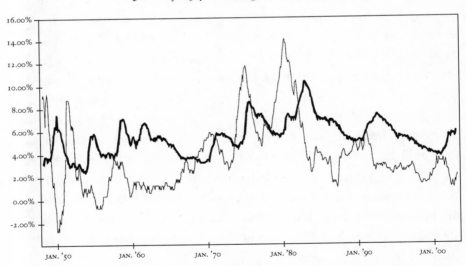

This figure shows monthly unemployment rates and monthly rates of inflation over the preceding 12 months. The unemployment rate, shown by the dark line, is for the civilian labor force 16 years and older, while the rate of inflation, shown by the lighter line, is the rate of change in the consumer price index for all urban consumers. Data are available at www.bls.gov.

enough to curb rising prices. Martin is best known for quipping that the Fed's job is to "take away the punch bowl just as the party is getting going," but he may not have recognized how raucous it was about to become. From less than 2 percent a year in 1965, the rate of inflation rose to about 6 percent by 1970, and then more than doubled to more than 12 percent in 1980, led in part by sharply higher oil prices, which spiked upward as a result of the Arab-Israeli War in 1973, the Iranian revolution in late 1978 and early 1979, and the associated restrictions imposed on oil production by OPEC. The unemployment rate also doubled during the 1970s, reaching 8 percent by the middle of the decade. This was contrary to our experience in the 1950s and 1960s, when inflation rose as unemployment fell, largely because increased spending strained the economy's capacity to produce, pushing up both wages and prices.

Unemployment peaked at more than 10 percent in late 1982, at the end of one of the most severe recessions since the depression of the 1930s. In fact, the setback to the economy was even worse than implied by this episode alone. The sixteen-month recession that lasted from July 1981 to November 1982, when the economy contracted by 2.8 percent, came just a year after a short but sharp recession in the first six months of 1980, when GDP fell by 2.2 percent. As a result, the economy did not regain the heights attained in 1979 until 1983, more than three years later. By then inflation had receded below 4 percent, where it stayed for most of the rest of the decade, even as the unemployment rate dropped below 6 percent. Following its rise in 1989–1990, and the relatively mild recession of 1990–1991, inflation averaged less than 3 percent over the next four years, and fell to slightly over 2 percent in the last four years of the decade, even though growth accelerated sharply and unemployment declined to just over 4 percent.

Paul Volcker became chairman of the Federal Reserve Board in August 1979 and was largely responsible for the turnaround in the economy and, as a consequence, for the Fed's vastly improved reputation. Volcker was an experienced and highly respected economic policy maker, having served as undersecretary for monetary affairs in the Nixon Treasury Department and in lesser Treasury posts in the Kennedy and Johnson administrations. He was president of the Federal Reserve Bank of New York when Jimmy Carter named him to lead the Board of Governors. The two preceding chairmen, G. William Miller and, before him, Arthur Burns, had done little to contain the buildup of inflation during the 1970s. Miller was appointed by Carter in early 1978 and served only eighteen months before Volcker replaced him. Miller had little experience in making economic policy and was burdened by the problems he had inherited from Burns. Before Nixon tapped him for the Fed chairmanship in 1970, Burns had been a professor of economics (and mentor to Alan Greenspan in the 1950s) at Columbia University, president of the National Bureau of Economic Research, and a highly regarded student of the business cycle. He had also served as an economic adviser to President Dwight D. Eisenhower.

According to observers as diverse as William Greider and Milton Friedman, Burns did not try hard enough to reduce inflation because he was playing politics. First, according to Greider, he collaborated with "the economic pump priming that helped Richard Nixon win a landslide victory in 1972," and then he tried to ingratiate himself with Carter, initiating a policy of "easy money" in late 1976, just after the election, and continuing it in 1977 in the hope that he would be reappointed the following year. Friedman, who had been a student of Burns's as an undergraduate at Rutgers, also thinks he deserves much of the blame for the "great inflation" of the 1970s, particularly since "he knew better." As Friedman put it in a recent interview:

> From the moment Burns got into the Fed, I think politics played a great role in what happened. So far as Nixon was concerned, there is no doubt, as I know from personal experience. I had a session with Nixon sometime in 1970 . . . might have been 1971, in which he wanted me to urge Arthur to increase the money supply rapidly and I said to the president, "Do you really want to

do that? The only effect will be to leave you with a larger infla- tion if you get reelected." And he said, "Well, we'll worry about that after we get reelected." Typical.[11]

The Fed began to raise interest rates in October 1979, just two months after Volcker was appointed, but it eased prematurely the fol- lowing spring, when the economy fell sharply under the pressures of higher rates and controls on consumer lending that President Carter authorized the Fed to impose in March 1980. Once the restraints were removed, however, the economy recovered briskly and inflation picked up again, averaging 12.5 percent for the entire year. The Fed responded vigorously in early November, just after Ronald Reagan's election, raising rates aggressively and keeping them very high for al- most two years before relaxing in August 1982. The federal-funds rate had risen six percentage points by the end of 1980 and remained above 15 percent for almost a year, much of the time near 20 percent. High interest rates stifled spending and pushed the economy into a severe recession, which choked off inflation. (OPEC also eased its production restrictions, because sales had fallen as oil prices ex- ploded.) The recession was so severe because inflation had become deeply embedded in the economy and was hard to dislodge. When negotiating wages, for example, workers insisted on a large "inflation premium" to protect themselves against expected price increases. So did the lenders who made mortgage loans. For the rate of inflation to fall, it was necessary to break the inflationary cycle in which a pro- longed period of accelerating inflation led people to expect even larger price increases in the future, which then became incorporated in wage bargains and other contracts, reinforcing inflationary expec- tations.[12]*

---

*With regard to the controls on consumer credit that were imposed in March 1980, Volcker points out that existing legislation allowed the president to authorize the Fed to impose controls, that he tried to dissuade Carter from doing so, but that once the pres- ident decided to proceed with the authorization, it would have been "awkward, to say the least," to refuse.

The recessions of the early 1980s broke the cycle of inflation but caused much hardship, reducing jobs and spending as well as prices; critically, the severe decline in economic activity convinced businesses and consumers that in the future, prices would no longer rise as rapidly as before. The 1981–1982 downturn lasted sixteen months, five months longer than the average postwar recession, and the economy not only fell by nearly 3 percent but, according to some estimates, produced about 10 percent less than it would have if it had grown at its long-term pace. Many workers and businesses never fully recovered what they lost. Industries with fundamental problems, such as the steel and automobile industries of the Rust Belt, were particularly hard hit. Nevertheless, even liberal economists such as James Tobin, another Nobel laureate who has been critical of the Fed's emphasis on controlling inflation at the expense of economic growth, think that Volcker did well under the circumstances. "I hope that history will give Paul and his colleagues the praise that they deserve," he wrote in 1994, "not only for fighting the war against inflation but also for knowing when to stop, when to declare victory. They reversed course in the summer of 1982, probably averting an accelerating contraction of economic activity in the United States and financial disasters worldwide."[13]

In *Changing Fortunes*, a book about economic policy in the 1980s that he coauthored, Volcker recalls sensing "substantial support in the country for a tough stand against inflation, for all the pain and personal dislocation that seemed to imply." "In the end," he concludes, "there is only one excuse for pursuing such strongly restrictive monetary policies. That is the simple conviction that over time the economy will work better, more efficiently, and more fairly, with better prospects and more saving, in an environment of reasonable price stability." Greider and other critics think that Volcker's policies were unnecessarily harsh, that he was too slow to ease in 1982, and that the Fed would have sought a better balance between inflation and unemployment had it been more "democratic," more directly accountable to elected government officials. Such an argument is hard to reject outright: we don't know what would have happened if Volcker had not raised interest rates, and we can't conduct a controlled experiment to find out. Even so, Greider's case is inconsistent and weak; he also argues, for example, that inflation in the 1970s was not contained largely because Arthur Burns was guilty of the most crass "political collusion in the Federal Reserve's history." Moreover, even if the Fed waited too long to relax its tight monetary policy in 1982, that delay accounted, as one analyst put it, for only a "modest fraction" of the cost of the recession, and the risks of relaxing too soon were high. "Perhaps that is true," Volcker writes about Greider's charge, "but those arguments do not impress me very much. It's not that our policies were perfection but that the far greater error at that point would have been to fail to follow through long enough to affect fundamental attitudes and really put inflationary expectations to rest."[14]

THE GREENSPAN ERA

As the economy improved during the 1980s and 1990s, making and evaluating monetary policy became, ironically, more difficult. When Volcker took over the Fed, the economy had what seemed to be the worst possible combination—high unemployment and high inflation—and there were no clear alternatives to the deeply restrictive policies he instituted. In the prosperous environment that Greenspan inherited, and has fostered, the main question was subtler: Could the economy have grown more rapidly without a lot more inflation? Because nobody knows the answer, and probably never will, Solow argues, the Fed should operate by trying to find out, pushing the economy as far toward full employment as it can go without setting off higher and higher inflation. "Monetary policy," he writes, "could afford to go in for a trial-and-error approach to finding a fair balance between the dangers of inflation and the benefits of high output and employment," a policy-making style consistent with the one Greenspan has followed, particularly since 1994.

In a broad sense, Greenspan's record at the Fed, like Volcker's before him, has been successful because of his pragmatism, flexibility, and shrewd judgments rather than because he was committed to particular rules or theories. "Policy rules anticipate that key causal connections observed in the past will remain fixed over time, or evolve only very slowly," he told a 1997 conference at Stanford University in a speech that outlined his more adaptable approach, showed how it could effectively confront contingencies that arose, and explained why he had come to believe that it was better able to accommodate changes in the economy. Although the Fed has tried to "exploit past patterns and regularities to operate in a systematic way," he explained, "we have found that very often [these] historical regularities have been disrupted by unanticipated change, especially in technologies." As a consequence, he continued, "in an ever changing world, some element of discretion appears to be an unavoidable aspect of policymaking."[15]

Perhaps Greenspan's emphasis on intuition and improvisation in making monetary policy, on a more subtle approach than strict rules permit, reflects his brief early career as a musician (in the Harry Jerome swing band that also included Leonard Garment, later a law partner and political aide to Nixon) or his longer one as head of his own economic consulting firm. According to Woodward, even in his much-cited 1950s relationship with the libertarian novelist and cult figure Ayn Rand, Greenspan was "never a complete Rand acolyte. He had a separate career and identity, which caused some to distrust him. He was a dedicated networker."[16] In making decisions, he appears to rely more on insights gleaned from studying detailed economic data, such as the volume of freight shipments or help-wanted advertising, than on those derived from abstract economic models. He also is willing to change his policies when they are not working. In 1987, for example, the Fed contributed to the October stock market crash by raising interest rates over the preceding six months in an attempt to trim inflation, which had doubled to just under 4 percent in the first six months of the year. Yet it was able to limit the effects of the crash by immediately providing funds to the strained financial markets and pledging that the Federal Reserve remained ready "to serve as a source of liquidity to support the economic and financial system." When it became clear in early 1988 that the danger had passed, the Fed quickly began withdrawing the "excess liquidity" it had provided.[17]*

Despite the acclaim he received, Greenspan considers the Fed's response to the crash one of its "easier decisions," there being "little question that the appropriate central bank action was to ease policy significantly," even though "we knew we would soon have to sop up the excess liquidity that we added to the system."[18]† The Fed was less successful in deciding how aggressively to cut interest rates in order to induce a strong recovery from the 1990–1991 recession. Although it may have contributed to the contraction by raising interest rates in 1989 in an attempt to lower inflation, which had risen to more than 5 percent by June, it could not have anticipated the Iraqi invasion of Kuwait in August 1990, which raised oil prices and helped to bring on the slump. July 1990 was later judged to be the start of the recession, but by the time this verdict was rendered in April 1991, the recovery had already started. The war was short and the recession relatively mild, but the Fed has been criticized for not cutting rates sooner and more aggressively, thus hindering a more vigorous recovery and possibly costing George Bush the 1992 presidential election.

From July 1990 through December 1991 the Federal Reserve cut

---

*In a review of monetary policy in the 1980s, Michael Mussa points out that in addition to restraining inflation, the Fed's tightening from April through early October 1987 was designed to limit further depreciation of the dollar, which the United States had agreed to do in the Louvre Accord signed that February. He also notes that the FOMC seemed to deny responsibility for the interest-rate increases in early October, claiming, as recorded in the minutes of the November 3, 1987, meeting, that rates rose because "market participants appeared to anticipate monetary tightening." But at the very least, he writes, the Fed "allowed market participants" to have such expectations, and the rise in rates in early October, which the Fed chose *not* to neutralize, surely was one of the factors that "contributed" to the market crash.

†The crash's end, however, remains puzzling. On Wednesday, October 21, 1987, there was a mysterious midday rally in the market for futures contracts geared to the Major Market stock market index, which appears to have stopped the stock market's hemorrhaging, but nobody Woodward interviewed would admit to knowing whether the trades resulted from "skillful calculation or serendipity," or perhaps were engineered.

the funds rate fifteen times, lowering it from 8.25 percent to 4 percent, mostly in increments of twenty-five basis points, but the economy did not respond very forcefully for two related reasons. First, since inflation was receding along with interest rates, the real federal-funds rate actually rose for part of the period and remained too high until early 1992. Second, the rate cuts occurred in the midst of a "credit crunch," a situation in which borrowing at prevailing interest rates was unusually difficult. The collapse of the commercial real-estate market from 1990 to 1992 had seriously impaired the capital of many banks and savings and loan institutions, making them less willing to extend new loans to corporations and consumers who were highly leveraged. And their reluctance to lend seems to have been encouraged by bank examiners who were very aggressive in questioning new lending, perhaps in an attempt to atone for their laxity in missing the buildup of questionable loans in the late 1980s. As these problems gradually became clearer, the Fed eased further, pushing the real federal-funds rate near zero by July 1992 and keeping it there until October 1993, well into the early phase of the record expansion. At the FOMC meeting that September, Greenspan exhaled, telling the committee, "We *finally* got it right and decided to sit with it."[19]

Unfortunately, the Fed abandoned its lenient stance too soon, or at least too forcefully, probably because it still had too much faith in outdated relationships and stale "regularities," particularly the idea then prevalent among economists that the unemployment rate could not fall below 6 percent without triggering an inflationary spiral. Thus, in February 1994, with the unemployment rate down to about 6.5 percent and no signs of a pickup in inflation—"it was difficult," Greenspan admits, "to discern any overt inflationary signals"—the Fed began raising interest rates in a "preemptive strike" against a feared rise in inflation. Over the next year the federal-funds rate doubled, rising from 3 to 6 percent in seven steps, cooling the economy and keeping it below its potential, even if only temporarily. This was probably the Greenspan Fed's greatest failure, and it seems attributable to the undue influence of the theory of the "nairu"—the nonaccelerating inflation rate of unemployment. The nairu, if such a rate exists, is the lowest unemployment rate the country can have without inflation continuously increasing. It is also called the "natural" rate of unemployment, an unfortunate label, which, Solow believes, "intends deliberately to claim more for that state of the economy than anyone has ever seriously argued it deserves."[20]

Economists used to think that as the economy approached its capacity to produce, inflation would rise gradually as goods and services became scarcer and unemployment fell. This tendency of inflation to rise as unemployment falls is known as the Phillips curve after the Australian economist A. W. H. Phillips, who first pictured it in a graph. Essentially, the nairu is a scary version of the Phillips curve; supposedly, if unemployment falls below this rate, then the rate of inflation will not simply rise but accelerate continuously. The theory was developed independently in the late 1960s by Friedman and Edmund S. Phelps, then a professor at the University of Pennsylvania, and it caught hold during the ensuing decade, in part because of the severe inflation and inept monetary policy of the 1970s. If it were true, limiting employment temporarily would be a small price to pay for not risking ever-accelerating inflation. But, Solow argues, the doctrine is "theoretically and empirically as soft as a grape." Not only does the nairu change too much, and in ways that are not well understood, to make it very useful as a guide to monetary policy; there also is little evidence that inflation accelerates continuously when the unemployment rate falls below the estimated natural rate. "The large body of work on these issues," Solow writes, "does not support the various popular metaphors of sudden catastrophe and subsequent irreversibility: the slippery slope, the yawning cliff, the genie that has escaped from the bottle."[21]*

---

*If the natural-rate doctrine were true, then monetary policy could not push unemployment below this rate, and attempts to do so would result only in accelerating inflation. Most economists who believe the theory, however, think that it holds only in the long run. They accept the principle that monetary policy can influence both unemployment and inflation in the short run but are reluctant in practice to risk pushing unemployment below what they think the natural rate is.

Although it is impossible to know what would have happened had the Fed eschewed preemption in favor of a wait-and-see approach, it seems quite evident that its fears were unwarranted. The unemployment rate continued to fall throughout the decade, reaching about 4 percent by its end, while the rate of inflation fell as well, to roughly 2 percent. Moreover, it later became clear that this extraordinary performance occurred in part because productivity growth was accelerating. To its credit, the Fed recognized its error and reversed course beginning in early 1995, when it started taking back some of the rate increases. (Economists were slower to admit that they had overestimated the inflationary effects of low unemployment, but by 1997 some had adjusted their estimates of the nairu downward by about one percentage point, although it still was probably too high.)* Even so, the Fed's overly cautious policies in the first half of the 1990s expansion help to explain why the early part of the boom was so much weaker than the recoveries from the 1960–1961 and 1981–1982 recessions.[22]

After 1994 the Fed was far more accommodating toward the expansion, doing very little to restrain it despite the marked acceleration in economic growth and significant decline in unemployment. Of course, inflation also was falling, and permissive policies were needed to defuse the financial crisis of 1998 and to ensure that the country's banking and financial system would not be disabled by technical problems resulting from the "Y2K" conversion at the end of the millennium. Nevertheless, the Fed's forbearance in the last half of the 1990s should be considered among its most successful actions, particularly since it went against conventional wisdom—and was right. To an extent, its new posture was owing to the lessons learned from its

---

*Robert Gordon has found that the nairu varied considerably over time, rising steeply in the 1960s, remaining high from about 1970 to 1990, and then falling sharply. He also argues that the apparent failure of Phillips curve and natural-rate models in the 1970s was due to their not accounting for other factors that affect inflation: if you don't allow for the oil price shocks of the 1970s, for example, the basic Phillips curve relationship appears to show that inflation and unemployment increase at the same time, and the nairu appears lower than it actually is, a result that may have fooled policy makers.

questionable preemptive move against inflation and the need to reverse some of those rate increases. The U.S. economy also benefited from outside factors, including declines in the prices of raw materials and other imported goods, which were caused in part by economic problems in Asia and Russia. But the Fed's attitude stems even more from Greenspan's sense, developed before it was evident in the data and far ahead of most economists, that something dramatically new was happening in the economy, that "what the American economy was experiencing," he later told the Economic Club of New York, might well be "a once-in-a-century acceleration of innovation, which propelled forward productivity, output, corporate profits, and stock prices at a pace not seen in generations, if ever."[23]

Greenspan's prescient view of the maturing new economy emerged gradually, beginning with the idea, as he expressed it in his semiannual monetary policy report to Congress in July 1996, that "new technologies" and "improvements of production techniques" were helping to keep inflation in check because the "fast and changeable currents" made workers "more worried about their own job security," thus willing to accept "smaller increases in their compensation." In fact, he had already made a much broader argument to the FOMC, suggesting at its December 1995 meeting that productivity growth might be increasing but that the acceleration was not yet evident because "the data are lousy" and because "we may be looking at the lag that Professor Paul David of Stanford has been talking about," the likelihood that "the global infrastructure has not yet adjusted" to computers and information technologies. In his speech at Stanford a year and a half later, Greenspan made essentially the same point, suggesting that "the persistence of *rising* profit margins in the face of stable or falling inflation" made it "difficult to avoid the conclusion that output per hour has to be rising at a pace significantly in excess of the officially published annual growth rate of nonfarm productivity."

Before accumulating evidence began to confirm these suspicions, however, Greenspan not only had to satisfy himself that his instincts were correct; he also had to convince more skeptical colleagues, including fellow governors and the Fed's research staff, that it was worth taking a chance that he might be right. At the 1995 FOMC meeting, for example, Alan Blinder, the board's vice chairman, agreed to cut the funds rate by twenty-five basis points but emphasized that he was doing so "without signing onto your brave new world scenario, which I am not quite ready to do." Like Blinder and most other economists, the Fed's staff put the economy's noninflationary "speed limit" near 2.5 percent for much of the decade even as growth accelerated to more than 4 percent. Despite the skepticism and opposing views of the other committee members, Greenspan was able to persuade them, Governor Edward Kelley recalled in an interview several years later, that they should "take a bit of a risk," let the economy "run and see if this thing is going to be real and have some legs and keep allowing us, for a while at least, to have a very strong [growth rate] and a declining inflation rate."[24]

In addition to following the chairman's sense that productivity growth was accelerating, the Fed after 1994 excluded as too risky measures such as raising interest rates or margin requirements in order to cool the stock market. Even when Greenspan cautioned investors in December 1996, asking whether "irrational exuberance" had raised share prices excessively, making them vulnerable to "prolonged contractions," he did not act to depress the stock market, though he appears to have thought it was seriously overvalued. Lawrence Lindsey, a Fed governor from November 1991 through January 1997 and one of President George W. Bush's principal economic advisers until he resigned in late 2002, was more concerned about a stock market bubble and more willing to risk the inevitable damaging consequences of deflating it, urging the FOMC in September 1996 to act while it "still resembles surface froth and before the bubble carries the economy to stratospheric heights." Greenspan agreed that "there is a stock-market bubble problem . . . that we should keep our eye on." But in raising the issue publicly two months later, he was much more circumspect, pointing out in response to his own question that even if stock prices were too high, "we as central bankers need not be concerned if a collapsing financial asset bubble does not threaten to impair the real economy, its production, jobs, and price stability."[25]

As the decade wore on, Greenspan softened his comments about stock prices, emphasizing how hard it is to know when shares are fairly valued and that the Fed's proper concern should be how the stock market affects the economy, not the market itself. As he told the Joint Economic Committee of Congress in June 1999, "bubbles generally are perceptible only after the fact," and if they burst, "the consequences need not be catastrophic for the economy" if monetary policy responds appropriately, as it did when the stock market crashed in 1987 but failed to do in Japan a few years later or in the United States following the great crash of 1929. "While the stock market crash of 1929 was destabilizing," he concluded, "most analysts attribute the Great Depression to ensuing failures of policy" rather than fault the Fed for not acting to restrain share prices. Concerned about the moral hazard that his posture inevitably entailed, Greenspan warned investors that it didn't mean the Fed would act to bail them out, and he continued to remind them that the "productivity acceleration does not ensure that equity prices are not overextended." But he believed—consistent with history if not with the second-guessers—that the bubble could not be deflated "short of the central bank inducing a substantial contraction in economic activity—the very outcome we would be seeking to avoid." In other words, "the notion that a well-timed incremental tightening could have been calibrated to prevent the late 1990s bubble is almost surely an illusion."[26]

Milton Friedman and Anna Schwartz, who studied monetary policy in the depression most intensively, consider the Fed's failure to provide enough money and credit to contain the banking panic and economic contraction that followed the market crash its greatest error, and attribute it to the lack of courageous and knowledgeable leadership. "The detailed story of every banking crisis in our history," they conclude in their *Monetary History of the United States, 1867–1960,* "shows how much depends on the presence of one or more outstanding individuals willing to assume responsibility and leadership." Benjamin Strong, who became head of the Federal Reserve Bank of New York when it was established and dominated the entire system until his death in October 1928, was one such exceptional leader, and Friedman and Schwartz ascribe the Fed's ineffectiveness in the 1930s to the "shift of power" after his death "and the lack of understanding and experience of the individuals to whom the power was shifted." As they explain:

> Strong, more than any other individual, had the confidence and backing of other financial leaders inside and outside the System, the personal force to make his own views prevail, and also the courage to act upon them . . . If Strong had still been alive and head of the New York bank in the fall of 1930, he would very likely have recognized the oncoming liquidity crisis for what it was, would have been prepared by experience and conviction to take strenuous and appropriate measures to head it off, and would have had the standing to carry the System with him.

Strong's experience, they also point out, came in part from his having served as J. P. Morgan's right-hand man during the 1907 financial crisis.[27]

Disastrous as its actions may have been in allowing the depression to develop, the Fed's failure to respond appropriately to the 1929 stock market crash and subsequent banking panic was only part of the problem. As Federal Reserve governor and former Princeton professor Ben Bernanke argued in an October 2002 speech, by trying to deflate the stock market bubble in the late 1920s, the Fed helped to precipitate the crash itself. Strong had opposed such actions because he feared they would weaken the economy—"I am wondering," he wrote, "what will be the consequences of such a policy if it is undertaken and who will assume responsibility for it"—but his death left the field open to what Bernanke terms "a coterie of aggressive bubble-poppers." Although the Board claimed that it "neither assumes the right nor has it any disposition to set itself up as an arbiter of security speculation or values," that is what it did. "There is no doubt," according to Friedman and Schwartz, that the Fed acted to "curb the stock market boom" in 1928 and 1929, raising interest rates substantially and slowing the economy, but not stock prices. However, "the slowing economy, together with rising interest rates," Bernanke concludes, was "a major factor in precipitating the stock market crash," an interpretation shared by Keynes, who wrote in 1930 that by raising interest rates, the Fed "played an essential role in bringing about the collapse," which it then failed to contain.[28]

Volcker and Greenspan were also unusually good leaders of the Fed, far better than any other directors since Strong, yet Friedman is strangely ungenerous in evaluating their contributions. Unlike, say, *The Economist*, which thinks "Mr. Volcker was a giant among pygmies," Friedman attributes much of his success to Reagan's commitment to end inflation, while Greenspan's performance leaves Friedman and other rules proponents in the dark. "I'm baffled," he replied to a question about what explains Greenspan's record. "What I'm puzzled about is whether, and if so how, they suddenly learned how to regulate the economy. Does Greenspan have an insight into the movements in the economy and the shocks that other people don't have?" Whatever the reasons for Greenspan's success—and luck cannot be ruled out, since the period was relatively short—his policies after 1994 were more conducive to economic growth than any rules-based policies would have been.[29]

The most plausible explanation for the superior monetary policies of the 1980s and 1990s is probably the obvious one—the presence, as Friedman and Schwartz emphasize in discussing the failures of the early 1930s, of "outstanding individuals willing to assume responsibility and leadership." Both the 1990s and the even more extensive long boom, which began at the end of 1982 and lasted for more than seventeen years, were periods of almost continuous growth, robust stock market returns, and low and stable rates of unemployment and inflation, as Figure 6 on page 246 shows quite clearly.[30]* And although monetary policies did not create the new technologies and new business methods that are the foundations of these impressive expansions, the economy's great runs were cared for and supported by two exceptional Federal Reserve chairmen who did not follow rules and appreciated the wisdom of a trial-and-error approach to monetary policy, especially when the economy was changing so dramatically. Superior leadership also helps to explain why the 2001–2002 recession, which resulted in part from the excesses that inevitably built up during the boom, has been reasonably contained, leaving the new economy in relatively good shape to resume its rise.

---

*During the 1990s, the economy grew by 3.2 percent a year (4 percent after 1994), the unemployment rate averaged 5.8 percent (5 percent after 1994), prices rose by 2.9 percent a year (2.4 percent after 1994), and stocks returned more than 18 percent a year (more than 28 percent in the second half of the decade). The years 1983 through 1989 were similarly impressive, with average rates of growth, unemployment, inflation, and total stock market returns of 4.2 percent, 6.5 percent, 3.7 percent, and 18.5 percent, respectively. Moreover, these measures of economic health were unusually stable.

Conclusion: Looking Forward

THE PRECEDING CHAPTERS have tried to show how the economy reinvented itself in the last few decades of the twentieth century, and why, many years from now, this transformation is likely to be seen as the beginning of one of those rare long waves of superior productivity growth and innovation-driven prosperity that have combined to produce the extraordinary increase in living standards of the last two centuries—why, in short, it is appropriate to call the economy of the early twenty-first century revolutionary or new. Like the two or three other major economic transformations that have occurred since the country was founded, such as the industrial revolution of the nineteenth century and the makeover based on electric power and mass production in the early years of the twentieth century, this one was propelled by powerful new technologies and complementary new business practices. Lean and flexible operating methods evolved in response to the pressures and opportunities created by new information and communications technologies, growing global competition, and important financial innovations, including the development of the junk-bond market and the spread of hostile corporate takeovers. Just as in the electric power revolution, it took more than a generation for the process to advance sufficiently to boost productivity growth materially as the technologies were refined and improved and as companies learned how to use them effectively and made necessary investments in new equipment and in training their workers to function in a new way. And throughout its formative years, the budding new economy was supported by superior monetary policy.

That the economy is new in this sense—that the technologies and business practices developed over the last twenty-five years have made it significantly more productive, and that heightened rates of productivity growth are likely to persist for some time—is a statement about its longer-term performance. Over shorter spans, it will inevitably be buffeted by less-lasting forces and the wild moods and expectations they sometimes bring about. The new economy was never capable of delivering unlimited prosperity, which the bubbly years of the late 1990s led many to anticipate or hope for; nor was it destroyed by the collapse of the stock market, investment spending, and economic growth in the first few years of the twenty-first century, which quickly turned the prevailing euphoria and optimism into deadening despondency and pessimism. The resulting crisis of confidence also owed much to the terrorist attacks of September 11, 2001, the subsequent campaign against terrorism, and burgeoning evidence that corporations' top managers had looted their companies, cheated investors, and misled them about the strength of their businesses. Debilitating as these blows may have been, however, with the exception of the terror-related ones, all were characteristic consequences of frenzied speculative booms and did little to undermine the economy's fundamental strength or long-term prospects, which remain exceptionally bright. If anything, the economy's resilience in the face of this combination of external shocks and internally generated corrections reinforces the sense that it has changed deeply in the last generation and that the technologies and business practices that have made it more productive and competitive are unusually powerful, likely, barring significant external problems, to propel it much further once the effects of the prior decade's excesses are worked off.

Major economic transformations generally stimulate unrealistic expectations, producing speculative frenzies, market bubbles, swin-

dling, fraud, and underhanded dealing, which end eventually in collapse, disillusionment, and recessions or depressions. Like the 1980s
and 1990s, the 1920s were years of dynamism and fanciful expectations when merger activity soared, scores of firms went public, and
hopes of unlimited prosperity flourished as corporate earnings grew
rapidly but stock and other asset prices grew even faster, reaching unsustainable heights. Dishonest accounting, misleading financial reporting, and other manipulations also were not unique to the 1980s
and 1990s; contemporary observers considered the 1920s "the greatest
era of crooked high finance the world has ever known," and the abuses
of that period led to the enactment of many of our securities laws,
which attempted to create an environment of full and fair disclosure in
which all investors could make informed decisions. But whereas
the stock market crash of 1929 soon became the Great Depression of
the 1930s, the collapse that began in the spring of 2000, like that
of the junk-bond market in late 1989, resulted in only a relatively mild
recession, largely because the policy errors of the 1930s, when the
Fed, notoriously, failed to contain the crash, were not repeated (and
because federal deposit insurance, which was enacted in 1933 in response to the banking panics of the early 1930s, has prevented subsequent panics). The relative mildness of the current recession is also
due to the operating flexibility and financial innovations of the new
economy that have allowed companies to better control their operations and diversify and manage their risks, thus helping maintain high
enough productivity growth to prevent the sustained drop in overall
economic activity typical of most recessions.[1]

Nevertheless, as the economy continued to struggle in the summer and fall of 2002, many people grew frustrated, blaming the Federal Reserve for not having acted to deflate the stock market bubble
before it got out of hand. Some also suggested that the U.S. economy, like Japan's in the early 1990s, might be sliding into a long deflationary slump. But unlike the bureaucratic Japanese economy,
which may have run out of gas in the late 1980s (much as our stagnant industrial state did twenty years earlier), the U.S. economy in

the late 1990s was just beginning to reflect the changes that had been percolating since at least the late 1960s. And ironically, concerns about the Fed's purported failure to control the stock market bubble, or to confront incipient deflation, derive from the economy's underlying strength combined with wishful thinking about what might have been and impatience with the seemingly slow pace of recovery from the recession. Economic growth fell off significantly in mid-2000 and stagnated after that, but because the innovations of the new economy had boosted the trend rate of productivity growth significantly, there was an emerging "deflationary gap" between actual economic output and the economy's growing capacity to produce. Yet while a sustained period of underutilized capacity and falling prices could eventually spiral out of control and frustrate the Federal Reserve's ability to stimulate the economy, especially with interest rates already so low, in September and October 2002 it still was premature to project the current shortfall of demand too far into the future. The economy had resumed growing in the fourth quarter of 2001, albeit sluggishly and erratically, and continued strong productivity growth, which had held up unusually well during the slowdown, was likely to boost corporate profits and stimulate investment spending once existing capacity was deployed more effectively and used more fully. In addition, "the chances of a serious deflation in the United States appear remote," Fed governor Ben Bernanke emphasized in November 2002, "because of the determination of the Federal Reserve and other U.S. policymakers to act preemptively against deflationary pressures," and because they have many ways to stimulate the economy even when short-term interest rates are near zero.[2]*

In sum, throughout most of 2002, the economy was straining to overcome the lingering effects of a classic speculative binge, whose

---

*The economy grew by 4.1 percent in 1999, 3.8 percent in 2000 (but just over 1.5 percent in the second half of the year), and 0.3 percent in 2001, even though GDP fell during the first three quarters of the year. Growth resumed in the fourth quarter of 2001 and fluctuated in 2002, averaging about 2.4 percent for the year. Similarly, productivity growth was 2.9 percent in 2000, 1.1 percent in 2001 (even though productivity fell in the first two quarters), and just under 5 percent in 2002.

impact was compounded by the terrorist attacks, the subsequent campaign against terrorism, and the likelihood of war with Iraq, and it was unrealistic to think that the accumulated dislocations and excesses would quickly be corrected. (Fiber-optic capacity, for example, was estimated to have increased five hundred–fold between 1998 and 2001, while demand rose only fourfold.) Moreover, something similar had happened just ten years earlier, during the 1990–1991 recession, which also followed a long expansion, complete with bubbles in the commercial real-estate market, a scandal-racked junk-bond market, and the outbreak of war in the Middle East. That recession was even milder, but economic growth was slow to recover, largely because banks and S&Ls were reluctant to lend before they rebuilt their balance sheets, which had been wrecked by the collapse of the real-estate and junk-bond markets. Then as now, many feared a "jobless recovery," but in a few years economic growth and stock prices began to take off, and by the middle of the decade Alan Greenspan was worrying famously about "irrational exuberance." The Fed later admitted that it could have done more to stimulate the economy in the early 1990s and—surprisingly, in light of that experience—was unwilling to cut interest rates between December 2001 and November 2002. Moreover, with prices barely rising, the consequences of providing an extra boost to the economy, even if it turned out not to be needed, were likely to be far less damaging than those that might result from holding back. Finally, on November 2, 2002, saying it was concerned about a "soft spot" in the economy, which it attributed largely to "greater uncertainty" resulting from "geopolitical risks" associated with the campaign against terrorism and a possible war with Iraq, the Fed lowered the federal funds rate by fifty basis points, to 1.25 percent. It would also have been helpful, and would have caused little harm, if Congress and the president had agreed on a plan for additional fiscal stimulus, perhaps by extending unemployment benefits (done on January 8, 2003) or making grants to the states to ensure that services such as medical care for the needy were maintained at reasonable levels.[3]

Although such policies would have eased many people's burdens, it is unlikely that these or other measures, including a preemptive strike against the stock market bubble by the Federal Reserve, would have greatly softened the recession or the slowdown in economic growth. Wild speculative fevers, such as those that enveloped the economy in the late 1980s and late 1990s, frequently occur during significant economic transformations and are almost impossible to cure painlessly. While it would have been wonderful had the Fed been able to pull it off, fine-tuning monetary policy is so difficult even in less tumultuous times that it is hard to believe the central bank could have limited the buildup of the stock market bubble, or the severity of its collapse, without short-circuiting the boom from which it sprang. The Fed's attempts to let the hot air out of share prices in 1928, for example, slowed the economy but did not calm the stock market, thus helping to precipitate the great crash less than a year later. But even if monetary policy could not have deflated the bubble in technology stocks without creating a recession—"the very outcome," Greenspan has emphasized, "we would be seeking to avoid"—were there changes in our laws, accounting rules, or in the way that companies are run ("corporate governance") that might have limited the abuses that exploded along with share prices in the late 1990s?[4]

As with the bubble itself, however, controlling the shady practices that accompany speculative manias is more complicated, and more difficult to do, than is suggested by the public debate or by most of the remedies that have been proposed. The transgressions at companies such as Enron and WorldCom are the most egregious manifestations of a far deeper problem that is inextricably linked to the stock-buying frenzy stimulated by the developing new economy. The *Financial Times* has estimated that the top executives of the twenty-five largest American companies that went bankrupt between January 1999 and December 2001, including Kenneth Lay, Jeffrey Skilling, and at least seven other Enron executives, walked away with more than $3 billion over those three years. But even these "barons of bankruptcy," a "privileged group of business people who made extraordinary personal fortunes even as their companies were heading for disaster," are less exceptional than we might hope. As stock prices took off in the 1990s, officers and directors of large American corporations generally rewarded themselves bountifully, and largely undeservedly, primarily through grants of stock options in amounts, and on terms, that bore almost no relationship to their effectiveness. In most instances these grants were made, accounted for, and reported to shareholders in accordance with the letter, if not the spirit, of accepted accounting rules, securities laws, and corporate charters and bylaws. Moreover, options were widely thought to be an effective means of aligning the interests of shareholders and managers, and even if the ways in which they were handed out made a mockery of this view, investors did not seem to care as long as they, too, were making money. As a result, in the mid-1970s the typical chief executive of a major American company was paid about 45 times as much as an average worker, but fifteen years later this "pay ratio" had risen to about 150, and by the end of the 1990s it had more than tripled again, to approximately 500, with most of the gains coming from executive stock options. According to one estimate, academic research on the subject grew even more rapidly than the compensation it was studying, but most of it was aimed at showing how the pay plans were designed to maximize shareholder value, a conclusion that defies both common sense and detailed scrutiny.[5]

While performance-based pay is overwhelmingly desirable, to be effective it should be geared both to realizing a company's long-term goals and to the beneficiaries' contributions to those accomplishments and should not reward windfalls, such as stock market gains that bear little or no relationship to their efforts. Yet a comprehensive review of corporate option-granting practices shows that American companies uniformly granted options to their executives that *do not* "filter out stock price rises that are due largely to industry and general market trends and thus are unrelated to managers' performance."

The authors could find only one publicly traded company that linked its executive options to share-price gains that exceeded those of the S&P 500, while only 5 percent of the largest 250 companies tied option vesting to performance targets. The value of such index options, unlike the fixed-price options that companies grant so abundantly, must be charged against the issuer's earnings, and the charges must be adjusted as the value changes, but these tougher accounting standards are probably less important than the more stringent achievement requirements in explaining the infrequent use of performance-based options. Even options that are linked to appropriate stock market indexes may not go far enough in tying compensation to executives' effectiveness, since they largely insulate the holders from share-price declines.[6]

In addition to not being indexed or performance-based, executive options are almost always granted "at-the-money," which means that their exercise prices are the market price of the issuer's shares at the time of the grant. In 1992, 95 percent of executive options were granted at-the-money, and since stock prices generally rise over time, such options are virtually guaranteed to pay off, regardless of how effectively the beneficiaries performed. As Warren Buffett has graphically pointed out, at-the-money options are really "a royalty on the passage of time." Even so, executive options frequently are "repriced" when the company's shares fall below the initial exercise price. "The lack of indexing on the upside and the use of repricing on the downside," the authors of the compensation study write, "ensures that managers receive both the full value of stock price increases that are due to market or sector rises *and* protection against market and sector declines," a combination whose incentives are laughably remote from ideal. If arrangements such as these were necessary to motivate superior performance, rather than being used to guarantee executive riches, why would they be more plentiful in companies whose managers are more protected from shareholder scrutiny? Yet executive compensation tends to be higher in companies with powerful CEOs who control their boards of directors, in companies that have enacted strong restrictions on takeovers, and in companies whose officers and directors don't have to answer to large and aggressive shareholders.[7]

Because the separation of ownership and control gives the modern corporation's officers and directors so much unchecked power, responsible governance rests in large part on their willingness and commitment to do the right thing. But in times such as the 1990s, the temptations and opportunities for undue self-enrichment expand enormously, and many people act badly, some criminally. In 1912 J. P. Morgan told a congressional committee investigating his influence in the economy that "moral responsibility" or "character" was the criterion he used in deciding with whom to do business, a prescription that is no less useful, or easier to apply, today than it was in his day.[8]* Failures of character in the face of outsize rewards made possible by the speculative mania both created the scandals and outrageous growth in executive compensation and make them hard to prevent. Since there is no perfect solution to the "agency problem" that shareholders face in trying to control the executives—their agents—who work for them, and since we can't establish moral responsibility through legislation, the best we can do is try to discourage improper behavior and encourage better conduct. Several useful proposals have been made, including repealing many of the state laws that unnecessarily inhibit hostile takeovers, an extremely "effective device for policing top managers of large, publicly traded companies," and changing accounting regulations and tax provisions that encourage option-related get-rich-quick schemes and share-price manipulations designed to make sure that they pay off handsomely. Particularly promising among the latter suggestions are those pro-

*In his testimony before the Pujo committee in 1912, Morgan emphasized the importance of character in his business dealings, while his partner Henry Davison told the investigators that Morgan partners sat on corporate boards because it was their "moral responsibility" to protect their investors' interests. "For a private banker to sit upon such a directorate," he wrote to them, "is in most instances a duty, not a privilege."

posing that we tax as well as expense the fair value of employee options when they are granted and that we end the corporate tax on dividends.[9]* But, most important, investors must penalize companies whose accounting and operating policies are opaque and untrustworthy, while those responsible for corporate malfeasance, particularly those at the top, should be punished appropriately. "Start sending some CFOs and CEOs to jail," one financial executive said, echoing sentiments expressed by former Treasury secretary Paul O'Neill, and "you'll see a real wake up call."[10]†

Nevertheless, because speculative manias typically beget swindling and fraud and tend to develop in response to significant economic change, widespread financial corruption is likely to be as common as new economies. This means that like the bubbly environment of which they were a part, the abuses of shareholders' trust during the 1980s and 1990s—whether outright fraud and theft or the

---

*This proposal would end the double taxation of dividends, which presently are taxed at both the corporate and the individual level: corporations cannot deduct the dividends they pay from their taxable income, yet individuals pay ordinary income taxes on the dividends they receive. And because corporate interest payments are tax deductible but dividends are not, companies are encouraged to take on debt and are discouraged from paying dividends, which are among the least ambiguous indications of their earnings. The asymmetrical tax treatment of dividends and interest payments also encourages option-based executive compensation and efforts to keep share prices rising, both to make the options pay off and to create capital gains for shareholders. In January 2003, as part of its "growth and jobs" plan, the Bush administration proposed ending the double taxation of dividends, but did so by excluding them from the personal income tax, a cumbersome and questionable approach that is likely to have a far smaller impact on corporate behavior than directly ending the corporate tax on dividends.

†Instead of trying to establish penalties that will deter bad behavior and incentives that will encourage better conduct, most of the programs that have been enacted or suggested, including the Sarbanes-Oxley Act of 2002, the recommendations of the Conference Board, and the suggestions of Henry Paulson of Goldman Sachs, identify desirable practices but generally do not provide mechanisms for effecting them. The Sarbanes-Oxley Act, for example, orders a company's chief executive and chief financial officer to pay back all incentive-based compensation earned in the year following an earnings report that is later restated materially, but only if the restatement is the result of "misconduct," a difficult hurdle to surmount. Paulson, on the other hand, would mandate a "one-year 'claw-back' in the case of bankruptcy, *regardless of the reason*" (emphasis added), and is appropriately critical of our faith in the efficacy of "complex, rules-based" accounting that is "lacking in underlying principle," but otherwise relies on more and better "outside" directors to restrain managerial power, the approach also taken by the Conference Board.

more pervasive and insidious explosion of executive compensation—probably could not have been prevented without slowing growth of the new economy. Unfortunate as they may be, such excesses—wild speculation, shady dealing, and unjustified pay—are the unseemly underside of important economic transformations. And although they have contributed to the 2000–2002 slowdown, they have not undermined the long-term prospects of the new economy and, in the absence of external calamities or inappropriate reactions by policy makers and investors, are not likely to impede its continued growth.

NOTES

ACKNOWLEDGMENTS

INDEX

Notes

INTRODUCTION

1. See, for example, Nathan Rosenberg, "Uncertainty and Technological Change," in *Technology and Growth: Conference Proceedings, June 1996* (Boston: Federal Reserve Bank of Boston, 1996) pp. 91–110.

2. See International Monetary Fund, *World Economic Outlook* (2000), pp. 150–51; and J. Bradford DeLong, "Cornucopia: The Pace of Economic Growth in the Twentieth Century," National Bureau of Economic Research, working paper no. 7602 (March 2000), esp. pp. 11–25.

3. See Alan S. Blinder and Janet L. Yellen, *The Fabulous Decade* (New York: Century Foundation Press, 2001), p. 3; and Moses Abramovitz and Paul David, "Two Centuries of American Macroeconomic Growth: From Exploitation of Resource Abundance to Knowledge-Driven Development," Stanford Institute for Economic Policy Research, discussion paper no. 01-005 (Aug. 2001), p. 100.

4. The comparison between electric power and information technology was first put forth by Paul David in a well-known 1990 article, "The Dynamo and the Computer: An Historical Perspective on the Modern Productivity Paradox," *American Economic Review* (May 1990), pp. 355–61.

5. When they have paid attention to Galbraith's writings, economists have generally criticized them for lacking precision and empirical support. For a contemporary assessment of *The New Industrial State*, see Robert M. Solow, "The New Industrial State or Son of Affluence," *Public Interest* (Autumn 1967), pp. 100–8, and the exchanges that followed, with Galbraith in the same issue and with Robin Marris in Spring 1968. Among the many unfortunate speculations about the rise of Japan and

the decline of the United States, see, for example, Paul Kennedy, *The Rise and Fall of the Great Powers* (New York: Random House, 1987); Lester Thurow, *Head to Head: The Coming Economic Battle Among Japan, Europe, and America* (New York: Morrow, 1992); and Alan S. Blinder, "Should the Formerly Socialist Economies Look East or West for a Model?" in Jean-Paul Fitoussi, ed., *Economic Growth and Capital and Labour Markets* (New York: St. Martin's Press, 1995), pp. 3–24.

6. See the committee's statements of April 10, 2002, and August 6, 2002, available at www.nber.org.

7. Joseph A. Schumpeter, *Capitalism, Socialism, and Democracy*, 3rd ed. (New York: Harper Torchbooks, 1950), pp. 84, 82–83.

8. The quotations are from Nathan Rosenberg, *Schumpeter and the Endogeneity of Technology*, The Graz Schumpeter Lectures (New York: Routledge, 2000), p. 2; and Schumpeter, *Capitalism, Socialism, and Democracy*, pp. 67–68.

ONE: IS THERE A NEW ECONOMY?

1. John Moody, "The New Era in Wall Street," *Atlantic Monthly* (Aug. 1928), p. 260.

2. Walter Bagehot, *Lombard Street* (London: Smith, Elder & Co., 1915), p. 150.

3. "A Booming Stock Market: Strength of the Underlying Conditions," *New York Daily Tribune* (April 6, 1901), p. 3; and Alexander Dana Noyes, *The Market Place: Reminiscences of a Financial Editor* (Boston: Little, Brown, 1938), pp. 195–96.

4. Charles P. Kindleberger, *Manias, Panics, and Crashes: A History of Financial Crises*, 4th ed. (New York: John Wiley & Sons, 2000), p. 2. On the history of financial bubbles, see also Edward Chancellor, *Devil Take the Hindmost: A History of Financial Speculation* (New York: Farrar, Straus and Giroux, 1999).

5. The term was coined by John Taylor, a Stanford economist currently serving as undersecretary of the Treasury for International Affairs. See his "Monetary Policy and the Long Boom," *Review*, Federal Reserve Bank of St. Louis (Nov./Dec. 1998), pp. 3–11.

6. See David S. Landes, *The Unbound Prometheus: Technological Change and Industrial Development in Western Europe from 1750 to the Present* (London: Cambridge University Press, 1972), chap. 1, esp. pp. 1–6.

7. On the transformation of the American economy in the nineteenth century, see Moses Abramovitz and Paul David, "Two Centuries of American Macroeconomic Growth: From Exploitation of Resource

Abundance to Knowledge-Driven Development," Stanford Institute for Economic Policy Research, discussion paper no. 01-005 (Aug. 2001), pp. 11–17, 37–39, 99–101; and for a livelier account, James M. McPherson, *Battle Cry of Freedom* (New York: Ballantine Books, 1989), pp. 6–15. (An earlier and much less comprehensive version of Abramovitz and David's paper appears in Stanley L. Engerman and Robert E. Gallman, eds., *The Twentieth Century*, vol. 3 of *The Cambridge Economic History of the United States* [New York: Cambridge University Press, 2000], pp. 1–92.)

8. See Moses Abramovitz, "Resource and Output Trends in the United States since 1870," *American Economic Review* (May 1956), pp. 5–23; Robert M. Solow, "Technical Change and the Aggregate Production Function," *Review of Economics and Statistics* (Aug. 1957), pp. 312–20, and his retrospective, "Perspectives on Growth Theory," *Journal of Economic Perspectives* (Winter 1994), pp. 45–54. The quotations are from the latter article, p. 46.

9. The quotation is from Joseph A. Schumpeter, *Business Cycles* (New York: McGraw-Hill, 1939), p. 167. Among the many books and articles emphasizing the unpredictable and extended process of developing and effectively deploying new technologies are Paul David, "Computer and Dynamo: The Modern Productivity Paradox in a Not-Too-Distant Mirror," in *Technology and Productivity*, OECD (1991), pp. 315–47; and Nathan Rosenberg, "Uncertainty and Technological Change," in *Technology and Growth: Conference Proceedings, June 1996* (Boston: Federal Reserve Bank of Boston, 1996), pp. 91–110. The examples cited in the text are from pp. 94–95 of Rosenberg's paper.

10. See, for example, James Kahn, Margaret M. McConnell, and Gabriel Perez-Quiros, "On the Causes of the Increased Stability of the U.S. Economy," *Economic Policy Review*, Federal Reserve Bank of New York (May 2002), pp. 183–202, which attributes much of the improvement to better control of business inventories made possible in part by new information and communications technologies; and "US Business Cycle Expansions and Contractions," available at www.nber.org.

11. Abramovitz and David, "Two Centuries of American Macroeconomic Growth," esp. pp. 5–20, E-1, and A11–A14.

12. This is not true of many other attempts to portray the long-term buildup of productivity growth. For example, the former Federal Reserve Board governor Laurence Meyer has impressionistically divided the last 110 years into six alternating periods of low- and high-productivity growth, which closely resemble Abramovitz and David's

long-swing intervals. Not surprising, he finds that productivity growth fluctuated from period to period, averaging approximately 3 percent in the high-growth years, 1.5 percent in the low ones, and about 2.15 percent for the entire time. See his "Remarks Before the New York Association for Business Economics and the Downtown Economists" (New York, June 6, 2001), which is available at www.federalreserve.gov.

13. North considers the wedding of science and technology in the nineteenth century the second economic revolution; the first, in his view, was the development of agriculture in the eighth millennium B.C. See Douglass C. North, "Institutions and Productivity in History" (Nov. 1994), pp. 5–6, available at the Economics Working Paper Archive at Washington University, St. Louis, econwpa.wustl.edu; and Alfred North Whitehead, *Science and the Modern World* (New York: Macmillan, 1925), p. 98.

14. Schumpeter, *Business Cycles*, pp. 166–68; and Jean Strouse, *Morgan: American Financier* (New York: Random House, 1999), p. 195.

15. See Alfred D. Chandler Jr., "The Information Age in Historical Perspective," in Alfred D. Chandler Jr. and James W. Cortada, eds., *A Nation Transformed by Information* (New York: Oxford University Press, 2000), pp. 6–15; and Alfred D. Chandler Jr., "Organizational Capabilities and the Economic History of the Industrial Enterprise," *Journal of Economic Perspectives* (Summer 1992), esp. pp. 80–82. Chandler considers the creation of the nation's "information infrastructure" in the second half of the nineteenth century an important part of an "industrial age" that grew out of the industrial revolution. Similarly, "A Survey of the New Economy," *Economist* (Sept. 23, 2000), pp. 7–11, adds a "railway age" to the two major industrial revolutions emphasized by Abramovitz and David, "Two Centuries of American Macroeconomic Growth," pp. 37–53, 129–35.

16. Abramovitz and David, "Two Centuries of American Macroeconomic Growth," pp. 99–100, 114–19.

17. Ibid., pp. 110–14. The skeptical view of long-term growth is presented in Robert J. Gordon, "U.S. Economic Growth Since 1870: One Big Wave?" *American Economic Review* (May 1999), pp. 123–28.

18. See Jacob M. Schlesinger and Nicholas Kulish, "As Paper Millionaires Multiply, Estate Tax Takes a Public Beating," *Wall Street Journal* (July 13, 2000); and Jeffrey Bell, Glenn Burkins, and Gregory L. White, "Why Labor Unions Have Grown Reluctant to Use the 'S' Word," *Wall Street Journal* (Dec. 16, 1999). Based on the findings of a 2000 survey by the Zogby organization for the American Shareholders Association, *The*

Economist suggested that a shareholder "class" might have grown up in the United States ("Al Gore's Investor Problem" [Oct. 21, 2000] p. 41).

19. Quoted in David Wessel, "American Economy Offers a Model Others Both Envy and Fear," *Wall Street Journal* (Jan. 18, 2001). See also Christopher Rhoads, "Behind the Crisis in Germany, a Past That Is Crippling," *Wall Street Journal* (Dec. 6, 2002).

20. Robert M. Solow, review of *Manufacturing Matters: The Myth of the Post-industrial Economy*, by Stephen S. Cohen and John Zysman, *New York Times Book Review* (July 12, 1987), p. 36.

21. See Kevin J. Stiroh, "Information Technology and the U.S. Productivity Revival: What Do the Industry Data Say?" *American Economic Review* (Dec. 2002), pp. 1562–1563 and fig. 1; and William Nordhaus, "Productivity Growth and the New Economy," National Bureau of Economic Research, working paper no. 8096 (Jan. 2001), pp. 7–8 and table 1.

22. On the data revisions, see Brent R. Moulton, Eugene P. Seskin, and Daniel F. Sullivan, "Annual Revision of the National Income and Product Accounts," *Survey of Current Business* (Aug. 2001), esp. pp. 10–14; and Eugene P. Seskin, "Improved Estimates of the National Income and Product Accounts for 1959–98: Results of the Comprehensive Revision," *Survey of Current Business* (Dec. 1999), esp. pp. 15–17. The comprehensive revisions are discussed in *The Economic Report of the President* (2000), pp. 80–82; and Nordhaus, "Productivity Growth and the New Economy," p. 8 and fig. 2.

23. Abramovitz, "Resource and Output Trends in the United States Since 1870," pp. 11, 14; Charles R. Hulten, "Total Factor Productivity: A Short Biography," National Bureau of Economic Research, working paper no. 7471 (Jan. 2000), pp. 31–32; and Gene M. Grossman and Elhanan Helpman, "Endogenous Innovation in the Theory of Growth," *Journal of Economic Perspectives* (Winter 1994), pp. 30–31.

24. See Martin Neil Baily, "The New Economy: Post Mortem or Second Wind?" *Journal of Economic Perspectives* (Spring 2002), pp. 3–22, which updates and reviews the three most prominent studies of productivity growth in the late 1990s. Baily was chairman of the Council of Economic Advisers when it conducted the productivity analysis reported in *The Economic Report of the President* (2001), one of the three important studies of the productivity acceleration. The other two are Stephen D. Oliner and Daniel E. Sichel, "The Resurgence of Growth in the Late 1990s: Is Information Technology the Story?" *Journal of Economic Perspectives* (Fall 2000), pp. 3–22; and Dale W. Jorgenson and Kevin J.

Stiroh, "Raising the Speed Limit: U.S. Economic Growth in the Information Age," *Brookings Papers on Economic Activity* 1 (2000), pp. 125–211. (Follow-up articles include Dale W. Jorgenson, Mun S. Ho, and Kevin J. Stiroh, "Projecting Productivity Growth: Lessons from the U.S. Growth Resurgence," published in the Federal Reserve Bank of Atlanta *Economic Review* [Third Quarter, 2002], pp. 1–13; and Stephen D. Oliner and Daniel E. Sichel, "Information Technology and Productivity: Where Are We Now and Where Are We Going?" Federal Reserve Board Finance and Economics Discussion Series, paper no. 2002-29 [June 2002].) In addition to these more extensive analyses, the Bureau of Labor Statistics publishes growth accounts, which allocate labor productivity growth among the various causes. See, for example, "Multifactor Productivity Trends, 2000," USDL 02-128 (March 12, 2002), which is available at www.bls.gov.

25. See Dale W. Jorgenson, "Information Technology and the U.S. Economy," *American Economic Review* (March 2001), esp. pp. 1–10; and on the collapse of the investment bubble that accompanied the bubble in technology stocks, see Greg Ip, "Amid Devastation, Many Still See Gains in Burst Tech Bubble," *Wall Street Journal* (March 20, 2001), which quotes the telecom-equipment analyst Paul Sagawa of Sanford C. Bernstein & Co.; and Scott Thurm, "The Broader Slowdown Isn't the Only Cause of Tech Industry's Ills," *Wall Street Journal* (March 21, 2001), which quotes the Mohawk executive Reid Batsel.

26. See Robert J. Gordon, "Technology and Economic Performance in the American Economy," National Bureau of Economic Research, working paper no. 8771 (Feb. 2002), esp. pp. 22–25 and table 2; and Robert J. Gordon, "Does the 'New Economy' Measure Up to the Great Inventions of the Past?" *Journal of Economic Perspectives* (Fall 2000), pp. 49–74.

27. See Susanto Basu, John G. Fernald, and Mathew D. Shapiro, "Productivity Growth in the 1990s: Technology, Utilization, or Adjustment?" (Nov. 2000), esp. pp. 3–5 and figs. 1–4 (subsequently published in the 2001 *Carnegie-Rochester Conference Series on Public Policy*, pp. 117–65); *Economic Report of the President* (2001), pp. 27–29, 77; and Kevin J. Stiroh, "Investing in Information Technology: Productivity Payoffs for U.S. Industries," *Current Issues in Economics and Finance*, Federal Reserve Bank of New York (June 2001), p. 3. The difficulty of measuring productivity growth in the service sector is discussed in more detail in the next chapter.

28. See Stiroh, "Information Technology and the U.S. Productivity Revival," esp. pp. 1559–60, 1574, fig. 3, and the tables; and Baily, "New

Economy," pp. 9–10, which highlights the importance of the new data in establishing these results.

29. See McKinsey Global Institute, *U.S. Productivity Growth 1995–2000: Understanding the Contribution of Information Technology Relative to Other Factors* (Oct. 2001); and *McKinsey Quarterly* 1 (2002), which summarizes the report's findings. Baily, "New Economy," pp. 11–12, points out that McKinsey developed its own measure of banking-industry productivity, which may explain why it finds that banking productivity growth fell. The data from the Commerce Department's Bureau of Economic Analysis, which he uses in his work, show a rise in banking productivity.

30. McKinsey Global Institute, *U.S. Productivity Growth 1995–2000*, chap. 4, "Retail Trade"; and Bradford C. Johnson, "Retail: The Wal-Mart Effect," *McKinsey Quarterly* 1 (2002), which discusses the report's main findings for the retail sector.

31. Specifically, the McKinsey report finds that industry productivity gains in the late 1990s were correlated with investments in information technology when the industry data were weighted by industry employment but not when they were unweighted. As Baily notes, weighting is appropriate, but using employment may not be the best way to do it ("New Economy," p. 11). Some of the ambiguity in these results may also arise because the McKinsey analysis is based on data for the period 1995–1999, unlike other industry studies, which include 2000, when productivity growth was particularly strong.

32. See McKinsey Global Institute, *U.S. Productivity Growth 1995–2000*, chap. 1, exhibits 11–13; Gene Epstein, "Why the Whiz Kids Got It Wrong on Productivity," *Barron's* (Oct. 22, 2001); and Louis Uchitelle, "Deepening Wrinkles in the New Economy," *New York Times* (Oct. 17, 2001).

33. David C. Mowery and Nathan Rosenberg, *Paths of Innovation* (New York: Cambridge University Press, 1999), pp. 117–18.

34. See Nicholas Crafts, "The Solow Productivity Paradox in Historical Perspective," London School of Economics (Nov. 2001), p. 2 and tables 1–3; J. Bradford DeLong, "Productivity Growth in the 2000s" (March 2002), pp. 24–25, 37–39, available at his Web site, www.j-bradford-delong.net; Baily, "New Economy," pp. 4–5; and Abramovitz and David, "Two Centuries of American Macroeconomic Growth," pp. 32–36, 54–56, 117–18.

35. Robert E. Litan and Alice M. Rivlin, *Beyond Dot.Coms: The Economic Promise of the Internet* (Washington, D.C.: Brookings Institution Press, 2001), pp. 4–6; Robert E. Litan and Alice M. Rivlin, "The Economy and

the Internet: What Lies Ahead?" Brookings Institution, conference report no. 4 (Dec. 2000); Baily, "New Economy," pp. 17–18; DeLong, "Productivity Growth in the 2000s," pp. 5–7, 32–37; and Jorgenson, Ho, and Stiroh, "Projecting Productivity Growth," esp. pp. 13–15, 18–19, and table 3.

TWO: WHY DID IT TAKE SO LONG?

1. Beginning with Paul David's 1990 article "The Dynamo and the Computer: An Historical Perspective on the American Productivity Paradox," which appeared in the *American Economic Review* that May, a growing body of research has further explored the argument. For example, see Moses Abramovitz and Paul David, "Two Centuries of American Macroeconomic Growth: From Exploitation of Resource Abundance to Knowledge-Driven Development," Stanford Institute for Economic Policy Research, discussion paper no. 01-005 (Aug. 2001), pp. 129–33, and the references they cite; Nathan Rosenberg and Manuel Trajtenberg, "A General Purpose Technology at Work: The Corliss Steam Engine in the Late 19th Century US," National Bureau of Economic Research, working paper no. 8485 (Sept. 2001), pp. 2–3; and Timothy F. Bresnahan and Manuel Trajtenberg, "General Purpose Technologies: 'Engines of Growth'?" *Journal of Econometrics* (1995), pp. 83–84, from which the brief quotation is taken.

2. Many people have emphasized the need for information and communications technologies to establish a critical presence in the economy before they could affect economic and productivity growth significantly. Oliner and Sichel, for example, begin their analysis of the productivity revival by recalling earlier research in which they found that the technologies had little impact on productivity in the first part of the 1990s because "computing equipment still represented an extremely small fraction of the total capital stock." But by the end of the decade, they point out, information and communications equipment had become far more prevalent, "boosting their contribution to growth." See Stephen D. Oliner and Daniel E. Sichel, "The Resurgence of Growth in the Late 1990s: Is Information Technology the Story?" *Journal of Economic Perspectives* (Fall 2000), pp. 3–4; and Dale W. Jorgenson, "Information Technology and the U.S. Economy," *American Economic Review* (March 2001), esp. pp. 1–10.

3. The idea that the value of a network can be approximated by the square of the number of users is called Metcalfe's law, after Robert Metcalfe, the computer scientist who developed the Ethernet method of computer

networking in 1973, and in 1979 formed 3Com Corporation, a company that provides computer networking products and services. See Richard L. Nolan, "Information Technology Management Since 1960," in Alfred D. Chandler Jr. and James W. Cortada, eds., *A Nation Transformed by Information* (New York: Oxford University Press, 2000), pp. 229–44.

4. See, for example, Jeff Hecht, "Fiber Crosses the 10-Trillion-Bit Barrier," *Technology Review* (March 27, 2001); David C. Mowery and Nathan Rosenberg, *Paths of Innovation* (New York: Cambridge University Press, 1999), pp. 172–73; David Denby, "The Speed of Light," *New Yorker* (Nov. 27, 2000), pp. 132–33; C. Michael Cox and Richard Alm, "The New Paradigm," annual report of the Federal Reserve Bank of Dallas (1999), pp. 6–9; *The Economic Report of the President* (2001), pp. 99–100; and "What Is a Laser?" available at www.bell-labs.com/history/laser.

5. The quoted fragments are from Gordon E. Moore, "Intel—Memories and the Microprocessor," *Daedalus* (Spring 1996), pp. 56–57. Moore never predicted that chip density would double every eighteen months. In 1975 he modified his original prediction, suggesting that for any given price, the power of processing chips would henceforth double every two years. The current version of the law is an average of Moore's two forecasts. See his comments in "Moore's Law," the second part of a 1997 interview with W. Wayt Gibbs, an editor of *Scientific American*, which was never published in the magazine but appears on its Web site at www.sciam.com/article.cfm?articleID=000C8D8B-7E63-1CDA-B4A 8809EC588EEDF. One reason to think the law is not yet in serious danger is the development of a new system for producing chips using shorter waves of "extreme ultraviolet" light to etch the circuits. See James Fallows, "New Life for Moore's Law," *Atlantic Monthly* (Oct. 2001), pp. 44–46.

6. "Moore's Law," and "Intel's Gordon Moore Donates $5 Billion for Research Center," *Wall Street Journal* (Nov. 17, 2000).

7. See "Bell Labs: More Than 50 Years of the Transistor," available at www.lucent.com/minds/transistor.

8. Mowery and Rosenberg, *Paths of Innovation*, pp. 123–26, 174–75; Nathan Rosenberg, "Uncertainty and Technological Change," in *Technology and Growth: Conference Proceedings, June 1996* (Boston: Federal Reserve Bank of Boston, 1996) pp. 94–95; and James W. Cortada, "Progenitors of the Information Age: The Development of Chips and Computers," in Chandler and Cortada, eds., *Nation Transformed by Information*, pp. 177–79.

9. In addition to the references in the preceding note, see Tom Wolfe,

"Two Young Men Who Went West," in *Hooking Up* (New York: Farrar, Straus and Giroux, 2000), esp. pp. 47–49, 55–56; and James Fallows, "The Computer Wars," *New York Review of Books* (May 24, 1994) p. 34.

10. Mowery and Rosenberg, *Paths of Innovation*, pp. 128–35.

11. Wolfe, "Two Young Men Who Went West," esp. pp. 19–20, 37–38, 58–60, 50–51.

12. See Charles Townes, "Quantum Electronics, and Surprise in Development of Technology," *Science* (Feb. 1968), pp. 699–701; Rosenberg, "Uncertainty and Technological Change," pp. 93, 99; and "Why Lasers Are Important Today," available at www.bell-labs.com/history/laser.

13. See Jean Strouse, *Morgan: American Financier* (New York: Random House, 1999), pp. 180–83, 230–35, who quotes *Engineering*; Rosenberg, "Uncertainty and Technological Change," pp. 93–95, 102; and Richard R. John, "Recasting the Information Infrastructure for the Industrial Age," in Chandler and Cortada, eds., *Nation Transformed by Information*, pp. 87–89.

14. Rosenberg, "Uncertainty and Technological Change," p. 95.

15. Alan S. Blinder and Richard E. Quandt, "Waiting for Godot: Information Technology and the Productivity Miracle?" Princeton University Center for Economic Policy Studies, working paper no. 42 (May 1997).

16. See Paul David, "Computer and Dynamo: The Modern Productivity Paradox in a Not-Too-Distant Mirror," in *Technology and Productivity*, OECD (1991), esp. pp. 325–32; and Paul David and Gavin Wright, "Early Twentieth Century Productivity Growth Dynamics: An Inquiry into the Economic History of 'Our Ignorance,'" Oxford Discussion Papers in Economic and Social History, no. 33 (Oct. 1999), esp. pp. 21–23. Other papers by Paul David on this theme include "Dynamo and Computer"; Abramovitz and David, "Two Centuries of American Macroeconomic Growth," esp. pp. 129–38; and Paul David and Gavin Wright, "General Purpose Technologies and Surges in Productivity: Historical Reflections on the Future of the ICT Revolution," in Paul David and Mark Thomas, eds., *The Economic Future in Historical Perspective* (Oxford: Oxford University Press, 2002).

17. Warren D. Devine Jr., "From Shafts to Wires: Historical Perspective on Electrification," *Journal of Economic History* (June 1983), p. 357. In addition, see David, "Computer and Dynamo," pp. 329–31; and David and Wright, "Early Twentieth Century Productivity Growth Dynamics," pp. 23–30.

18. David and Wright, "Early Twentieth Century Productivity Growth Dynamics," p. 24.

19. David, "Computer and Dynamo," pp. 322–29, 334, app. A, and n. 17; and David and Wright, "Early Twentieth Century Productivity Growth Dynamics," pp. 8–11, 15–19, 21–23. Following David, many people have noted that the penetration of personal computers in the United States, generally measured as the number of PCs per 100 Americans, passed 50 percent at about the time that productivity growth began to accelerate in the second half of the 1990s. See, for example, "Survey of the New Economy," *Economist* (Sept. 23, 2000), pp. 11–12.

20. Mowery and Rosenberg, *Paths of Innovation*, pp. 117–18, esp. n. 73.

21. Gary's comments at the 1923 annual meeting of the shareholders of U.S. Steel are quoted by David Brody, *Workers in Industrial America: Essays on the Twentieth Century Struggle* (New York: Oxford University Press, 1980), p. 55. Also see David, "Computer and Dynamo," pp. 322–23; and David and Wright, "Early Twentieth Century Productivity Growth Dynamics," pp. 32–36.

22. Mowery and Rosenberg, *Paths of Innovation*, pp. 105–7; and David, "Computer and Dynamo," p. 331.

23. See Kevin J. Stiroh, "Information Technology and the U.S. Productivity Revival: What Do the Industry Data Say?" *American Economic Review* (Dec. 2002), pp. 1563–64; and Jack E. Triplett and Barry P. Bosworth, " 'Baumol's Disease' Has Been Cured: IT and Multifactor Productivity in U.S. Services Industries," Brookings Institution (May 2002), p. 12.

24. John Cassidy of *The New Yorker* is one of those who think our measures of productivity are too generous; see, for example, "The Productivity Mirage," *New Yorker* (Nov. 27, 2000), esp. p. 118. He also endorses the hypothesis advanced by Stephen Roach, chief economist of Morgan Stanley, which attributes part of the productivity revival to the possibility that hours of work have been underestimated. Recent research has shown, however, that although hours tend to be underestimated, the undercount has been shrinking rather than growing as it would have to be to inflate productivity growth rates. See Alan B. Krueger, "Economic Scene: Despite Real Concerns, Gauging Work Hours Is Not a Problem in Measuring Productivity Growth," *New York Times* (June 21, 2001).

25. Zvi Griliches, "Productivity, R&D, and the Data Constraint," *American Economic Review* (March 1994), p. 14.

26. Lucy Eldridge, "How Price Indexes Affect BLS Productivity Measures," *Monthly Labor Review* (Feb. 1999), pp. 35–46; and Barry P. Bosworth and Jack E. Triplett, "The U.S. Statistical System and a Rapidly Changing Economy," Brookings Institution, policy brief no. 63 (July 2000).

27. See Martin Neil Baily, "The New Economy: Post Mortem or Second

Wind?" *Journal of Economic Perspectives* (Spring 2002), pp. 9–10, esp. table 3. If productivity is measured somewhat differently, using an industry's gross output rather than its "value added" in the numerator, the results also differ slightly, with health-care productivity growing slowly and that of insurance carriers falling. See Triplett and Bosworth, " 'Baumol's Disease' Has Been Cured," esp. table 3.

28. Jack E. Triplett and Barry P. Bosworth, "Productivity in the Services Sector," Brookings Institution (Jan. 2000), pp. 16–17, which appears as chapter 2 of Robert M. Stern, ed., *Services in the International Economy* (Ann Arbor: University of Michigan Press, 2001).

29. See "The Swaps Emperor's New Clothes," *Economist* (Feb. 10, 2001), pp. 71–72; Henry Sender, "A Market Backfires, and Investors Pay," *Wall Street Journal*, Dec. 5, 2002; and William Gullickson and Michael J. Harper, "Bias in Aggregate Productivity Trends Revisited," *Monthly Labor Review* (March 2002), p. 36.

30. William D. Nordhaus, "Do Output and Real Wage Measures Capture Reality? The History of Lighting Suggests Not," Cowles Foundation, discussion paper no. 1078 (Sept. 1994), later published in Robert J. Gordon and Timothy F. Bresnahan, eds., *The Economics of New Goods* (Chicago: University of Chicago Press, 1997), pp. 29–66.

31. Robert J. Gordon, "The Boskin Commission Report and Its Aftermath," National Bureau of Economic Research, working paper no. w7759 (June 2000); and Gullickson and Harper, "Bias in Aggregate Productivity Trends Revisited," esp. table 7.

32. See, for example, Charles Steindel, "The Impact of Reduced Inflation Estimates on Real Output and Productivity Growth," *Current Issues in Economics and Finance*, Federal Reserve Bank of New York (June 1999); and Abramovitz and David, "Two Centuries of American Macroeconomic Growth," pp. 125–28.

THREE: THE CHANGING OF THE GUARD

1. John Kenneth Galbraith, *The New Industrial State* (Boston: Houghton Mifflin, 1967). The quoted fragments are from pp. 9, 1, 26, and 6.

2. See Peter H. Lindert, "U.S. Foreign Trade and Trade Policy in the Twentieth Century," in Stanley L. Engerman and Robert E. Gallman, eds., *The Twentieth Century*, vol. 3 of *The Cambridge Economic History of the United States* (New York: Cambridge University Press, 2000), pp. 408, 454–58; and Peter Temin, "The Great Depression," pp. 304–6, ibid.

3. On the labor-management "accord," see Barry Bluestone and Irving Bluestone, *Negotiating the Future: A Labor Perspective on American Business* (New York: Basic Books, 1992), esp. chap. 2; and Steven A. Marglin, "Lessons of the Golden Age: An Overview," in Steven A. Marglin and Juliet B. Schor, eds., *The Golden Age of Capitalism* (Oxford: Clarendon Press, 1991), pp. 4–6.

4. Galbraith, *New Industrial State*, pp. 71, 49–50.

5. Adolf A. Berle and Gardiner C. Means, *The Modern Corporation and Private Property*, rev. ed. (New York: Harcourt, Brace & World, 1967), p. xxv, first published by Macmillan in 1932; Peter F. Drucker, *The Pension Fund Revolution* (New Brunswick, N.J.: Transaction Publishers, 1996), pp. 5–7 (originally published as *The Unseen Revolution: How Pension Fund Socialism Came to America* [New York: Harper & Row, 1976]); and Mark J. Roe, *Strong Managers, Weak Owners* (Princeton, N.J.: Princeton University Press, 1994), which emphasizes the institutional and political factors that constrained financial intermediaries from getting involved in corporate governance. Roe discusses GM's pension-fund policies on pp. 124–32.

6. David M. Gordon, *Fat and Mean: The Corporate Squeeze of Working Americans and the Myth of Managerial "Downsizing"* (New York: Free Press, 1996), pp. 42–49, esp. fig. 2.2 on p. 47. As noted in the Introduction, economists have generally criticized Galbraith's writings for lacking precision and empirical support. See, for example, Robert M. Solow, "The New Industrial State or Son of Affluence," *Public Interest* (Autumn 1967), pp. 100–8, and the exchanges his review elicited.

7. Paul Kennedy, *The Rise and Fall of the Great Powers* (New York: Random House, 1987). The quotations in the text are from pp. 533 and 467, and that in the footnote from pp. 462–63. On MITI, also see James P. Womack, Daniel T. Jones, and Daniel Roos, *The Machine That Changed the World: The Story of Lean Production* (New York: HarperPerennial, 1991), pp. 50–51, which is the source of the other quotation in the footnote (emphasis added).

8. Alan S. Blinder, "Should the Formerly Socialist Economies Look East or West for a Model?" in Jean-Paul Fitoussi, ed., *Economic Growth and Capital and Labour Markets* (New York: St. Martin's Press, 1995), pp. 3–24.

9. "Corporate America's Woes, Continued," *The Economist* (November 30, 2002); "The Price of Atonement," *The Economist* (November 16, 2002); Glen R. Simpson and Jathon Sapsford, "Banks' Enron Deals Draw Scrutiny," *Wall Street Journal* (Dec. 9, 2002); Charles Gasparino, "Mer-

rill Is Paying in Wake of Analyst's Call on Tech Stock," *Wall Street Journal* (July 20, 2001); "Merrill Lynch and New York State's Attorney-General Declare a Truce," *Economist* (May 23, 2002); and "Credit Suisse First Boston Agrees to Pay $100 Million Settlement," *Wall Street Journal* (Jan. 23, 2002).

10. Joseph A. Schumpeter, *Capitalism, Socialism, and Democracy*, 3rd ed. (New York: Harper Torchbooks, 1950), p. 84.

11. See Joan Robinson, *The Economics of Imperfect Competition* (London: Macmillan, 1933); and Edward H. Chamberlin, *The Theory of Monopolistic Competition* (Cambridge, Mass.: Harvard University Press, 1936).

12. Schumpeter, *Capitalism, Socialism, and Democracy*, pp. 79–80, 83–84, 106.

13. Paul Volcker and Toyoo Gyohten, *Changing Fortunes: The World's Money and the Threat to American Leadership* (New York: Times Books, 1992), pp. 288–89, 3–4, 49. Also see Lindert, "U.S. Foreign Trade and Trade Policy in the Twentieth Century," pp. 454–55; and Barry Eichengreen, "U.S. Foreign Financial Relations in the Twentieth Century," in Engerman and Gallman, eds., *Twentieth Century*, pp. 488–92.

14. David C. Mowery and Nathan Rosenberg, *Paths of Innovation* (New York: Cambridge University Press, 1999), pp. 56–59; Lindert, "U.S. Foreign Trade and Trade Policy in the Twentieth Century," pp. 407–8, 432–37; and Womack, Jones, and Roos, *Machine That Changed the World*, pp. 43–47.

15. Jean Strouse, *Morgan: American Financier* (New York: Random House, 1999), pp. 395–407, 447.

16. On the problems of the U.S. steel industry, see my statement in *Steel Imports and the Administration of the Antidumping Laws*, hearings before the Commerce, Consumer, and Monetary Affairs Subcommittee of the House Committee on Government Operations, Dec. 20, 1979, esp. pp. 51–60; Lindert, "U.S. Foreign Trade and Trade Policy in the Twentieth Century," pp. 419–32; Aaron Tornell, "Rational Atrophy: The US Steel Industry," National Bureau of Economic Research, working paper no. 6084 (July 1997), esp. pp. 6–14; and Robert Guy Matthews, "Retiree Costs Drive Big Changes in Steel; Retirees Are Losers," *Wall Street Journal* (April 25, 2002).

17. Thomas J. Prusa, "On the Spread and Impact of Antidumping," Rutgers University (Jan. 19, 2001), which will be published in the *Canadian Journal of Economics*; and Bruce A. Blonigen and Thomas J. Prusa, "Antidumping," National Bureau of Economic Research, working paper no. 8398 (July 2001), esp. pp. 1–6, which will appear in *Handbook of International Economics*, published by Basil Blackwell.

18. See the statement of Robert Crandall at the 1979 hearings in the House of Representatives, *Steel Imports and the Administration of the Antidumping Laws*, pp. 34–36.

19. "Steely Resolve," *Economist* (June 9, 2001), p. 30; Robert Guy Matthews, "Man of Steel: Bush Shows His Mettle," *Wall Street Journal* (July 2, 2001); Leslie Wade, "Ex-Alcoa Boss May Become a Man of Steel," *New York Times* (July 17, 2001); and Gene Epstein, "The Tariff Trap," *Barron's* (July 15, 2002).

20. Tornell, "Rational Atrophy," esp. fig. 5; Donald F. Barnett and Robert Crandall, "Remembering a Man of Steel," *Wall Street Journal* (April 23, 2002); "Meltdown," *Economist* (Jan. 6, 2001), p. 56; and *The Economic Report of the President* (Feb. 2000), p. 104, and (Feb. 2001), pp. 122, 125.

21. Richard Preston, "Hot Metal," *New Yorker* (Feb. 25, 1991), pt. 1, and (March 4, 1991), pt. 2. The quoted fragments are from part 1, pp. 43, 60, 65, 44, and the changes at U.S. Steel are discussed on pp. 63–64. Preston reports that at the time Nucor's overall accidental death rate was troublingly high, roughly three times the average for Big Steel (pp. 54–55).

22. The discussion of the early history of the computer industry in the next few pages relies heavily on the essays by Chandler and Cortada in Alfred D. Chandler Jr. and James W. Cortada, eds., *A Nation Transformed by Information* (New York: Oxford University Press, 2000), esp. pp. 17–37, 177–98; and on Mowery and Rosenberg, *Paths of Innovation*, esp. pp. 135–56.

23. Bill Gates, *The Road Ahead* (New York: Penguin Books, 1996), pp. 41–42.

24. Stephen Manes and Paul Andrews, *Gates* (New York: Touchstone, 1994), pp. 62, 99, 181.

25. Benjamin Rosen, "Visicalc: Breaking the Personal Computer Bottleneck," *Morgan Stanley Electronics Letter* (July 11, 1979), available at www.bricklin.com/history/rosenletter; James Fallows, "The Computer Wars," *New York Review of Books* (March 24, 1994), p. 34; and J. Bradford DeLong, "Productivity Growth in the 2000s" (March 2002), pp. 34–37, available at his Web site, www.j-bradford-delong.net.

26. See Fallows, "Computer Wars," esp. pp. 34–36 and Manes and Andrews, *Gates*, pp. 186–88.

27. See Manes and Andrews, *Gates*, pp. 165–68, 307; and "PARC's Legacy," at www.parc.xerox.com/hist.

28. Alfred D. Chandler Jr., "Introduction: Entrepreneurial Achievements," *Daedalus* (Spring 1996), p. xvi.

29. Gates, *Road Ahead*, p. 63; and Intel and IBM's joint news release, "IBM to Buy Minority Interest in Intel" (Dec. 22, 1982). For photographs, see *Inside Out: Microsoft—in Our Own Words* (New York: Warner Books, 2000), p. 7.

30. Manes and Andrews, *Gates*, pp. 154–62; and Fallows, "Computer Wars," esp. pp. 38–40.

31. Gates, *Road Ahead*, pp. 54–55; and *Inside Out*, pp. 18–19.

32. James B. Stewart, "Whales and Sharks," *New Yorker* (Feb. 15, 1993), pp. 37–43.

33. See William M. Bulkeley, "These Days Big Blue Is About Big Services Not Just Big Boxes," *Wall Street Journal* (June 11, 2001); William M. Bulkeley and Kemba Dunham, "IBM Speeds Move to Consulting with $3.5 Billion Acquisition," *Wall Street Journal* (July 31, 2002); and Steve Lohr, "I.B.M. to Acquire Rational in Big Move into Software," *New York Times*, Dec. 7, 2002.

34. "A Survey of Software," *Economist* (April 14, 2001), esp. pp. 8–10, 15–19; Steve Lohr, "Code Name: Mainstream: Can 'Open Source' Software Bridge the Software Gap?" *New York Times* (Aug. 28, 2000); and Steve Lohr, "Some I.B.M. Software Tools to Be Put in Public Domain," *New York Times* (Nov. 5, 2001).

35. See Galbraith, *New Industrial State*, esp. p. 71 n. 6; and Schumpeter, *Capitalism, Socialism, and Democracy*, pp. xiii, 112, 132–33.

36. See Robert Heilbroner, "Analysis and Vision in the History of Modern Economic Thought," *Journal of Economic Literature* (Sept. 1990), pp. 1098–1100; Alvin H. Hansen, *A Guide to Keynes* (New York: McGraw-Hill, 1953); Schumpeter, *Capitalism, Socialism, and Democracy*, pp. 111–12, 117–18; and David S. Landes, *The Unbound Prometheus: Technological Change and Industrial Development in Western Europe from 1750 to the Present* (London: Cambridge University Press, 1972), pp. 480–83.

37. Oskar Lange, "On the Economic Theory of Socialism," in Oskar Lange and Fred M. Taylor, *On the Economic Theory of Socialism* (New York: McGraw-Hill, 1938), pp. 72–98.

38. See Don Lavoie, *Rivalry and Central Planning: The Socialist Calculation Debate Reconsidered* (New York: Cambridge University Press, 1985), esp. pp. 175–77.

39. Nathan Rosenberg, *Schumpeter and the Endogeneity of Technology*, The Graz Schumpeter Lectures (New York: Routledge, 2000), p. 15.

40. Schumpeter, *Capitalism, Socialism, and Democracy*, pp. 172, 163, 61, 132–34, 143–46; and Galbraith, *New Industrial State*, p. 399.

FOUR: NEW WAYS OF WORKING

1. David A. Hounshell, *From the American System to Mass Production, 1800–1932: The Development of Manufacturing Technology in the United States* (Baltimore: Johns Hopkins University Press, 1984), p. 1.

2. Ibid., pp. 260–61; and David C. Mowery and Nathan Rosenberg, *Paths of Innovation* (New York: Cambridge University Press, 1999); pp. 48–55, which quotes the magazine *Autocar*.

3. The discussion of mass production in the next few pages relies on James P. Womack, Daniel T. Jones, and Daniel Roos, *The Machine That Changed the World: The Story of Lean Production* (New York: Harper-Perennial, 1991), pp. 26–29.

4. Hounshell, *From the American System to Mass Production*, pp. 250–53.

5. Daniel M. G. Raff, "Wage Determination Theory and the Five-Dollar Day at Ford," *Journal of Economic History* (June 1988), pp. 388–91; Hounshell, *From the American System to Mass Production*, pp. 11, 256–59; and Irving Bernstein, *The Lean Years: A History of the American Worker, 1920–1933* (Boston: Houghton Mifflin, 1960), pp. 179–80. The Ford biographer is Keith Sward, *The Legend of Henry Ford*, who is quoted by Hounshell, p. 257.

6. See Henry Ford (in collaboration with Samuel Crowther), *Today and Tomorrow* (New York: Doubleday, Page & Company, 1926), pp. 8–10; Raff, "Wage Determination Theory," pp. 387, 397–99; Hounshell, *From the American System to Mass Production*, pp. 258–59; Bernstein, *Lean Years*, pp. 179–81; and Stuart D. Brandes, *American Welfare Capitalism, 1880–1940* (Chicago: University of Chicago Press, 1976), pp. 88–89. According to Raff, Joseph Galamb, chief designer of the Model T and one of Henry Ford's close associates, recalled Ford saying he established the five-dollar day to ward off the Wobblies.

7. Womack, Jones, and Roos, *Machine That Changed the World*, pp. 33–35, 38–39; and Hounshell, *From the American System to Mass Production*, pp. 267–68. The term "industrial colossus," which is from Allan Nevins and Frank Ernest Hill, *Ford: Expansion and Challenge, 1915–1933* (New York: Scribner, 1957), is quoted on p. 267 of Hounshell's book.

8. Mowery and Rosenberg, *Paths of Innovation*, pp. 54–55; and Irving Bernstein, *Turbulent Years: A History of the American Worker, 1933–1941* (Boston: Houghton Mifflin, 1969), pp. 734–51.

9. Joan Magretta, "The Power of Virtual Integration: An Interview with Dell Computer's Michael Dell," *Harvard Business Review* (March–April 1998), pp. 74–76; and John Schwartz, "Dell Computer Is in the Catbird

Seat, for Now," *New York Times* (Sept. 11, 2001). The emphasis has been added to Michael Dell's remarks.

10. All the quoted remarks in this paragraph, as in the prior one, are Michael Dell's and are from the Margretta interview, pp. 76–79.

11. James Kahn, Margaret M. McConnell, and Gabriel Perez-Quiros, "On the Causes of the Increased Stability of the U.S. Economy," *Economic Policy Review*, Federal Reserve Bank of New York (May 2002), esp. pp. 184–87 and chart 3.

12. Mani Agrawal, T. V. Kumaresh, and Glenn A. Mercer, "The False Promise of Mass Customization," *McKinsey Quarterly* (2001); and "Mass Customization: A Long March," *Economist* (July 14, 2001), pp. 63–65.

13. "Incredible Shrinking Plants," *Economist* (Feb. 23, 2002); "All Yours," *Economist* (April 1, 2000), pp. 57–58; and Fred Andrews, "Dell, It Turns Out, Has a Better Idea," *New York Times* (Jan. 26, 2000).

14. Paul Milgrom and John Roberts, "The Economics of Modern Manufacturing: Technology, Strategy, and Organization," *American Economic Review* (June 1990), esp. pp. 511–15.

15. UPS and Baxter ASAP are discussed in Erik Brynjolfsson and Loren Hitt, "Beyond Computation: Information Technology, Organizational Transformation, and Business Performance," *Journal of Economic Perspectives* (Fall 2000), pp. 28, 30; Eastman Chemical's procurement practices are discussed in Scott Thurm, "Technology Spurs Economic Expansion," *New York Times* (Jan. 31, 2000).

16. Julie Holland Mortimer, "The Effects of Revenue-Sharing Contracts on Welfare in Vertically-Separated Markets: Evidence from the Video Rental Industry," mimeo (Jan. 2001), esp. pp. 1–10, 27–30; and Hal R. Varian, "Economic Scene: With Evolving Technology, Good Monitors Make for Better Contracts," *New York Times* (Aug. 23, 2001). Three Texas video-rental companies brought a lawsuit against Blockbuster, its parent, Viacom, and most of the major film studios, alleging that revenue-sharing arrangements were designed to drive them out of business, but it was dismissed by the judge in mid-2002. See "Judge Tosses Out Suit Against Blockbuster," *Wall Street Journal* (June 28, 2002).

17. Thomas Hubbard, "Information, Decisions, and Productivity: On-Board Computers and Capacity Utilization in Trucking," mimeo (March 26, 2001); Varian, "Economic Scene"; and Daniel Machalaba and Carrick Mollenkamp, "Companies Struggle to Cope With Chaos, Breakdowns, and Trauma," *Wall Street Journal* (Sept. 13, 2001).

18. Steve Liesman, "Better Machine Tools Give Manufacturers Newfound

Resilience," *Wall Street Journal* (Feb. 15, 2001). The discussion in the next two paragraphs also relies on this article.

19. Womack, Jones, and Roos, *Machine That Changed the World*, pp. 13, 48–49. The authors attribute the term "lean production" to John Krafcik, a researcher on the project that led to the book and, before that, the first American engineer hired at the Toyota–General Motors joint venture discussed on pp. 143–146.

20. Ibid., p. 99. The book is based on the MIT International Vehicle Program—a comprehensive study of the world automobile industry that was conducted at MIT in the 1980s. The authors were the three senior managers of the project.

21. Ibid., pp. 56–57.

22. Taiichi Ohno, *Toyota Production System* (Cambridge, Mass.: Productivity Press, 1988), pp. 26–27; and Womack, Jones, and Roos, *Machine That Changed the World*, pp. 60–62, 66–68.

23. Womack, Jones, and Roos, *Machine That Changed the World*, pp. 57–58, 65–69, 79–82, 119–21.

24. On NUMMI, see David I. Levine, *Reinventing the Workplace: How Business and Employees Can Both Win* (Washington, D.C.: Brookings Institution, 1995), pp. 10–35; and Womack, Jones, and Roos, *Machine That Changed the World*, pp. 82–84.

25. See, for example, Gabriella Stern and Rebecca Blumenstein, "GM's Saturn Division Plans to Build a Midsize Car to Keep Customers Loyal," *Wall Street Journal* (Aug. 6, 1996); "Saturn Workers Vote to Scale Back Risk and Reward Program," *Wall Street Journal* (Dec. 20, 1999); and Keith Bradsher, "The Reality Behind the Slogan: Saturn Unit, Once a Maverick, Is Looking a Lot More Like G.M.," *New York Times* (Aug. 23, 2001).

26. See, for example, Brandes, *American Welfare Capitalism*, pp. 83–91; and David Brody, *Workers in Industrial America: Essays on the Twentieth Century Struggle* (New York: Oxford University Press, 1980), pp. 48–81. Gallatin is quoted by Richard Nadler, "The Rise of Worker Capitalism," Cato Institute, policy analysis no. 359 (Nov. 1, 1999).

27. On the problems of downsizing and the evidence referred to in the footnote on page 147, see "When Slimming Is Not Enough," *Economist* (Sept. 3, 1994), pp. 59–60; and Martin Neil Baily, Eric J. Bartelsman, and John Haltiwanger, "Downsizing and Productivity Growth: Myth or Reality?" Center for Economic Studies, Bureau of the Census, discussion paper no. CES 94-4 (May 1994).

28. Steven Spear and H. Kent Bowen, "Decoding the DNA of the Toyota

Production System," *Harvard Business Review* (Sept.–Oct. 1999), pp. 97–98.

29. *Human Resource Practices for Implementing Advanced Manufacturing Technology* (Washington, D.C.: National Academy Press, 1986), pp. 1–4 (emphasis added).

30. David H. Autor, Frank Levy, and Richard J. Murnane, "Upstairs, Downstairs: Computers and Skills on Two Floors of a Large Bank," MIT Department of Economics, working paper no. 00-23 (July 1999, revised Aug. 2001), available at econ-www.mit.edu/faculty/dautor.

31. See David H. Autor, Frank Levy, and Richard J. Murnane, "The Skill Content of Recent Technological Change: An Empirical Exploration," MIT Department of Economics, working paper no. 01-22 (Jan. 2000, revised Sept. 2002), available at econ-www.mit/edu/faculty/dautor); *The Economic Report of the President* (Feb. 2000), pp. 25–27, 132–36; and Bureau of Labor Statistics, *Current Population Survey*.

32. *The Economic Report of the President* (Jan. 2001), pp. 126–27; and David Lebow, Louise Sheiner, Larry Slifman, and Martha Starr-McCluer, "Recent Trends in Compensation Practices," Federal Reserve Board Finance and Economics Discussion Series, paper no. 1999-32 (July 1999), esp. tables 2 and 3.

33. Casey Ichniowski, Kathryn Shaw, and Giovanna Prennushi, "The Effects of Human Resource Management Practices on Productivity: A Study of Steel Finishing Lines," *American Economic Review* (June 1997), pp. 291–313. Two papers by Sandra E. Black and Lisa M. Lynch also found that the extent to which new working methods are used, rather than their mere presence, is what matters for productivity. See "How to Compete: The Impact of Workplace Practices and Information Technology on Productivity," *Review of Economics and Statistics* (Aug. 2001), pp. 434–45; and "Human-Capital Investments and Productivity," *American Economic Review* (May 1996), pp. 263–67.

34. Brent Bolling, Casey Ichniowski, and Kathryn Shaw, "Opportunity Counts: Teams and the Effectiveness of Production Incentives," National Bureau of Economic Research, working paper no. 8306 (May 2001). The early studies include Douglas L. Kruse, *Profit Sharing: Does It Make a Difference?* (Kalamazoo, Mich.: W. E. Upjohn Institute for Employment Research, 1993), esp. chaps. 3 and 5; and those surveyed in a report Kruse prepared with Linda A. Bell, "Evaluating ESOPs, Profit-Sharing, and Gain Sharing Plans in U.S. Industries: Effects on Worker and Company Performance," Office of the American Workplace, U.S. Department of Labor (March 1995), esp. pp. 16–22.

35. Timothy F. Bresnahan, Erik Brynjolfsson, and Lorin M. Hitt, "Technology, Organization, and the Demand for Skilled Labor," in Margaret M. Blair and Thomas A. Kochan, eds. *The New Relationship* (Washington, D.C.: Brookings Institution Press, 2000), pp. 145–93; and Timothy F. Bresnahan, Erik Brynjolfsson, and Lorin M. Hitt, "Information Technology, Workplace Organization, and the Demand for Skilled Labor: Firm-Level Evidence," *Quarterly Journal of Economics* (Feb. 2002), pp. 339–76. Along the same lines, see Sandra E. Black and Lisa M. Lynch, "What's Driving the New Economy: The Benefits of Workplace Innovation," Federal Reserve Bank of New York, staff report no. 118 (March 2001).

36. Laurence Zuckerman, "Divided, an Airline Stumbles: Employee-Ownership Experiment Unravels at United," *New York Times* (March 14, 2001); and Laurence Zuckerman, "UAL Board Ousts Chief Unexpectedly," *New York Times* (Oct. 29, 2001).

37. Quoted in Laurence Zuckerman, "Challenges Abound for New Chief at Beleaguered United Airlines," *New York Times* (Oct. 30, 2001). Also see Floyd Norris, "Pilot Woes: Why Employee Ownership Didn't Help UAL," *New York Times* (Aug. 8, 2000).

38. Louis O. Kelso and Patricia Hetter Kelso, *Democracy and Economic Power: Extending the ESOP Revolution Through Binary Economics* (Lanham, Md.: University Press of America, 1991), pp. 4–7, 51–53; and Joseph R. Blasi, *Employee Ownership: Revolution or Ripoff?* (New York: Harper & Row, 1988), pp. 18–29.

39. The data are from the "Employee Ownership Fact Sheet" (1994), put out by the National Center for Employee Ownership in Oakland, California. See also "A Statistical Profile of Employee Ownership" (April 2002), available at www.nceo.org. As noted in Chapter 3, legal, regulatory, and institutional constraints have generally prevented pension funds and other financial intermediaries from exercising much control over the companies whose shares they hold on behalf of their clients. See Mark J. Roe, *Strong Managers, Weak Owners* (Princeton, N.J.: Princeton University Press, 1994), esp. chap. 9.

40. See "Gordon Cain (A)," Harvard Business School, case no. N9-391-112 (Dec. 12, 1990), esp. pp. 6–7. Javits is quoted by Blasi, *Employee Ownership*, p. 25.

41. See "Changes at ASI 'Poorly Understood,' " *Sault Star* (June 14, 1995); Robert Oakshott, "The United Steelworkers of America & Employee Ownership," research report for Partnership Research Ltd., London (October 1994); James B. Lieber, *Friendly Takeover: How an Employee Buyout Saved a Steel Town* (New York: Viking, 1995); and "Weirton Steel

Corp.: Union Ratifies 3 Contracts as Part of Restructuring," *Wall Street Journal* (Sept. 17, 2001).

42. Kelso and Kelso, *Democracy and Economic Power*, esp. chaps. 2 and 12; Peter F. Drucker, *Post-Capitalist Society* (New York: HarperBusiness, 1993), pp. 76–81; and Peter F. Drucker, *The Pension Fund Revolution* (New Brunswick, N.J.: Transaction Publishers, 1996), pp. 5–11.

43. On the changing nature of pension funds, see Alicia H. Munnell, Annika Sunden, and Elizabeth Lidstone, "How Important Are Private Pensions?", Center for Retirement Research at Boston College, Issue in Brief, no. 8 (Feb. 2002). On the history of pensions, see Drucker, *The Pension Fund Revolution*, pp. 5–6; and Bernstein, *The Lean Years*, pp. 181–82.

FIVE: THE STOCK MARKET AND THE NEW ECONOMY

1. On the difference between the indexes discussed in the footnote, see Jeremy Siegel, *Stocks for the Long Run: The Definitive Guide to Financial Market Returns and Long-Term Investment Strategies*, 2nd ed. (New York: McGraw-Hill, 1998), pp. 55–61.

2. See ibid., pp. 12–13, 23–24; and, on the difference between compound and average returns that is discussed in the footnote, John Y. Campbell, "Forecasting US Equity Returns in the 21st Century," which appears in *Estimating the Real Return on Stocks over the Long Term* (Washington, D.C.: Social Security Advisory Board, Aug. 2001).

3. Joseph de la Vega, *Confusion de Confusiones* (repr., Boston, Mass.: Harvard Graduate School of Business Administration, 1988; originally published 1688), p. 10; the introduction to this volume by Hermann Kellenbenz; and "Mr. Buffett on the Stock Market," *Fortune* (Nov. 22, 1999).

4. Siegel, *Stocks for the Long Run*, pp. 18–21.

5. Ibid., pp. 5–15, 26–33.

6. See Burton G. Malkiel, *A Random Walk Down Wall Street* (New York: Norton, 1996), pp. 188, 162; Roger Lowenstein, "How Tisch and NYU Missed Bull Run," *Wall Street Journal* (Oct. 16, 1997); and Richard Wilner, "Tsk, Tsk, Tisch: NYU Loses Out on Millions with Larry as Leader," *New York Daily News* (Oct. 17, 1997).

7. Burton G. Malkiel, "Are Markets Efficient? Yes, Even If They Make Errors," *Wall Street Journal* (Dec. 28, 2000); Malkiel, *Random Walk Down Wall Street*, pp. 177–84, 442–43; Josef Lakonishok, Andrei Shleifer, and Robert Vishny, "What Do Money Managers Do?" presented at conference on "The Power and Influence of Pension and Mutual Funds," NYU Salomon Center for the Study of Financial Institutions, Feb. 21,

1997; Josef Lakonishok, Andrei Shleifer, and Robert Vishny, "The Structure and Performance of the Money Management Industry," *Brookings Papers on Economic Activity* (1992), pp. 339–91; "Henry Hindsight," *Economist* (Feb. 12, 2000), p. 81; and "The Foresight Saga," *Economist* (Dec. 18, 1999), pp. 59–61.

8. Warren E. Buffett, "The Superinvestors of Graham-and-Doddsville," app. 1 of Benjamin Graham, *The Intelligent Investor*, 4th rev. ed. (New York: Harper Business, 1997), p. 294.

9. Ibid., p. 300. Buffett discusses intrinsic value in *An Owners' Manual*, which he issued to shareholders of Berkshire Hathaway Inc. in June 1966 and reprinted in the company's 1996 annual report; the quote is on pp. 64–65 of the annual report.

10. The quotation about USAir is from the 1997 annual report of Berkshire Hathaway, p. 17. In addition, see the 1994 and 1996 reports, pp. 17–18 and 16–17.

11. Buffett discusses risk in the 1993 annual report of Berkshire Hathaway, pp. 14–15 and in "The Superinvestors of Graham-and-Doddsville," pp. 299–300. Morgan is quoted in Malkiel, *Random Walk Down Wall Street*, p. 321. According to Peter Bernstein, Harry Markowitz, who won the Nobel Prize in economics in 1990, was the first person to identify risk with the variability of returns, in large part because it was easy to measure. See Bernstein, *Against the Gods: The Remarkable Story of Risk* (New York: John Wiley & Sons, 1996), pp. 247–61.

12. Josef Lakonishok, Andrei Shleifer, and Robert Vishny, "Contrarian Investment, Extrapolation, and Risk," *Journal of Finance* (Dec. 1994), pp. 1541–78. As in other such studies, the authors adjusted their portfolios for company size because there is evidence that shares of small companies outperform those of larger ones. In addition to measuring a stock's riskiness in the usual way, by the standard deviation of its returns, they considered how it performed in bad economic times such as recessions.

13. See *Stocks, Bonds, Bills, and Inflation: 2001 Yearbook*, Ibbotson Associates, pp. 139–61.

14. Narasimhan Jegadeesh and Sheridan Titman, "Returns to Buying Winners and Selling Losers: Implications for Stock Market Efficiency," *Journal of Finance* (1993), pp. 65–91; and Narasimhan Jegadeesh and Sheridan Titman, "Profitability of Momentum Strategies: An Evaluation of Alternative Explanations," National Bureau of Economic Research, working paper no. 7159 (June 1999).

15. The quotations are from John Maynard Keynes, *The General Theory of*

Employment, Interest, and Money (New York: Harcourt, Brace, 1936), pp. 156–58. Also see Andrei Shleifer and Robert Vishny, "The Limits of Arbitrage," *Journal of Finance* (1997), pp. 35–55; and Andrew Barry, "What's Wrong Warren?" *Barron's* (Dec. 27, 1999).

16. Keynes, *General Theory of Employment, Interest, and Money*, p. 151 (emphasis added).

17. Warren E. Buffett, "Who Really Cooks the Books?" *New York Times* (July 24, 2002); Steve Liesman and Jonathan Weil, "Disappearing Act: Spate of Write-Offs Calls into Question Lofty 1990s Profits," *Wall Street Journal* (July 13, 2001); and Patricia McConnell, "Pension and Other Retirement Benefits," Bear Stearns Equity Research (Nov. 2001).

18. The quotation is from a book by Joseph R. Blasi, Douglas L. Kruse, and Aaron Bernstein, *In the Company of Owners: The Truth About Stock Options and Why Every Employee Should Have Them*, which was published by Basic Books in Jan. 2003. It was taken from Michael Lewis, "In Defense of the Boom," *New York Times Magazine* (Oct. 27, 2002), p. 49.

19. Lucian Bebchuk, Jesse M. Fried, and David I. Walker, "Managerial Power and Rent Extraction in the Design of Executive Compensation," *University of Chicago Law Review* (Summer 2002), esp. pp. 765–66, 809–10, and 817–20; and Gretchen Morgenson, "When Options Rise to Top, Guess Who Pays," *New York Times* (Nov. 10, 2002), which is based in large part on data from Blasi, Kruse, and Bernstein, *In the Company of Owners*.

20. Bebchuk, Fried, and Walker, "Managerial Power and Rent Extraction," pp. 753–54.

21. On core earnings and options, see Standard & Poor's, "Measures of Corporate Earnings" (May 14, 2002); "Standard & Poor's Core Earnings Market Review" (Oct. 24, 2002); and the data for the S&P 500 companies, all of which are available at www.coreearnings.com; Pat McConnell and Janet Pegg, "Employee Stock Options: Is the Time Right for Change?" Bear Stearns Equity Research (July 2002); Jeremy Siegel, "Stocks Are Still an Oasis," *Wall Street Journal* (July 25, 2002); and Gary Schieneman, "Quality of Technology Earnings," Merrill Lynch (June 19, 2001).

22. Zvi Bodie, Robert S. Kaplan, and Robert C. Merton, "Options Should Be Reflected in the Bottom Line," *Wall Street Journal* (Aug. 1, 2002); Don Clark, "Contrary Intel Won't Expense Options," *Wall Street Journal* (Aug. 8, 2002); Rachel Emma Silverman, "GE to Expense Stock Options Held by 12% of Its Employees," *Wall Street Journal* (Aug. 1, 2002);

and Jonathan Weil and Theo Francis, "The Options-Value Brain Teaser," *Wall Street Journal* (Aug. 6, 2002).

23. See Rebecca Smith, "A Blockbuster Deal Shows How Enron Overplayed Its Hand," *Wall Street Journal* (Jan. 17, 2002); John R. Emshwiller and Rebecca Smith, "Murky Waters: A Primer on Enron Partnerships," *Wall Street Journal* (Jan. 21, 2002); and David Barboza, "Ex-executives Say Sham Deal Helped Enron," *New York Times* (Aug. 8, 2002).

24. Dan Ackman, "Enron the Incredible," Forbes.com (Jan. 17, 2002); Gretchen Morgenson, "How 287 Turned into 7: Lessons in Fuzzy Math," *New York Times* (Jan. 20, 2002); and David Cay Johnston, "Enron Avoided Income Taxes in 4 of 5 Years," *New York Times* (Jan. 17, 2002).

25. The quotations have been pieced together from Charles P. Kindleberger, *Manias, Panics, and Crashes: A History of Financial Crises*, 4th ed. (New York: John Wiley & Sons, 2000), chaps. 1 and 5, esp. pp. 2, 73, 76, 90.

26. See Burton G. Malkiel, "Don't Sell Out," *Wall Street Journal* (Sept. 26, 2001), who believes that reported earnings today are no less inaccurate than in the 1970s, when high inflation gave rise to misleading gains on business inventories and caused companies to depreciate their plant and equipment at rates that were too low.

27. Ibid.; and Siegel, "Stocks Are Still an Oasis."

28. Jeremy Siegel, "Big-Cap Tech Stocks Are a Sucker Bet," *Wall Street Journal* (March 14, 2000); Jeremy Siegel, "Not-Quite-So-Big-Cap Tech Stocks Are Still a Bad Bet," *Wall Street Journal* (March 19, 2001); and Burton G. Malkiel, "Nasdaq: What Goes Up . . . ," *Wall Street Journal* (April 14, 2000).

29. Robert J. Shiller, *Irrational Exuberance* (Princeton, N.J.: Princeton University Press, 2000), pp. 4–13; Campbell, "Forecasting US Equity Returns in the 21st Century"; and John Y. Campbell and Robert J. Shiller, "Valuation Ratios and the Long-Run Stock Market Outlook: An Update," National Bureau of Economic Research, working paper no. 8221 (April 2001), esp. pp. 8–19.

30. Milton Friedman and Anna Jacobson Schwartz, *A Monetary History of the United States, 1867–1960* (Princeton, N.J.: Princeton University Press, 1963), pp. 304–6, 351; John Kenneth Galbraith, *The Great Crash, 1929* (Boston: Houghton Mifflin 1972), pp. 93–112; Edward Chancellor, *Devil Take the Hindmost: A History of Financial Speculation* (New York: Farrar, Straus and Giroux, 1999), pp. 211–20; and David M. Kennedy,

Freedom from Fear: The American People in Depression and War, 1929–1945 (New York: Oxford University Press, 1999), pp. 34–41.

31. Shiller, *Irrational Exuberance*, pp. 8–10; and *Stocks, Bonds, Bills, and Inflation: 2001 Yearbook*, pp. 139–61.

32. Campbell and Shiller, "Valuation Ratios and the Long-Run Stock Market Outlook," p. 2.

33. Investors' expectations about future returns are from a 1997 survey conducted by Montgomery Asset Management, a San Francisco firm, but the way that some questions were posed may have caused the respondents to conflate cumulative and average annual returns. See David Barboza, "Bull Market's Glitter May Be Blinding Investors," *New York Times* (Oct. 27, 1997); and Robert McGough, "Was Investor Survey a Rush to Judgment?" *Wall Street Journal* (Oct. 27, 1997).

34. John Y. Campbell, "Strategic Asset Allocation: Portfolio Choice for Long-Term Investors," *NBER Reporter* (Fall 2000), pp. 8–10; and Campbell, "Forecasting US Equity Returns in the 21st Century."

35. Milton Friedman, "The 1990s' Boom Went Bust, What's Next?" *Wall Street Journal* (Jan. 22, 2002); and Kennedy, *Freedom from Fear*, pp. 40–41.

36. The quoted fragments are from Ron Chernow, "A Market in Need of a Broker," *New York Times* (April 16, 2000).

37. On the growth in stock ownership, see James M. Poterba, "The Rise of the 'Equity Culture': US Stockownership Patterns, 1989–1998," MIT Department of Economics (Jan. 2001), pp. 1–5 and tables 1–6; and Arthur B. Kennickell, Martha Starr-McCluer, and Annika Sunden, "Family Finances in the US: Recent Evidence from the Survey of Consumer Finances," *Federal Reserve Bulletin* (Jan. 1997), pp. 11–12.

38. The data on pension wealth are from Edward Wolff, "Income, Wealth, and Late-Life Inequality in the U.S.," NYU Department of Economics (Jan. 2002), especially table 3, as supplemented by correspondence with the author.

39. See Alicia H. Munnell and Annika Sunden, "401(K)s and Company Stock: How Can We Encourage Diversification?" Center for Retirement Research at Boston College, Issue in Brief no. 9 (July 2002); "When Labour and Capital Don't Mix," *Economist* (Dec. 15, 2001); Ellen E. Schultz, " 'Lockdowns' of 401(k) Plans Draw Scrutiny," *Wall Street Journal* (Jan. 16, 2002); Gretchen Morgenson, "Beware Those One-Note 401(k)'s," *New York Times* (Dec. 2, 2001); and Kathy Chen, "Fight Looms over Pension-Plan Changes," *Wall Street Journal* (Jan. 22, 2002).

40. Paul A. Gompers and Andrew Metrick, "Institutional Investors and Equity Prices," *Quarterly Journal of Economics* (Feb. 2001), pp. 229–59.

41. See "Aggressive Growth Equity Funds: Could a Selling Panic Erupt?" Bank Credit Analyst Research (Oct. 29, 2000); and Ken Brown, "Profits from Bull Market of '90s Are Leaving Fast," *Wall Street Journal* (Oct. 2, 2001).

42. The discussion of creative destruction in the stock market draws on the work of Boyan Jovanovic and various collaborators, particularly Peter L. Rousseau. See Jovanovic, "Technology and the Stock Market," *NBER Reporter* (Summer 2000), pp. 19–22; Jovanovic and Rousseau, "Vintage Organizational Capital," National Bureau of Economic Research, working paper no. 8166 (March 2001); and Jovanovic and Rousseau, "Stock Markets in the New Economy," Vanderbilt University Department of Economics, working paper no. 01-W18 (Aug. 2001).

43. Greg Ip, "Look at Roaring '20s Finds Optimistic Parallels," *Wall Street Journal* (June 12, 2000), and Siegel, *Stocks for the Long Run*, pp. 105–14.

SIX: JUNK BONDS AND TAKEOVERS

1. Although merger activity has tended to peak at about the same times as stock prices or earnings multiples, the relative heights of the different merger peaks are not the same as the rankings of the stock market peaks. On the wavelike character of merger activity, see Devra L. Golbe and Lawrence J. White, "Catch a Wave: The Time Series Behavior of Mergers," *Review of Economics and Statistics* (1993), pp. 493–99; and Devra L. Golbe and Lawrence J. White, "A Time-Series Analysis of Mergers and Acquisitions in the U.S. Economy," in Alan J. Auerbach, ed., *Corporate Takeovers: Causes and Consequences* (Chicago: University of Chicago Press, 1988), pp. 265–302.

2. See F. M. Scherer, *Industrial Market Structure and Economic Performance* (Chicago: Rand McNally, 1970), pp. 103–6, from which the quotation is taken, and George J. Stigler, "Monopoly and Oligopoly by Merger," in *The Organization of Industry* (Homewood, Ill.: Richard D. Irwin, 1968), pp. 95–107. (The article first appeared in *American Economic Review* in May 1950.) Stigler believes the first merger wave did not occur earlier because modern corporate structures and financial markets did not develop sufficiently until about the 1880s, but it is at least as likely that new organizational forms and new financial markets developed to meet companies' evolving needs.

3. Jean Strouse, *Morgan: American Financier* (New York: Random House, 1999), pp. 312–15, 395–409.

4. On Insull, who had once been Thomas Edison's personal secretary, see Edward Chancellor, *Devil Take the Hindmost: A History of Financial Speculation* (New York: Farrar, Straus and Giroux, 1999), pp. 207–8; Charles P. Kindleberger, *Manias, Panics, and Crashes: A History of Financial Crises*, 4th ed. (New York: John Wiley & Sons, 2000), p. 85; and Strouse, *Morgan*, p. 312. On mergers and antitrust law, see Stigler, "Monopoly and Oligopoly by Merger," pp. 100–6; Scherer, *Industrial Market Structure*: pp. 106–7; and Richard A. Posner, *Antitrust Law* (Chicago: University of Chicago Press, 1976), pp. 23–28, which is quoted in the footnote.

5. See *Covert Action in Chile 1963–1973*, Staff Report of the Select Committee to Study Government Operations with Respect to Intelligence Activities, United States Senate (December 18, 1975).

6. On the conglomerates of the 1960s, see John Brooks, *The Go-Go Years* (New York: Weybright and Talley, 1973), pp. 150–81.

7. See Gregor Andrade, Mark Mitchell, and Erik Stafford, "New Evidence and Perspectives on Mergers," *Journal of Economic Perspectives* (Spring 2001), pp. 103–20; Bengt Holmstrom and Steven N. Kaplan, "Corporate Governance and Merger Activity in the U.S.: Making Sense of the 1980s and 1990s," *Journal of Economic Perspectives* (Spring 2001), pp. 121–44; and Andre Shleifer and Robert Vishny, "Stock Market Driven Acquisitions" (June 2001), available at post-economics.harvard. edu/faculty/shleifer/papers.

8. See Mark L. Mitchell and J. Harold Mulherin, "The Impact of Industry Shocks on Takeover and Restructuring Activity," *Journal of Financial Economics* (1996), pp. 193–229; Sanjai Bhagat, Andrei Shleifer, and Robert Vishny, "Hostile Takeovers in the 1980s: The Return to Corporate Specialization," *Brookings Papers on Economic Activity: Microeconomics* (1990), pp. 1–72; and Brian J. Hall and Jeffrey B. Liebman, "Are CEOs Really Paid Like Bureaucrats?" *Quarterly Journal of Economics* (Aug. 1998), pp. 653–91.

9. On the relationship between the acquisitions of the 1980s and 1990s, see Holmstrom and Kaplan, "Corporate Governance and Merger Activity in the U.S.," esp. pp. 32–37; and Andrei Shleifer and Robert Vishny, "The Takeover Wave of the 1980s," *Science* (Aug. 17, 1990), esp. pp. 746–48. On the similarity between the mergers of the 1960s and 1990s, see Robert Frank, "More and More, Mergers of '90s Are Becoming Today's Spinoffs," *Wall Street Journal* (Feb. 6, 2002).

10. Connie Bruck, *The Predators' Ball: The Inside Story of Drexel Burnham and the Rise of the Junk-Bond Raiders* (New York: Penguin Books, 1989), p. 39.

11. James B. Stewart, *Den of Thieves* (New York: Touchstone, 1992), p. 51; and Martin S. Fridson, "What Caused the 1977–1978 Takeoff in High Yield Finance?" *Extra Credit*, Merrill Lynch Journal of High Yield Research (Nov./Dec. 1993), pp. 6–9.

12. Bruck, *Predators' Ball*, pp. 23–24; Stewart, *Den of Thieves*, pp. 51–53; and Jesse Kornbluth, *Highly Confident: The True Story of the Crime and Punishment of Michael Milken* (New York: Morrow, 1992), pp. 39, 42.

13. W. Braddock Hickman, *Corporate Bond Quality and Investor Experience* (Princeton, N.J.: Princeton University Press, 1958), pp. 15–16, 26. Martin Fridson, former director of high-yield research at Merrill Lynch, thinks that Milken knowingly ignored Hickman's cautions and Fraine's more skeptical view of high-yield bonds. See Martin Fridson, "Fraine's Neglected Findings: Was Hickman Wrong?" *Financial Analysts Journal* (Sept.–Oct. 1994), p. 53.

14. On Milken's compensation arrangements, see Stewart, *Den of Thieves*, pp. 48–51. The miner's helmet story is from Bruck, *Predators' Ball*, p. 23, and the objections to it are from Kornbluth, *Highly Confident*, pp. 9, 46.

15. James Grant, *Money of the Mind: Borrowing and Lending in America from the Civil War to Michael Milken* (New York: Farrar, Straus and Giroux, 1992), p. 369.

16. See Martin S. Fridson and Michael A. Cherry, "Penn Central Transportation Rides Again," *Extra Credit*, Merrill Lynch Journal of High Yield Research (March 1991), pp. 4–17.

17. On Saul Steinberg and his bid for Chemical Bank, see "Why Leasco Failed to Net Chemical," *Business Week* (April 26, 1969), from which the quotation in the footnote is taken.

18. The story of Texas International is told by Harlan D. Platt, *The First Junk Bond: A Story of Corporate Boom and Bust* (Armonk, N.Y.: M. E. Sharpe, 1994). Milken did another junk-bond offering for it in July 1978, and the company prospered during the oil boom, merging in 1982 with Phoenix Resources, a company created in the bankruptcy reorganization of King Resources in 1977. Texas International fell on hard times as oil prices dropped sharply in the mid-1980s, however, and declared bankruptcy later in the decade. It emerged in April 1990 as Phoenix Resource Companies, which Apache acquired in May 1996. Both companies had operations in the Western Desert of Egypt. On the growth of the junk-bond market in the late 1970s, see Fridson, "What Caused the 1977–1978 Takeoff in High Yield Finance?" pp. 9, 20–23.

19. Linton is quoted by Cary Reich, "Milken the Magnificent," *Institutional Investor* (Aug. 1986), p. 97. Similarly, roughly six years later, Milken was

described as "the original control freak" by a senior editor of *Forbes*, who conducted a lengthy, largely favorable interview with him. See "Sidelines," *Forbes* (March 16, 1992), pp. 78–100. On the decision to finance hostile takeovers, see Bruck, *Predators' Ball*, pp. 98–102; Kornbluth, *Highly Confident*, pp. 55–59; and Stewart, *Den of Thieves*, pp. 132–35.

20. See Grant, *Money of the Mind*, pp. 370–72, 379–81; and Stewart, *Den of Thieves*, p. 200. The Beatrice transaction was the basis for the felony plea of Robert Freeman, head of risk arbitrage at Goldman Sachs, in one of the insider-trading cases that arose a few years later (Stewart, pp. 201–2).

21. On the proper way to measure default rates, which is discussed in the footnote, see Paul Asquith, David W. Mullins Jr., and Eric D. Wolff, "Original Issue High Yield Bonds: Aging Analyses of Defaults, Exchanges, and Calls," *Journal of Finance* (Sept. 1989), pp. 923–52.

22. On the post-1985 decine in the quality of junk bonds, which is discussed in the footnote, see Barrie A. Wigmore, "The Decline in Credit Quality of New-Issue Junk Bonds," *Financial Analysts Journal* (Sept.–Oct. 1990), pp. 53–62; and Steven N. Kaplan and Jeremy C. Stein, "The Evolution of Buyout Pricing and Financial Structure in the 1980s," *Quarterly Journal of Economics* (May 1993), pp. 313–57.

23. See the indictment *USA* v. *Michael R. Milken, Lowell J. Milken, and Bruce L. Newberg* (S89 Cr. 41, KBW), for example, pp. 22–24, 101–3.

24. See Stewart, *Den of Thieves*, pp. 511, 523; and "The Global Settlement Closing Stipulation and Order," U.S. District Court for the Southern District of New York, MDL docket no. 924.

25. See Marshall E. Blume and Donald B. Keim, "The Risk and Return of Low-Grade Bonds: An Update," *Financial Analysts Journal* (Sept.–Oct. 1991), pp. 85–89.

26. See General Accounting Office, *High Yield Bonds: Issues Concerning Thrift Investments in High Yield Bonds* (March 1989).

27. See Kaplan and Stein, "Evolution of Buyout Pricing," especially the tables, and Gregor Andrade and Steven N. Kaplan, "How Costly Is Financial Distress?", *Journal of Finance* (Oct. 1998), pp. 1443–94.

28. See *Letters to the Shareholders of Berkshire Hathaway, 1987–1990*, p. 82, issued by Berkshire Hathaway, Omaha, Nebr.

29. See Kaplan and Stein, "Evolution of Buyout Pricing," pp. 340–44, esp. fig. 3.

30. For an overview of the high-yield market, see Martin S. Fridson, "The High Yield Asset Class," *Extra Credit*, Merrill Lynch Journal of Global High Yield Research (May/June 2001), pp. 3–18. In 2001, high-yield

bonds issued by telecommunications companies lost almost 30 percent, worse than junk bonds issued by companies in any other industry. See "Returns and Issuance: Full Year 2001," *This Week in High Yield*, Merrill Lynch (Jan. 4, 2002), p. 10.

31. Recall the discussion in the first part of this chapter and the references cited there, especially Bhagat, Shleifer, and Vishny, "Hostile Takeovers in the 1980s"; Hall and Liebman, "Are CEOs Really Paid Like Bureaucrats?"; Holmstrom and Kaplan, "Corporate Governance and Merger Activity in the U.S."; and Shleifer and Vishny, "Takeover Wave of the 1980s."

32. "My Story—Michael Milken," *Forbes* (March 16, 1992), p. 80.

33. See James Stewart, "The Milken File," *New Yorker* (Jan. 22, 2001), pp. 47–61; Michael Schroeder, "Clinton Pardons Two Traders, but Not Milken," *Wall Street Journal* (Jan. 22, 2001); and Neil A. Lewis, "Protests May Have Kept Milken from Pardon Roll," *New York Times* (Jan. 21, 2001).

34. For example, see Benjamin J. Stein, *A License to Steal: The Untold Story of Michael Milken and the Conspiracy to Bilk the Nation* (New York: Simon and Schuster, 1992).

SEVEN: BETTER MONETARY POLICY

1. Gerard Baker, "Man of the Year Alan Greenspan, Guardian Angel of the Financial Markets," *Financial Times* (Dec. 25/26, 1998); and Joshua Cooper Ramo, "The Committee to Save the World," *Time* (Feb. 15, 1999).

2. See John B. Taylor, "Monetary Policy and the Long Boom," *Review*, Federal Reserve Bank of St. Louis (Nov./Dec. 1998), p. 3.

3. For the gripping story of the 1907 crisis, and Morgan's role in resolving it, see Jean Strouse, *Morgan: American Financier* (New York: Random House, 1999), chap. 28.

4. See Board of Governors of the Federal Reserve System, *The Federal Reserve System: Purposes and Functions* (Washington, D.C.: Board of Governors, 1994), esp. chaps. 1 and 7.

5. See Alan S. Blinder, *Central Banking in Theory and Practice* (Cambridge, Mass.: MIT Press, 1998), pp. 54–59; and "Is Government Too Political?" *Foreign Affairs* (Nov./Dec. 1997), pp. 115–26.

6. Starting from the end of the paragraph, see Paul Krugman, *The Return of Depression Economics* (New York: Norton, 2000), pp. 69–82; Lawrence Summers, "How Should Long-Term Monetary Policy Be Determined?" *Journal of Money, Credit, and Banking* (Aug. 1991), pp. 625–31; George A.

Akerlof, William T. Dickens, and George L. Perry, "The Macroeconomics of Low Inflation," *Brookings Papers on Economic Activity* 1 (1996), pp. 1–76; and William Greider, *Secrets of the Temple: How the Federal Reserve Runs the Country* (New York: Touchstone, 1989).

7. On the distinction between rules and objectives, see Alan S. Blinder, *Central Banking in Theory and Practice* (Cambridge, Mass.: MIT Press, 1998), pp. 36–40. On inflation targeting, see Laurence Meyer, "Inflation Targets and Inflation Targeting," remarks at the University of California at San Diego Economics Roundtable (July 17, 2001), esp. pp. 7–11; and Ben S. Bernanke, Thomas Laubach, Frederic S. Mishkin, and Adam S. Posen, *Inflation Targeting* (Princeton, N.J.: Princeton University Press, 1999). The Friedman and Taylor rules were proposed in Milton Friedman, *A Program for Monetary Stability* (New York: Fordham University Press, 1959), pp. 90–94, 98–99; and John B. Taylor, "Discretion versus Policy Rules in Practice," *Carnegie-Rochester Conference Series on Public Policy* (Dec. 1993), pp. 195–214.

8. Robert M. Solow, "How Cautious Must the Fed Be?" in Benjamin M. Friedman, ed., *Inflation, Unemployment, and Monetary Policy*, The Alvin H. Hansen Symposium on Public Policy (Cambridge, Mass.: MIT Press, 1998), pp. 1–28.

9. See Paul Volcker, "Taking on Inflation," in Paul Volcker and Toyoo Gyohten, *Changing Fortunes: The World's Money and the Threat to American Leadership* (New York: Times Books, 1992), p. 176; and Alan Greenspan, "Transparency in Monetary Policy," remarks at the Federal Reserve Bank of St. Louis Economic Policy Conference (Oct. 11, 2001) (emphasis added).

10. See Friedman, *Program for Monetary Stability*, pp. 87, 90–99; Blinder, *Central Banking in Theory and Practice*, p. 38; and on the gaps in economic understanding that continue to hinder monetary policy making, see Alan S. Blinder, "Is There a Core of Practical Macroeconomics That We Should All Believe?" *American Economic Review* (May 1997), pp. 240–43.

11. On Burns's inflationary policies, see Greider, *Secrets of the Temple*, pp. 66–67, 342–47; and "An Interview with Milton Friedman," *Macroeconomic Dynamics* 5 (2001), p. 106. The interview was conducted by John B. Taylor at Stanford University on May 2, 2000.

12. For the details of Volcker's actions in these years, see Michael Mussa, "Monetary Policy in the 1980s," in Martin Feldstein, ed., *American Economic Policy in the 1980s* (Chicago: University of Chicago Press, 1994), pp. 95–107; and Volcker's "Comment" on Mussa's article, p. 147.

13. James Tobin, "Comment on Monetary Policy in the 1980s," in Feldstein, ed., *American Economic Policy in the 1980s*, p. 152. The estimate of the recession's costs is from Mussa, "Monetary Policy in the 1980s," pp. 113–14.

14. See Volcker and Gyohten, *Changing Fortunes*, pp. 176–77; Greider, *Secrets of the Temple*, pp. 67, 527–34; and Mussa, "Monetary Policy in the 1980s," p. 114.

15. Alan Greenspan, "Rules vs. Discretionary Monetary Policy," remarks at the Fifteenth Anniversary Conference of the Center for Economic Policy Research at Stanford University (Sept. 5, 1997), pp. 1–2.

16. Bob Woodward, *Maestro: Greenspan's Fed and the American Boom* (New York: Simon & Schuster, 2000), pp. 55–56.

17. On the Fed's policies prior to th 1987 crash and its disingenuous portrayal of the tightening in early October, which are summarized in the footnote, see Mussa, "Monetary Policy in the 1980s," pp. 125–27.

18. Greenspan, "Rules vs. Discretionary Monetary Policy," p. 4; and, on the mysterious reversal of the stock market crash, Woodward, *Maestro*, pp. 36–47.

19. See Greenspan, p. 4; and Alan S. Blinder and Janet L. Yellen, *The Fabulous Decade* (New York: Century Foundation Press, 2001), pp. 9–13, who also quote his comment at the September FOMC meeting (without the emphasis, which has been added).

20. Solow, "How Cautious Must the Fed Be?" p. 17.

21. Ibid., esp. pp. 17–27.

22. For a comparison of the 1990s expansion with those of the 1980s and 1960s, see Victor Zarnowitz, "The Old and the New in the U.S. Economic Expansion of the 1990s," National Bureau of Economic Research, working paper no. 7721 (May 2000), esp. pp. 6–8 and chart 1. On the nairu, see Robert J. Gordon, "The Time-Varying Nairu and Its Implications for Economic Policy," *Journal of Economic Perspectives* (Winter 1997), pp. 11–32.

23. Alan Greenspan, "Technology and the Economy," remarks before the Economic Club of New York (Jan. 13, 2000), p. 1.

24. See Alan Greenspan, "The Federal Reserve's Semiannual Monetary Policy Report," testimony before the Committee on Banking, Housing, and Urban Affairs, U.S. Senate, July 18, 1996, p. 3; Greenspan, "Rules vs. Discretionary Monetary Policy," p. 5; and Greg Ip and Jacob Schlesinger, "Did Greenspan Push High-Tech Optimism Too Far?" *Wall Street Journal* (Dec. 28, 2001) (they interviewed Kelley and quote Blinder's statement from the Dec. 19, 1995, FOMC meeting).

25. See Alan Greenspan, "The Challenge of Central Banking in a Democratic Society," remarks at the Annual Dinner and Francis Boyer Lecture of the American Enterprise Institute (Dec. 5, 1996). The quotations from the minutes of the 1996 FOMC meetings, which were made public in early 2002, are from Joseph Rebello, "Minutes from 1996 Fed Meetings Bear Out Governor's Presentiments of Market Slump," *Wall Street Journal* (Feb. 22, 2002).

26. See Alan Greenspan, "Monetary Policy and the Economic Outlook," testimony before the Joint Economic Committee, U.S. Congress, June 17, 1999; and Alan Greenspan, "Economic Volatility," remarks at a symposium sponsored by the Federal Reserve Bank of Kansas City (Jackson Hole, Wyo., Aug. 30, 2002). On his attitude toward the stock market and his concern about moral hazard, see Jacob Schlesinger, "How Alan Greenspan Finally Came to Terms with the Stock Market," *Wall Street Journal* (May 8, 2000); and Jacob Schlesinger, "Fed Won't Rescue the Markets, Greenspan Warns," *Wall Street Journal* (May 5, 2000).

27. Milton Friedman and Anna Jacobson Schwartz, *A Monetary History of the United States, 1867–1960* (Princeton, N.J.: Princeton University Press, 1963), pp. 410–19; the quoted passages are from pp. 418 and 412–13. These extracts are also quoted by Strouse, *Morgan*, p. 595.

28. Ben S. Bernanke, "Asset-Price Bubbles and Monetary Policy," remarks before the New York Chapter of the National Association of Business Economists (Oct. 15, 2002), esp. pp. 7–8, 11, where he discusses the late 1920s and quotes Strong, the Fed, Friedman and Schwartz, and Keynes. The speech is available at www.federalreserve.gov.

29. See "A Very Big Shoe to Fill," *Economist* (March 9, 2002), p. 40; "An Interview with Milton Friedman," pp. 105, 107–8; and, on the relative ineffectiveness of rules in the second half of the 1990s, Laurence Ball and Robert Tchaidze, "The Fed and the New Economy," National Bureau of Economic Research, working paper no. 8785 (Feb. 2002).

30. See Blinder and Yellen, *Fabulous Decade*, pp. 1–2; N. Gregory Mankiw, "Monetary Policy during the 1990s," Harvard University (May 2001); and Taylor, "Monetary Policy and the Long Boom."

CONCLUSION: LOOKING FORWARD

1. The quotation about the 1920s is from Watson Washburn and Edmund S. De Long, *High and Low Financiers: Some Notorious Swindlers and Their Abuses of Our Modern Stock Selling System* (Indianapolis: Bobbs-Merrill, 1932), p. 13, who are cited by Charles P. Kindleberger, *Manias, Panics,*

and Crashes: A History of Financial Crises, 4th ed. (New York: John Wiley & Sons, 2000), p. 84. Also see Bob Davis, "Past Crises Offer Hope for Economy, Warnings to Watch," *Wall Street Journal* (Sept. 26, 2002); and on the importance of deposit insurance, Milton Friedman and Anna Jacobson Schwartz, *A Monetary History of the United States, 1867–1960* (Princeton, N.J.: Princeton University Press, 1963), pp. 11–12, 342–59, 437–40.

2. See Ben S. Bernanke, "Deflation: Making Sure It Doesn't Happen Here," remarks before the National Economists Club (Nov. 21, 2002), esp. pp. 8–9, available at www.federalreserve.gov. On economic and productivity growth from 1999 through 2002, the Bureau of Economic Analysis's GDP release of February 28, 2003, available at www.bea.doc.gov; and the Bureau of Labor Statistics' productivity release of March 6, 2003, available at www.bls.gov.

3. On the crisis in the telecom industry, see "Too Many Debts; Too Few Calls," *Economist* (July 20, 2002). On the risks of deflation and measures that might have been taken, see J. Bradford DeLong, "America's Date with Deflation," *Financial Times* (Aug. 21, 2002); Paul Krugman, "Mind the Gap," *New York Times* (Aug. 16, 2002); Paul Krugman, "My Economic Plan," *New York Times* (Oct. 4, 2002); and "The Unfinished Recession: A Survey of the World Economy," *Economist* (Sept. 28, 2002).

4. See Alan Greenspan, "Economic Volatility," remarks at a symposium sponsored by the Federal Reserve Bank of Kansas City (Jackson Hole, Wyo., Aug. 30, 2002), p. 3; and Ben S. Bernanke, "Asset-Price Bubbles and Monetary Policy," remarks before the New York Chapter of the National Association of Business Economics (Oct. 15, 2002), esp. pp. 7–8.

5. The *Financial Times* series "Barons of Bankruptcy" was published in three parts on July 31, Aug. 1, and Aug. 2, 2002. On the growth of executive compensation in the 1990s, see Lucian Bebchuk, Jesse M. Fried, and David I. Walker, "Managerial Power and Rent Extraction in the Design of Executive Compensation," *University of Chicago Law Review* (Summer 2002), esp. pp. 753, 842–45; Kevin J. Murphy, "Explaining Executive Compensation: Managerial Power versus the Perceived Cost of Stock Options," *University of Chicago Law Review* (Summer 2002), pp. 847–49; and John Cassidy, "The Greed Cycle," *New Yorker* (Sept. 23, 2002), esp. the comments of the compensation expert Graef Crystal, which are quoted on p. 76.

6. On the desirability of performance-based pay, see the Conference Board Commission on Public Trust and Private Enterprise, "Findings and

Recommendations; Part I: Executive Compensation" (Sept. 17, 2002); Henry M. Paulson Jr., "Restoring Investor Confidence: An Agenda for Change," speech to the National Press Club (June 5, 2002); and Bebchuk, Fried, and Walker, "Managerial Power and Rent Extraction," esp. pp. 791–93. On the lack of indexing, see pp. 757, 801–2 in this article.

7. Bebchuk, Fried, and Walker, "Managerial Power and Rent Extraction," esp. pp. 759–60, 801–2, 809–10, 817, 819–20, which quotes Buffett. The longer quotation is from pp. 759–60 (emphasis added).

8. See Jean Strouse, *Morgan: American Financier* (New York: Random House, 1999), pp. 12–13, 675.

9. The three specific proposals cited in the preceding sentences were made by Henry G. Manne, "Bring Back the Hostile Takeover," *Wall Street Journal* (June 26, 2002); Floyd Norris, "Time to Change the Way Options Are Taxed," *New York Times* (Sept. 20, 2002); and Paul Gompers, Andrew Metrick, and Jeremy Siegel, "This Tax Cut Will Pay Dividends," *Wall Street Journal* (Aug. 13, 2002).

10. The quotation about sending white-collar crooks to jail is from "How to Fix Corporate Governance," *Business Week* (May 6, 2002), p. 76, and closely resembles suggestions made by O'Neill. See "Treasury Secretary: Crooked Execs Should Get Jail," usatoday.com (June 27, 2002). On the approach of the Sarbanes-Oxley Act, see Roger Lowenstein, "Make Pinocchio CEOs Pay," *Wall Street Journal* (Aug. 16, 2002).

Acknowledgments

Most of all, and most deeply, I am grateful to my family—my wife, Helen Bodian, and our children, David and Mara—for their love, understanding, and support, not only during the preparation of this book, but throughout our much longer time together.

In addition, I am grateful to the following:

My partners at Mount Lucas Management, Paul DeRosa, Tim Rudderow, and Frank Vannerson, with and from whom I learned a tremendous amount about financial markets and how to exploit the opportunities they present to investors. They also read drafts of the text and gave me helpful comments and suggestions, continuing a collaboration Frank and I began when we were graduate students at Princeton.

My editors: Robert Silvers of *The New York Review of Books*—where parts of the last four chapters first appeared—who gave me an opportunity to write about these issues and taught me so much about how to do it; and Jonathan Galassi of Farrar, Straus and Giroux, who was indispensable in helping me structure a book incorporating portions of those earlier writings into a much broader argument.

Two friends, Michael Edelstein and Jean Strouse, who read the entire manuscript, some parts more than once, and improved it greatly. Michael was hugely helpful in making me aware of the literature in economic history and in catching potential errors and omissions, sometimes recalling discussions we had when we were colleagues at Columbia.

I also am grateful to my agent, Lynn Nesbit, who helped me sort through my options and settle in the right place; to Jerry Prior of Mount Lucas, who dragged me into the microelectronic age by setting me up with ever-better computers, software, and connections, coaching me through countless problems with them, and assisting me with various calculations and with the charts; and to Larry Kauvar, a biophysicist and biotechnology entrepreneur, who sharpened my understanding of the basic technologies of the new economy. Finally, I want to thank Maria Santana for her gracious and varied assistance over the last four years; Miriam Bodian, a scholar of post-expulsion Spanish Jewry, for sending me a copy of Joseph de la Vega's pamphlet, which is thought to be the first written commentary on the stock market; Peggy Crowley of Microsoft and Rachel Stewart of Intel, for sending me material on their companies; and Stacey Barney and James Wilson of Farrar, Straus and Giroux, who coordinated my activities with those of the many other people at FSG who worked on the book.

Index